Unfinished Business

A volume in
Adult Learning in Professional, Organizational, and Community Settings
Carrie J. Boden, *Series Editor*

Unfinished Business

*Compelling Stories
of Adult Student Persistence*

Matt Bergman
University of Louisville

Joann S. Olson
University of Houston-Victoria

and Associates

INFORMATION AGE PUBLISHING, INC.
Charlotte, NC • www.infoagepub.com

Library of Congress Cataloging-in-Publication Data

A CIP record for this book is available from the Library of Congress
http://www.loc.gov

ISBN: 978-1-64113-854-3 (Paperback)
       978-1-64113-855-0 (Hardcover)
       978-1-64113-856-7 (ebook)

Contents

Foreword

Learning in adulthood is an intensely personal activity.
—Sharan Merriam, Rosemary Caffarella, and Lisa Baumgartner

In my time as the department head for an online, degree-completion program for adult learners, I have experienced compelling instances of the human spirit overcoming barriers, both real and perceived, to attain an undergraduate degree. As examples, three personal stories are ever present: the World War II veteran who first enrolled in the university in 1941 and graduated 71 years later at the age of 89, the academically underprepared transfer student-athlete who persisted to graduation after his eligibility and financial support expired, and the retired law enforcement officer who overcame repeated challenges from post-traumatic stress disorder and uncontrolled Type 1 diabetes. These three students are merely representative illustrations among the nearly 1,700 adult learners in whose degree-completion endeavors I have been fortunate enough to play some small role.

Matt Bergman and Joann Olson's *Unfinished Business: Compelling Stories of Adult Student Persistence* explores critical perspectives, practices, and initiatives affecting adult learners, as well as the institutions they attend, in the ever-changing higher education landscape in the United States. As noted in Chapter 1, the traditionally defined college student now reflects approximately 25% of higher education enrollment in the United States. We are at a crossroads, influenced by declining enrollment, increased competition, and public questioning of the value of a college degree. The proliferation of credential and degree programs available to adult learners in the virtual space alone creates an overwhelming environment, requiring those with limited knowledge to discern topics such as accreditation, quality delivery, cost, and reputation. Matt and Joann provide a precise charge: "Higher education professionals must develop a common language that strives to convey commitment to quality academics, educational workforce opportunity, affordability, personal growth, and advancement of social responsibility."

While grounded in the contemporary research of the adult learner and the pursuit of degree completion, this volume centers on the voices of those who returned, persisted, and achieved the goal. No two learner journeys are the same. Matt and Joann identify common threads of motivation for returning adult learners: providing for the family, personal fulfillment, career advancement, beating the odds, and reigniting the love of learning. Those of us who recognize our daily work in these stories will be reminded of why we do what we do and our impact on individual lives. If you are new to the field of degree completion in higher education, *Unfinished Business* provides you with foundational knowledge of one of the most rewarding paths one could choose as a career.

—**Jeff Aulgur**
President, Adult Higher Education Alliance
Arkansas Tech University

Preface

For at least the last 100 years, more than 40% of all students who enroll in American colleges and universities have not persisted to graduation at 4-year institutions. The stories of these noncompleters are wide and varied, and those stories explain the reasoning for students giving up on their goal of obtaining a college degree. Yet, hundreds of thousands of college students stop out or drop out entirely, from all types of universities, across the world, every year. While the factors are wide-ranging and complex, one fact remains for these individuals: They are connected to nearly 36 million other Americans who have some college but no degree.

This subject is taboo among friends, coworkers, and family members. For many, the embarrassment of not finishing college is often a closely held secret that weighs on them as they discuss, engage, and compete to meet the challenges of the workforce in the 21st century. Many have excelled despite their lack of a college credential. Some weren't ready at age 18 for the focus and commitment that academic studies require. Other noncompleters found opportunities that created income to meet immediate familial needs or requirements. Many are competent and high performing but bear the burden of not having the standard credential—a bachelor's degree—that many of their co-workers and fellow leaders can fall back upon in times of transition.

The idea for this book spawned from my (Matt's) time as an academic counselor at the University of Louisville. I was inspired on a daily basis by the sacrifices and commitment of the people who walked in my door in

Unfinished Business, pages xiii–xiv
Copyright © 2019 by Information Age Publishing
xiii

the Education Advising and Student Services office. I have sat with adult students, ranging from 24 to 77, as they shared their wide-ranging reasons for returning to school. This book encapsulates a very simple idea. It is past time to tell the stories of some of these outstanding professionals who just so happened to make a commitment to return to complete a long-held goal of a bachelor's degree. Needless to say, it was very easy to identify and recruit impressive and compelling stories from these adult learners from across the country.

The book in your hands cuts to the heart of what matters in education. The personal value that students hold for finishing their education makes them the most enjoyable population to serve in the in-person and online environment. They are extremely high-quality students because of their mission-driven approach to academics. The self-direction and commitment demonstrated by these adults is not only compelling, it is truly inspiring. While these narratives provide only a glimpse into the perspective of these incredible adult learners, they provide beautiful snapshots that will hopefully resonate with the readers of this book.

Over the past 15 years, I have laughed, cried, challenged, yelled at, and celebrated pure joy with adult students as they have sacrificed so much to complete a long-held goal that may have started as long as 30 years ago. We hear of the challenges all too often; this book allows you to rejoice in the success stories.

Yours truly,
Matt Bergman

Acknowledgments

We would like to thank our "and Associates" authors—the amazing adult learners who contributed to this book. Without their commitment and sacrifice to pursue a long-held dream to finish a degree, this book would not exist. While there are many adults with some college and no degree on the sidelines of education, this book highlights those who re-engaged in college classes and ultimately finished what was started last year or long ago. American college students of every age are balancing multiple responsibilities. In an ever-connected world, the adults whose stories you find here carved out space in their busy lives to pursue a degree to improve their quality of life. Whether this was driven by personal motivation, to move their career forward, or to set an example for the next generation, these inspiring adults fulfilled a vision that eluded them the first time they enrolled in college.

Unfinished Business: Compelling Stories of Adult Student Persistence is dedicated to all adult learners who have some college and no degree. There is no perfect time to finish what you started. Consequently, today is as good a day as any to re-start. Find a program, degree, certificate, or resource that can connect you with the most appropriate credential that will directly improve your quality of life. We promise, that program exists, and there are many people who are ready, willing, and able to help you find an efficient and do-able pathway for your future.

Colleges and universities have evolved to become more adult friendly in their practices. The days of standing in lines on campus to schedule classes

Unfinished Business, pages xv–xvi
Copyright © 2019 by Information Age Publishing
xv

and dealing with a litany of on-campus requirements have disappeared, and many institutions are ready to accommodate the competing responsibilities of working adults with online and evening services that are both stream-lined and effective. As our friend Sarah Ancel at Student Ready Strategies states, "Universities are now prepared to stop saying we will give you another chance and instead say please give us another chance to help you finish." Colleges and universities have changed and now provide pathways that hon-or your life experiences and adapt to your crazy life schedule. Jump in and see. The path to graduation may be much shorter than you expect.

—**Matt J. Bergman**
Joann S. Olson

1

Embracing the New "Traditional" Student in Higher Education

There is a common misconception in our country. It is perpetuated by popular culture through movies, television, streaming services, and even social media. When Americans picture "college students," they think of a young 18- to 21-year-old kid walking around a beautiful, country club-like, green-grassed campus heading to a class, a sporting event, a fraternity or sorority party; others envision some iconic and nostalgic vision of what it must be like to be a college student in America. This perception couldn't be farther from the reality of today's college landscape. Only roughly 25% of America's college-going population are traditional-age, residential students. The remaining 75% exhibit some form of nontraditional characteristic(s) including, but not limited to, being over 25 years old, having children, working full time, serving in the military, being financially independent, living off-campus, or attending classes part-time. In 2018, nearly 37% of college students were 25 or older, 38% attended part time, 26% were parents, and roughly 41% attended 2-year or non-bachelor's granting institutions (NCES, 2018).

Unfinished Business, pages 1–13
Copyright © 2019 by Information Age Publishing
All rights of reproduction in any form reserved.

These changes in higher education have not occurred overnight. Many campuses became friendlier to adult and military learners over the past 40+ years. For-profit institutions adopted practices to welcome working learners with online, evening, and other flexible approaches for adults to attend part time as early as the 1990s. At its peak, the University of Phoenix had a total enrollment of nearly 600,000 students. However, their retention and graduation rates were abysmal compared to many well-recognized traditional institutions, and there has been a sharp decline in enrollment at University of Phoenix and other for-profit universities. While for-profit institutions have seen a dramatic enrollment decline since their peak because of these shortcomings, their impact on higher education recruitment and adult-friendly best practices are evident across the country. Universities of all types are now more cognizant of the multiple challenges their incoming and current students face while trying to progress toward a degree or credential. In fact, the overall graduation rate of 59.1% has not varied much over the past century in American higher education (NCES, 2018). Consequently, there are nearly 36 million adults who have started a degree but haven't made it to the finish line (Graduate! Network, 2019). These individuals enrolled at some point in their lives, but life intervened to the detriment of their persistence to degree.

The changing landscape of higher education is not actually a bad thing. The millions of individuals who were often underserved in their first attempt at a degree are now finding that their former institutions have shifted policies, programs, and procedures to serve them much better this time around. Higher education is becoming more inclusive and accessible to people from all socioeconomic backgrounds. While it remains true that tuition is not affordable to all members of our society, there are many avenues for interested students to access and enroll in diverse types of institutions that provide flexible and more affordable options to a wide array of under-resourced adults.

The pace of change in higher education is likely to increase even further due to a declining population of high school graduates over the next 8–12 years. During the Great Recession, many families seemingly became more cautious about growing their families. As a result, fewer babies were born, which has had an impact on the educational pipeline. By 2027, there will simply not be enough traditional-age learners transitioning from high school to college to maintain the current enrollment of nearly 21 million students across the universities and colleges in America. While there has been a slow decline in overall American college enrollment, this birth rate decline will manifest in 15% fewer traditional-age students to enter universities as 18-year-old high school graduates.

However, this specific demographic shift could be positive from economic, social, public health, and workforce development perspectives. A broadly educated citizenry is critical for continued growth as a prosperous nation. Having well-educated and highly skilled members of society increases civic engagement, public health, and life expectancy. Moreover, encountering new ideas, philosophies, and epistemologies in higher education promotes more social and interpersonal growth through exposure to diverse ideas and contexts (Gurin, Dey, Hurtado, & Gurin, 2002). The collective growth in critical thinking and analytical thought develops the ability to exhibit empathy and reason in all aspects of life. College graduates, in aggregate, commit less crime, are more philanthropic, contribute more tax revenue, and cost less in overall healthcare (Baum & Ma, 2007; Perna, 2005). Consequently, the demographic shift of recruiting, retaining, and graduating more working adults could infuse higher education with self-directed, high-performing students who can make a more immediate impact on the performance of the American workforce.

Merriam, Caffarella, and Baumgartner (2007) outlined five primary purposes that drive educational programs for adults: encouraging ongoing individual development and growth, enabling people to respond to the issues and pragmatic problems that are part of adult life, preparing individuals for work opportunities—both current and future, facilitating organizational change and achievement, and providing opportunities to examine issues within their communities and societies. As Kuh (2008) highlighted, the well-being of individuals and society is dependent—at least in part—on shaping and reshaping undergraduate education to more effectively close the gap between theory and practice. Best practices in adult educational programs include providing better outreach, career and life planning, financing options, learning outcome assessment, teaching-learning processes, student support systems, technologies, and strategic partnerships. Improving these services will help both traditional and adult learners pursue their educational goals.

The Economics of Education

And yet, a college degree is not a silver bullet to address all of the world's problems. Public esteem for higher education is diminishing for a whole host of reasons including skyrocketing costs, political tension, and a perceived dip in overall quality. While it is true that Americans overwhelmingly believe that college degrees are essential to landing good jobs and reaching higher levels of income, research from the Federal Reserve Bank of New York shows that many people still have doubts about the quality and value of a college education, especially when compared to the cost (Abel & Deitz, 2014). These challenges should not be discounted, but the bigger picture displays a more compelling argument for seeking postsecondary degrees. During the most recent recession, the unemployment rates for those with a four-year degree increased but never exceeded 6.3%, compared to the peak 13.4% unemployment rate for those with no more than a high school education. Furthermore, economists at the Georgetown Center on Education and the Workforce estimate that a bachelor's degree is worth $2.8 million, on average, over a person's lifetime (Carnevale, Jayasundera, & Gulish, 2016). As the economy grows in a post-recession environment, both college and high school graduates are seeing decreases in unemployment rates. Yet, many of the jobs lost in the recession for high school graduates have not returned, and their rate of unemployment is still double that of four-year college graduates.

While higher education credentials are correlated with greater quality of life, it cannot be discounted that more than 44 million Americans hold nearly $1.5 trillion in student debt. Students are graduating with an average debt load of $37,172, up $20,000 since 2005. This massive loan repayment, coupled with the fact that more than 40% of students aren't graduating within six years, helps explain why the public perception of higher education has declined during the past 30 years. A myriad of factors has shifted the burden of paying higher costs to our students. First, higher education is a human-driven enterprise. Labor costs are large in an industry driven by human interaction to produce the product (that product being a college degree). In addition, universities are employing highly trained professionals (faculty and, to a large degree, staff) to impart knowledge to the future leaders of the workforce. Consequently, paying educators to convey knowledge will always cost a "pretty penny." To make matters more complicated, there has been a sharp decline in state and federal funding for higher education. According to the Hechinger Report, over the past 10 years, states have collectively scaled back their annual education funding by $9 billion in overall funding when adjusting for inflation (Marcus, 2019). In other words, the government is making educational attainment less of a priority, shifting the burden onto the consumer. This decrease in subsidy is a large reason for the spike of student debt to the astronomical figure of $1.5 trillion. Tuition has increased by more than 210% over the past 30 years. This has created a perfect storm of reduced government subsidy alongside a growing cost of paying administrators, faculty, and staff. In addition, calls for greater accountability for institutions of higher education have often led to the creation of new administrative positions (e.g., assessment coordinator, director of institutional effectiveness, etc.), further increasing the overhead of colleges and universities. While most members of society readily acknowledge the need for an educated citizenry to meet the demands of contemporary workforce, the trap of enabling students to get the requisite credentials to find a decent paying job without simultaneously digging a deep hole of debt remains. Thus, another chicken-and-egg scenario faces many under-resourced members of society. Degrees are generally seen as the path to higher-paying jobs and greater financial margin, but without those financial resources, it is challenging to pay for the degree. For millions of American homes, it is a foregone conclusion that the family will scramble to find the resources to make sure their children make it to and through college. Yet, rising costs are making it increasingly difficult, often impossible, for under-resourced Americans to reap the benefits from earning a baccalaureate or graduate degree.

The student debt issue is particularly acute for those students who find their pursuit of postsecondary education stopped or interrupted for some reason when "life intervenes" and they drop out or stop out. These students often leave college with debt and no credential to show for it because of nonacademic factors. Therefore, they have the increased financial pressures of paying back student loans without the increased economic opportunity that was an anticipated result of that education. Furthermore, when they attempt to return to finish what they started, they experience greater financial pressures, issues with child care, transportation, housing, food insecurity, lower job flexibility, and any number of other competing responsibilities that can quickly upend their ability to focus and finish college courses. As Jamie Merisotis (2018) from the Lumina Foundation stated:

> More and more students need help to gain access to college and to stay on the path that leads to a credential. Traditional financial aid such as grants and loans can offset some of the cost. But huge numbers of today's students—many of them older adults with children, jobs, and other responsibilities—have needs that outstrip such aid. For these students to succeed, colleges and universities must commit to a more holistic approach. They must provide wraparound services, a network of supports designed to meet students' individual, real-life needs. (para. 9)

The good news is that a broad support network is possible in the shifting climate of higher education. External agencies, degree-completion networks, foundations, and colleges and universities are increasingly employing models that incorporate best practices that have been proven to increase attainment and reduce further debt load on graduates. These systems have provided a blueprint for institutions to ensure a better life for those seeking and achieving higher levels of educational attainment.

At its core, what is higher education truly about? The authors of this book would posit that education is designed to develop human capital and talent. It's about sending students into the world prepared to be more productive and successful than they were before earning their degrees. To justify society's investment in higher education, graduates must not only secure gainful employment. They must also bring knowledge and skills that spur organizational growth and opportunity for others.

The focus of this book is to explore those campus and external agency strategies by sharing real-life stories of students who have been helped by those agencies and strategies. This will provide a window into what innovative educators are doing to drive this agenda forward. Within this book, you will find success stories from students at Morgan State University, University of Memphis, Georgia State University, University of Louisville, Gwinnett College, Wilmington University in Delaware, Empire State University, Thomas Edison State University, and Charter Oak. These institutions are pioneering new methods of recruiting, retaining, and graduating more adults with some college and no degree. The impact of these programs is evident in the narratives of the adult degree completers highlighted here.

The Skills Gap and Adults in Higher Education

Meeting the educational needs of the contemporary workforce requires painting a more accurate picture of students in American colleges and universities. While many institutions already recognize that adults are going to be crucial to the viability of higher education, not all have embraced the idea that programs and services catering to adults will be the engine that drives 21st century colleges and universities forward. Relevant, rigorous, and research-based curriculum will help address the skills gap that exists in the American workforce in a way that meets the needs of adults and responds to demographic changes. This will necessitate funding and focused attention on the needs of adult learner to serve the needs of adult learners, those who are beginning their education and those who are returning to complete a degree begun long ago. Prioritizing the needs of "come-backers" will be a worthy investment, and will likely reap benefits—and reduced barriers—for all students (Klein-Collins, 2018). The goal should be to create a pipeline backward and forward that educates incumbent workers and provides a pathway to current students through internships and apprenticeships to address the immediate needs of respective industries. In this way, graduates will complete their studies having gained real-world skills and ready to fully engage in their chosen professions. Likewise, institutions of higher education will have developed a more finely tuned understanding of the needs of the various organizations where graduates find employment.

Aligning curriculum with market needs and the changing nature of the American workforce is no easy feat. It is harder than coaching a traditional student or a returning adult to engage and become a more dynamic employee. However, employees and new graduates play an instrumental part in creating a "learning organization" culture in the U.S. workforce. Colleges and universities are now creating intentional partnerships with industries they serve. Although traditionally, industry came to higher education to ask for specific programming, institutional leaders are increasingly reaching out to elements in the corporate, government, military, and nonprofit sectors to formalize partnerships that address the immediate needs of their respective workforce. The shortage of talent in a booming economy is evidenced in the historic low unemployment rate across the country. There are currently 0.91 unemployed individuals per each job opening in today's economy (Bureau of Labor Statistics, 2018). In other words, there are more jobs than unemployed workers in the United States. If higher education institutions can become agile enough to ask appropriate questions about human capital needs from a wide array of corporate and professional partners, they will have a pipeline of full- and part-time students who will be purpose-driven and fully engaged in pursuit of advanced certificate and degree programs.

This adaptive and collaborative approach to curriculum development is attractive to leaders within industry. While some faculty may argue that this move diminishes the "academic freedom" of institutions of higher learning, others argue that this taps into the essence of what learners need to be prepared to thrive in a dynamic economy. Without diminishing the importance of academic freedom and the value of pursuing new knowledge, we would agree with the latter point of view: Amplifying professional and corporate partner collaborations can help institutions of higher education extract relevant learning outcomes that students must reach to be successful in the workforce. This does not, however, discount the importance of research-based curriculum rooted in academic rigor. These ideas can co-exist effectively. Rather than operating from an "either/or" framework, the skills gap calls for a "both/and" approach to capture both industry needs and discipline-specific fundamentals.

A certain complacency has always existed in the "Ivory Towers" of higher education. The insular notion of what it means to be an "educated person" is no longer defined at an elite selective group of campuses with perfectly manicured lawns and beautiful brick cathedrals. The open-source nature of information has challenged the status quo in higher education, leading to a re-evaluation of how business is done. The growing pressure to commoditize learning into job skills and tangible competencies consequently exerts a level of pressure on universities to demonstrate that students are actually developing knowledge, skills, and abilities that have value and utility in the workforce. This is a relatively new pressure, and reluctance to embrace change in all levels of higher education will diminish the viability of those institutions that resist it. Resisting this change will also leave a hungry public that desires to learn and innovate to advance the economy ill-equipped and underserved. When universities incorporate curricular elements that speak directly to the needs of an organization, the workers thrive with greater engagement, production, and retention (Klein-Collins, 2018). When industry partners with universities, the rigor and relevance of the research produced will advance the knowledge to a place it otherwise could not achieve. Consequently, both entities reach greater levels of prosperity, and the American and world economies benefit.

While just 6% of people surveyed in the United States believe the world is getting better, there is distinct and tangible proof that the health and prosperity of the entire population of the globe is improving. In a recent book, *Factfulness: Ten Reasons We're Wrong About the World—and Why Things Are Better Than You Think*, Hans Rosling (2018) outlined positive developments in areas including poverty, life expectancy, birth rate, and economy. Specifically, over the past 20 years, the proportion of the world living in extreme poverty has almost halved (the fastest drop ever in world history). Also, over the last 200 years, life expectancy has more than doubled (from 30 years to 72 years); it is also 10 years longer than it was 40 years ago. The average birth rate is actually declining (the world's total population is expected to peak around 11 billion people in 2050 and then stabilize). Rosling (2018) posited that the biggest contributor to these shifts is communities worldwide becoming less poor through increased education, better access to health care, and improved infrastructure like plumbing and electricity for a wider number of global citizens. Simultaneously, more innovation is improving the quality and access of transformative technologies spreading to the most impoverished areas on earth.

There is no doubt that higher education has played an influential role in this positive aggregate improvement in our world. However, public perception and costs have resulted in an overall enrollment decrease of 1.5% in the past year. Moreover, for-profit institutions have seen more than a 10% drop in overall enrollment (NCES, 2018). Some of these fluctuations in the higher education market are natural and have been happening over the past 100 years, but administrators and faculty alike are alarmed at the current perception and viability of this industry. Consequently, top-tier institutions such as Harvard, University of Pennsylvania, Stanford, MIT, and others are finding new ways to meet the needs of busy professionals through continuing and credit-bearing courses offered in multiple modalities. Just like many for-profit institutions, various traditional colleges and universities are acknowledging that adults balance an abundance of life and career responsibilities, which limits the amount of time that they have to engage with the formal learning environment. However, there is no mistaking the fact that additional educational attainment is a key to advancing in an ever-changing and dynamic workforce. These adaptations of an otherwise stagnant industry have opened the doors for innovation and service to a population that would not otherwise have had any opportunity to engage in additional formal learning. Online courses (credit and noncredit) have become increasingly diverse in practically every way possible. Courses and programs have diversity in age, race, region, people with disabilities, veterans on active duty in different countries, and beyond. This leads to a wide-ranging context of prior experience being brought into the online discussion forum, opening up a deeper learning opportunity and exposure to a more diverse array of perspectives among students and the instructor.

The Rise of Degree-Completion Programs

There has been significant growth in adult degree-completion programs across the nation (Bergman, 2016; Hoyt & Allred, 2008; Taylor, 2000), and these programs are growing in relevance and acceptance. As employers call for workers with "21st century skills" (Gallup, 2013) such as knowledge construction, skilled communication, and real-world problem solving, increasing baccalaureate attainment rates is offered as a strategy for equipping the workforce; helping adult students complete bachelor's degrees may be one of the fastest and most effective ways to increase baccalaureate attainment (Bragg, Townsend, & Ruud, 2009). In many cases, students may be closer to completing a degree than they realize (Murphy, 2012).

The North Central Association's Higher Learning Commission Task Force on Adult Degree-Completion Programs (Taylor, 2000) defined an adult degree-completion program as a program designed to meet the needs of working adults who have earned 60 or more college credit hours in previous attempts and who are now seeking to obtain a baccalaureate degree following an extended absence from school. In most cases, the institution employs several strategies to enable students to finish their program within two years of continuous study: alternative class schedules, accelerated course offerings (e.g., 8-week sessions rather than a 16-week semester), student cohorts, and credit for prior learning experiences. These programs also often include options for distance (online) learning, evening courses, weekend class schedules, test-out programs (CLEP or DSST), and college credit for prior workplace learning (that may account for approximately 25% of the required credits).

An individual may be drawn to an adult degree-completion program for a variety of reasons: desiring to change careers, seeking advancement and needing additional credentials, moving into middle management in business or industry, aspiring to advance in public service (e.g., customs/border patrol, legal, or court systems), or intending to move into government positions (local, state, or federal). In some cases, professional organizations are now calling for more education and credentials than in the past. Most notably, this is a strong trend in nursing; whereas an Associate Degree Nurse (ADN/RN) was once the standard credential, organizations such as the Institute of Medicine (IOM, 2010) and the American Association of Colleges of Nursing (AACN, n.d.) are now strongly recommending that the "entry-to-practice" credential be a Bachelor of Science in Nursing (BSN). These shifts, changes, and transitions create opportunities that can be met by adult degree-completion programs, as they prepare individuals to assume increased responsibility in business, industry, healthcare, public sector occupations, and other related fields.

Adults who return to complete a degree make significant investments of time and money to pursue their goals, and these pursuits often require significant sacrifices, as you will read in later chapters. In an effort to provide guidelines to protect these learners from being taken advantage of, The Adult Higher Education Alliance (1998) outlined the following Principles of Good Practice for Alternative and External Degree Programs for Adults:

1. The program's mission statement complements the mission of the institution and reflects clearly defined educational philosophies, goals, and purposes.
2. Those working in alternative and external degree programs (e.g., faculty and academic professionals) are highly committed to serving adult learners and they are trained, capable and competent to reach, advise, counsel, and assist these students.
3. Both specific learning experiences and the overall curriculum are framed around clearly articulated learning outcomes; general student goals are incorporated into the development of these outcomes.
4. The program maintains established and rigorous academic standards while also seeking to provide diverse learning experiences that consider the characteristics and contexts of adult learners.

5. Comprehensive and specific learning outcomes are intentionally and rigorously assessed to determine student learning and achievement. (pp. 6–8)

These statements are taken from *Principles of Good Practice for Alternative and External Degree Programs for Adults*, published by the American Council on Education and the Alliance: An Association for Alternative Degree Programs for Adults (1998). The organizational name of the Alliance was changed to the Adult Higher Education Alliance in 1998.

The Value of Compelling Stories

Americans are working more hours and taking less vacation than they did 40 years ago, putting in an average of nearly four more weeks of work annually, with the average climbing from 43 weeks per year in 1980 to 46.8 weeks in 2015 (Pew Research Center, 2016). Consequently, Americans feel more overwhelmed, more stressed, and increasingly as though they are working more than people of the past generations. In this ever-connected digital age, the vast amount of information being produced is never ending. Both working adults and young children face a plethora of outlets for receiving, processing, synthesizing, and conceptualizing information at all hours of the day. The so-called "time-saving" devices connect people to the farthest corners of the planet while individuals tend to lose track of connection to each other and their own goals. At work, we face hundreds of emails every day and seemingly endless meetings in our on-demand lives. At home, we are just looking for a break from work by scanning social media or binge-watching television or other streaming services. How then are working adults supposed to reconnect to the academic setting to complete a degree they started many years ago?

This presents both an opportunity and challenge for higher education. The perceived value of a college degree has diminished, yet is still seen as a requirement to advance in the workforce. Conveying value in today's world has become more complicated, and higher education—just like every other business—struggles to establish a distinct value proposition for its existence. Consequently, institutions of higher education must do more to reconnect learners (Klein-Collins, 2018). It is no longer about seeking knowledge for knowledge's sake in education. It is imperative to demonstrate return on investment for the tuition dollars collected. Fortunately, higher education does not need to view this as an either/or situation. Administrators and educators must master the art of developing a narrative about postsecondary education that makes it easier for students to relate to who we are and what we do. This encourages greater engagement on an emotional level while showing that a college degree is also a good choice from a practical point of view. Higher education professionals must develop a common language that strives to convey commitment to quality academics, educational and workforce opportunity, affordability, personal growth, and advancement of social responsibility. Promoting these values reinforce reasons for our existence and will make all the difference when it comes to recruiting the next generation of learners.

While there are no quick fixes to the public perception of a college degree, the stories contained in this book lay out a compelling picture of the emotional and practical value of finishing a college degree. The human brain is wired to engage with and enjoy stories. In fact, research suggests that stories are 22 times more memorable than straight facts alone (Aaker, 2013). The stories of these and many other successful returning adults could set the stage for a mass migration back to academics for many others who have some college and no degree. While many adults return to increase their earning potential, many would not be doing so without the more emotional element of personal fulfillment and inspiration of their children and other family members. As demonstrated in the following chapters, the compelling nature of their reasons for return outweighs any statistics that could be presented about the workforce needs of the 21st century. There are common misconceptions about the individuals who have dropped out of American colleges and universities: that they failed out, that they couldn't hack it, or that they are poor and couldn't afford the tuition. Similarly, higher education professionals are spouting similar misconceptions about who is being recruited back to their institutions. The "same old story" about adult students is that they are likely to be first generation, come from lower socioeconomic backgrounds, have low grades, and need developmental education. While those perceptions may be supported in some ways, the real story about adults paints a more appreciative picture of their qualities. The real story about returning adults includes strong and long-term performance in the workforce, strong familial connections and support systems, large networks, a laundry list of success and accomplishments in life, a self-directed approach to learning, and an achievement orientation and independence in the learning environment. If we take a more appreciative view point of these working learners, they will engage at a much deeper and more profound level. In an age of constant movement, nothing is more important than reflection and planning to achieve a better quality of life through intentionality. Research and the stories that follow demonstrate the fact that content relevance and active learning environments, alongside all of the positive external influences, have a great impact on adults' ability to fit education into an otherwise busy life schedule.

The following stories are meant to help the academy, industry, and society as a whole understand the impact of adult learning programs that have helped transform these people's lives and the impact that new and innovative approaches to serving working learners can have on the 21st century workforce. The stories outlined in the following chapters demonstrate a new era in higher education where students are at the center of the educational exchange.

2

Providing for Family

Often, the reason for leaving college is the same reason for returning. Families are the source of great pride and joy in life. Also, they encompass the greatest portion of worry, anxiety, and fear about health and happiness. People want the best for their families, specifically for their children. Nearly 25% of all college students in the United States are parents (Cruse, Holtzman, Gault, Croom, & Polk, 2019; NCES, 2018). That is a dramatic growth in students who are parents from past generations. Consequently, students with children do not generally consider academics their first priority. They identify as a parent, worker, community member, and then maybe a student. This creates challenges when life intervenes during their academic pursuits. Student-parents are less likely to persist to graduation as a result of the competing influences that naturally occur in life. Their progression through freshman, sophomore, junior, and senior status is less linear and more varied through part-time, stop-in, and stop-out behavior. The stories in this chapter have a common thread that family provided the inspiration to manage the daunting task of pursuing education while being a parent. In this chapter, adult completers promote education as a solid

Unfinished Business, pages 15–26
Copyright © 2019 by Information Age Publishing
15

path to a bright future, which led them to reflect that commitment with their own academic achievement. This theme is woven throughout the fabric of this book. Adult students are driven to be the model for their families, and while they may have put their ambitions on the shelf while they raised young kids, the desire to complete a degree never disappeared.

Being the Example for a Young Family

Joe Trainer

Xavier University, Ohio

So…was it worth it to return and finish my degree? Without hesitation my answer is a resounding, "Yes!" The road to finishing my degree was quite challenging and filled with many obstacles. Overcoming these obstacles was certainly why it was so fulfilling on graduation day, but definitely not the only reason why I say that the effort was worth it.

Many things had happened in my life in the cross section of time from when I first began college, dropped out, started again, and ultimately finished. These were things like starting a career, getting married, becoming a father, being a father, getting divorced, being a single father, getting promoted, buying houses, getting remarried, and being a stepfather. All of these are significant obstacles for any adult to finish a degree, but they are also all great motivators.

The primary motivation for me to go back to school was a significant chip I had developed on my shoulder. I had entered a career where I could make a decent living without a degree as a supervisor for a trucking company. This was and is a job that has a very high turnover rate. The shifts were 12½ hours—day shifts for 3 months, and then night shifts for 3 months. The concrete docks where we walked all day were not temperature controlled. If it was 5 or 100 degrees outside, it was 5 or 100 degrees inside. From a management standpoint, it was challenging as my subordinates were often three times my age, unionized, and challenging me was their favorite form of entertainment. While the starting pay was great, the daily grind was either something you were going to concede to or something that was going to motivate you to better yourself. I chose the latter. I knew that where I found myself in my early 20s was not the best that I could do, and I was going to have to prove it. It took 14 more years of hard work to complete my degree, and it was worth every second.

It took 14 years to finish because I took quarters and years off. When I did take classes, I took them on the weekends, at a pace I could handle with my career and my family life. I also had to take some time off to save money for classes as my company could no longer offer tuition reimbursement after 9/11. During those 14 years, I found a number of things to keep me motivated. My friends were finishing college and starting their lives. I had student loans to pay back with no degree. I had a family and a profound desire to provide more for them. I had little eyes that looked up to me, and I felt like I was letting them down. One of the more painful motivators was when a family member told my father that I would never finish college. Later in my life, one of the most powerful motivators for me was fear. There were opportunities within my career field for promotion, and I was terrified that my lack of a degree would hold me back. I have worked very hard throughout my career, and I have been tapped as one of the future leaders of my organization. However, there were times that I was concerned that my superiors did not know that I had not finished my degree, so I did not mention that my Saturdays were filled with 8 hours of classes. When I was in my last year of classes, I put in for a significant promotion. My resume stated that I was within 8 credit hours of receiving my degree, and that I currently held a 3.85 GPA. The hiring manager for the position discussed this with me during the interview. While the hiring manager was someone I had known and worked with for several years, this was a chapter of my life that he did not know. He was extremely impressed at my persistence and my resolve to complete my degree in a way that is significantly harder than traditional students. I got the job, and it was a huge relief that my education status no longer seemed like a secret. I am happy to say that I excelled in this position, and I have been promoted again. The interview process for my current job was completely free from the anxiety of not having finished my degree.

As a grown man, I cannot articulate how hard it was not to cry when my 8-year-old daughter, my wife, and my father told me they were proud of me at the graduation ceremony. And while that day alone was amazing, the real payoff has been the doors it has opened for my career, my increased ability to provide for my family, and my effectiveness as a role model and educational ambassador to my children. I hope that my story will help motivate other adults with no or some college to take real steps toward going back to school. I was fortunate to have a lot of cheerleaders along the way. My father, my wife, and my daughter were all extremely supportive. I would, however, be remiss if I did not mention the support I received from my friend of nearly 30 years, Dr. Matt Bergman. Matt and I were friends in high school and roommates after he had finished his undergraduate degree and I had not. Matt continues to be a true friend and a wellspring of positive support. He and many other adult-friendly faculty and staff are truly suited to helping working adults fulfill their dreams of completing their degrees. I hope that sharing my journey can play a part in others choosing their own journey back to finish a degree.

Even Super Bowl Champions Can Come Back to Finish Degrees

Joe Jacoby

University of Louisville

I was born and raised in Louisville, Kentucky. I was originally committed to Vanderbilt University in Nashville, Tennessee, but I just could not commit to leaving Louisville since my father had passed away when I was in high school. You could say I was a mama's boy because I wanted to be there for my mom and the rest of my family. It was also appealing to have my family there for home games to support me during my football career. The University of Louisville (U of L) had recently built a new stadium, and it was an exciting time in the college's history. It all worked out well, and I had a wonderful time being a student athlete at the U of L. After my senior year, I had an opportunity to sign with the Washington Redskins as a free agent. It was 1981 and although I wasn't drafted, I worked hard and made the team. I was less than an academic year from completing my degree but I knew this was my shot to go after a career in the National Football League.

Shortly after starting my NFL career, I met a young lady who became my wife, and we were blessed with two wonderful daughters, Lauren and Jenna. During my career, I played for Joe Gibbs and a great number of outstanding teammates. Under the leadership of our coach, we went to four Super Bowls and won three of those appearances in 1983, 1988, and 1992. My fellow offensive linemen and I became known as the "Hogs" and still receive a lot of attention and affection for those great years in Redskins history. I was also fortunate to be selected to four consecutive Pro Bowl appearances from 1983–1986.

After football, I had more time for family and business. I started a car dealership and made a nice career after football in the car business. However, football was always a great love of my life so I returned to coaching because I thought life was too short. I decided to get back in the game. During that time, I felt the pull to consider finishing my degree, because I wanted to be a good mentor for those young men I was coaching. I was telling them a degree was important, but I didn't have one myself. Also, as a father, I wanted to show my girls that education was an important part of making themselves successful. So, I went back to prove something to myself, to be a good model for my daughters, and to show the young men I was coaching that I was willing the walk the walk when it came to education. All that led me back to the U of L. There was a competition between myself and my girls to see who could finish first. Unfortunately, I came up 6 months short of beating my eldest daughter to graduation. She still rubs it in, and she has gone on to make me proud with three degrees of her own. Her last degree was from Georgetown, and it has helped her become a nurse practitioner. My youngest daughter has also made me proud by receiving her master's degree from Johns Hopkins University.

It has been inspiring to see so many of my NFL teammates and other players I played against come back to finish their degrees as well. I was able to talk with several guys, and I said that if I can do it, I think they can step back in and make it to the finish line. It is certainly not easy, but it is worth the effort to reach that long held goal of having a degree. It has helped me as I have moved forward in my career into insurance. I am currently in classes for continuing education to maintain my license in the insurance industry. You never stop learning, and there is always something out there that intrigues you enough to stay active and engaged. My daughters have helped their mother and I through some of the changing technology over the years. I would have never guessed that I would be sitting in front of a computer, with an iPad and two iPhones for the multiple businesses that I am managing. It has become my new normal.

As an athlete, I have always enjoyed competing. So, this long career beyond football and finishing my degree during that process has provided a platform to keep winning. That competition is kind of bred into your overall normal operation as a human. Although the degree happened 30 years after the first time around, it means a lot to me and my family. It is just another competition I was able to jump into and win in the end. It was definitely interesting going from walking around campus as an 18-year-old to navigating the academic process online. From uploading, downloading, listening to podcasts and lectures, and learning the technology, I was learning more than just the relevant content from the online classes. It was an interesting process, and it prepared me well to adapt to these devices that sustain us in our workforce. It has certainly helped me adapt to the business that I work in today. I also gained experience connecting with people from other industries who shared very similar viewpoints. We would throw our two cents into the mix on discussion boards and were very in sync with one another, even though we came from different worlds. In one instance, I expected one particular classmate to be similar to my stature because we thought a lot alike in the classes we shared. Then, when we finally met in person, I was face to face with a guy who is 5'9", and the visual image of him is much different than I constructed online. I am sure he felt the same staring up at me because I am 6'7".

So, if you are on the sidelines, don't make assumptions that you are not able to finish what you started. There are so many opportunities and avenues that open up when you jump back in and engage in academics. You are able to grow personally and unlock a lot of knowledge that was waiting to be opened up. There are a lot of people who get to a certain age and they don't believe they can develop any more. I believe you develop and learn until you pass away. Being active with our minds can prevent issues later in life. I am active in the insurance field, with my faith, and now back into the automotive industry to make sure I stay agile and active. It keeps me from getting bored and makes life more fun overall. Make sure you continue winning life's competitions and challenge yourself to be a lifelong learner for the rest of your days.

A Promise Fulfilled

Amobi Okugo

Major League Soccer Player
University of California–Los Angeles and University of Louisville

When I first decided to pursue my dream of playing professional soccer after one season at UCLA, my parents were against it. They didn't sacrifice and work so hard as immigrants from Nigeria for their firstborn son to leave a prestigious school like UCLA after one quarter. "Waste a full ride scholarship?" "What if you break your leg?" It took some convincing, but because of the way my contract was structured and the promise to continue my education, I was able to sell my parents on the once-in-a-lifetime opportunity.

Personally, I always knew I wanted to return and finish my degree. Not just because I promised my parents I would, but because it's something no one can take away from you. My parents valued education all throughout my childhood and taught me that education can take you further than any soccer or basketball would. I knew, long-term, that my degree and education would help me ultimately in the long run. But the good thing about school is that it's not running away. You can do school at any age, unlike a sports career where you only have a set amount of prime years. Fortunately for me, I was able to play a sport I love and pursue my education at the same time.

I knew I could go back and finish my degree and balance the workload because I had experience doing it all my life. Many times, people feel overwhelmed, but I grew up going to school and playing two sports (soccer and basketball). I think in my senior year of high school, I missed school

3 months due to traveling for soccer and still graduated with above a 3.5 GPA. I knew that if I stayed disciplined, made sacrifices, and was good with my time management, I would be able to complete my degree. The biggest thing for me was understanding it was a marathon and not a sprint. I took two or three classes per semester and never overworked myself with my soccer schedule. Granted, I didn't have to worry about kids or family like other individuals that I was in class with; this also made me take advantage of the opportunity and complete my degree.

The one thing that happened that I didn't expect along the way was how much I grew by continuing my education. When I first enrolled after I left and was just in the mindset of completing it; toward the end of the process, when I was close to graduating, I found that I was passionate about other things outside of sports. Thanks to the classes and the major I chose, I was able to find other passions that motivated me. I didn't expect completing my degree would do that, but now I'm in the process of researching graduate schools. Continuing my education was probably one of the best decisions I made for myself and will forever be grateful for my family and everyone who helped me achieve that feat.

A Path to a Better Life

Latrivia Guinn

Western Governors University–Texas

I went to Job Corps at the age of 16. After a wide range of life events, I finally returned to school when I turned 30. I wanted to prove to myself and to those around me that I had what it took to complete my degree. Sometimes people look down on you and expect you to be the same as when you were a young, rebellious, naïve teenager. They begin to speak negativity into your life. I was bound and determined to show my children they can complete their dream if they go after it, despite the difficulties they may face. I wanted to instill perseverance into my children and other members of my family!

I thought I could make it to the finish line because my "why" was bigger than the challenges I faced. My children were watching me. I didn't want them to become a statistic so I had to be the model they deserved. The environment we lived in was not promoting education. All around through family, friends, and just our natural surroundings produced lots of felons, young teenage pregnancies, and drug addicts. I've always said I might live in poverty, but I am not of a poverty mindset! I knew I had to keep striving for more so that my kids could see what it takes to be successful and maintain the healthy mindset that gives you opportunity in life.

My degree holds a high value. It symbolizes courage, strength, perseverance, overcoming, resilience, freedom, and so much more. With my degree, I was able to move my family out of the environment we were in and into a healthier setting. I was able to show my children what perseverance looks like through my dedication to my studies. With a ton of hard work and persistence, I was able to land a six-figure position. My degree is not just about title or the job; it was my way out. It is and always will be security for me and my family. No one can ever take away the education I earned.

There were so many things that happened along the way that I didn't expect when I came back as an adult learner. I left my home church of 17 years after a major split, which was quite devastating, due to shunning from the community that was not warranted in any way. My 15-year-old daughter got pregnant while I was trying to do everything I could to prevent such things from happening. I was on the verge of a divorce. Then God led me to move to Texas without any preplanning or substantial foundation in place for me. We had never been to Texas, and within three weeks we packed up, leaving our home, friends and family, and many belongings behind. To put it plainly, we moved to pursue a better life and gain a fresh start. After all of these trials, I could have given up. I could have said it was too much. I chose to remember my "why" and keep moving. I thought about my children, my marriage, my own desires, and dreams.

So, my encouragement to those who have just started or thinking about returning but have all these negative thoughts that may prevent or stop you is to remember that you can do all things through Christ who strengthens you. I honestly don't know how I made it sometimes, but I kept going. Even when the grades don't reflect the best of your abilities, you must not quit. This too shall pass, and you will be so glad you overcame the challenges.

I look back and I can just cry because I think, God, you helped me to the finish line! The Lord helped me persist to complete my degree when it looked so dark. I'm on the other side of the challenges, and I plan to make a difference in somebody's life because they read about my struggle and they are watching me and saying, "If she did it, then I can do it!"

Musician and College Graduate

Jeffrey A. Crane

University of Louisville

In 1987, after graduating from high school, I immediately went into college at the U of L. I was cultivating a talent for music during my first semester of college and opportunity presented itself to make music full time, and I took it. The opportunity required me to leave school. As my musical career played out, I attended classes at U of L when possible. However, my priorities were always with music first. Therefore, my grades suffered. At that point in my life I was not willing to give college the full-time commitment it requires. As a result, I took my last class in the fall of 1991 and didn't return until the spring of 2008. Seventeen years later.

My music career ran its course throughout the 1990s. By the end of the 1990s, things had changed drastically for me and in my professional life. I had become a successful businessman, and had a prosperous career in sales. I married my wife, Andrea, in 2002 and had everything I could imagine, except a college education. I mentioned to my wife numerous times over a few years that I would like to finish my college degree (she holds two degrees from U of L, an undergraduate degree as well as a graduate degree). One day when I brought it up (as I had so many times before) she said, "If you had started back when you first started talking about it you would be done by now." With that gentle encouragement I enrolled in my first class at U of L for the first time in 17 years.

My first class back to school was History of Civilizations. I was very anxious to return to campus, and the experience was as awkward as I had expected it would be. I was, by far, the oldest student in class and going back to campus was time consuming. College campus schedule didn't coincide with my professional schedule. That made it difficult to take and complete a simple general education class.

Dr. Bergman and I had developed a relationship socially. We became good friends and business partners. When he became involved in the Workforce Leadership program at U of L, he knew the program was a perfect fit for me so he reached out to tell me about the program. After telling me about the prior learning assessment offered within the material make-up of the degree focus, I thought it sounded too good to be true. Here I am taking general education courses, struggling to find my way after returning to college from a 17-year hiatus. I was more than twice the age of typical campus students, and I had a work schedule that demanded more than 75% of my time. Given all the challenges, I was wrestling with the realization that completing my degree wasn't a realistic goal. Then Dr. Bergman called and basically laid out a path for me that made completing my degree not only realistic but set me on a fast track to fulfill my requirements for the Organization Leadership and Learning degree in matter of a few years.

My wife and I had our son, Seth, in August of 2009. My degree now didn't just fulfill personal satisfaction. I wanted my son to have parents who are both college graduates. The demand of being a father coupled with the demands of my job made it necessary to take semesters off throughout my educational journey. But Dr. Bergman never let me stray too far from the path of completion. He would always gently encourage me to enroll in a class when that time came around but respected the challenges I faced and the time constraints I was trying to manage. He never gave up on me to get back in there and I owe him for that! Prior learning assessment allowed me to qualify for 37 credit hours and saved me $20,000 in tuition. I recently learned that other students from around the country in other institutions don't have prior learning assessment offered to them as a means to obtain college level credits for professional experience they have acquired in their adult life.

There are two things that had an undeniable impact on me realizing my dream of being a college graduate. Without prior learning assessment and the steadfast encouragement from Dr. Bergman, I am positive that I would have given up and not gotten to the end. I believe that to be successful in today's environment you need someone cheering for you who wants "it" as much—if not more—than you want "it" for yourself. Having a mentor throughout your life for whatever goals you try to achieve is something that can't be valued. Dr. Bergman was that cheerleader for me as I know he is for all of his students. I have witnessed it. Go Cards!

Comeback Student Athlete of the Year: From the Majors to Graduation

Sean Green

University of Louisville

I was born and raised in Louisville. I went to Male High School and had a great career as a pitcher. After high school, I was fortunate to get drafted in the late rounds of the major league baseball draft. However, I knew I needed to grow and get stronger to have a good chance of making it to the majors. I was able to grow physically and mentally between the ages of 17–21 and looking back, I think that was the best decision to delay going into the minors at age 18. Since I grew up a U of L fan, I thought staying close to home was a good option. The program was on the rise, and I knew there would be an opportunity to play for a great coach and a great team. So, I enrolled and then attended U of L for 3 years before getting drafted. I was fortunate to travel the country playing the game I loved and getting paid to do it along the way.

I was drafted in the 12th round by the Colorado Rockies and I went to the Single-A team in Portland, Oregon for a short season. From there, I went to Virginia and played for 2 years, and then to California for a season and a half making my way up through the minor league system. I was traded to the Seattle Mariners in 2005, and by 2006 I got an opportunity to pitch in the major leagues. Through hard work and some good fortune, I was blessed with a 6-year career in the majors, finishing up my career in 2012 with the New York Mets.

I was lucky to leave the game in good health without any major injuries. As we started our family, having kids, and traveling for the long 162-game season became difficult. Getting the family settled and established in Louisville provided an opportunity to make an easier transition to life outside of baseball. No matter how long you play, how high you go, everyone has a similar kind of exit from the game. I knew that my time was coming to a close when a coach asked me if I had ever considered coaching.

Initially, after I left my junior year in college to pursue a major league baseball career, I always told myself I would finish my degree. Then, year after year, my career progressed as I worked my way up to the big leagues, and I kept putting it off. Later in my career, I started to see fellow players trying to figure out what was next after their time in baseball with and without their degrees. Some had to just find jobs that didn't require a degree and others pursued their degree after finishing. I felt compelled to find ways to finish my degree while I was still playing so that when I was done, I was prepared for the future and didn't have a big delay in that transition. I wanted to map out the future before I left the game.

It was important that I finished because of the mindset that I had as an athlete. I didn't have one of those careers where I didn't have to work after baseball. I knew I was going to have to transition into the workforce and find a career I enjoyed. I knew I had limited work experience and unless I was going to be a baseball coach, I needed a degree to open the doors to jobs I was really interested in. So, I knew having a degree as a 33-year-old with limited industry experience would be the right move. I found the online program at U of L that counted most of my previous credit, and I knew it was a good fit with my family commitments and the mental transition from baseball.

I knew I was going to be telling my kids that an education was important so how could I not finish my degree after completing 3 previous years and being so close to graduation. I told myself that it would be worth it not just for a paper but for the knowledge. The academic setting got my mind moving again and introduced concepts and topics that were very relevant to my career interests. I consider myself somewhat well read, but I wasn't really educating myself for future employment. When I first went to school in 1998, I didn't have a grand idea of what I wanted to do. But when I got out of baseball, I thought about a more immediate major that would help me transition. The Workforce Leadership program helped me learn concepts like project management that I am using on a daily basis in my current job. So, learning the business acumen and practical application of organizational development concepts made an immediate impact on my ability to do well in my new role. The content and the classmates I studied with were both welcome and surprising. Studying alongside other adults in the military helped me see the direct benefit the content would give us as we explored the transition to another life.

The experience as an adult learner is night and day. It was a little bit intimidating being in courses with impressive military students who were strong writers and impressive leaders. I felt a little behind the curve. But, my motivation to get through it and do a good job was much higher than when I was an 18-year-old the first time around. I went to school because everyone else was taking that route and it was just the thing to do. I wasn't focused on my major and didn't have the same perspective I did the second time around as an adult learner.

I didn't expect my prior experiences to help as much as they did. I was amazed at how much I was able to take from my experience in baseball and apply it to the content in my classes. There are a lot of lessons I learned along the way, and I was shocked that I was able to bring experiences from baseball and apply them to academics and research to practice in the workforce.

There is no doubt that it is a challenge getting back into the swing of academics as an adult. It wasn't an easy process, but it was very much worth the effort. It gave me a resurgence of confidence, and I felt competent to handle the workload while having kids and balancing a lot of life events going on. I would recommend going back to finish what you started to anyone who wanted to feel a renewed sense of confidence and inspiration to fulfill their ambitions in life and work.

3

Finding Personal Fulfilment

American colleges and universities often market the idea that their school can advance one's earning potential and lead to a better job. While this may be a byproduct of achieving a degree, often it is not the key reason adults want to return. There is a much greater emotional component that drives a desire for many adults who have some college and no degree. The sense of "unfinished business" lingers and never truly goes away no matter how many years have passed since the most recent attempt at attaining a college degree. Many studies have confirmed the fact that adults rank personal fulfillment as an overarching reason for their return to finish a degree. Many cite the fact that they did not end their academic careers the first time around because of bad grades. Rather, life had a way of intervening with job opportunity, birth of a child, military deployment, moving from one place to another, and a whole host of nonacademic reasons for stopping out of that original degree plan. Thankfully, higher education has made great strides in transfer articulation, convenient and flexible programing, and streamlined admissions practices to welcome adults back into the academic setting. Below are a set of stories that outline the

Unfinished Business, pages 27–53

central theme of personal fulfillment as the driving factor for the return to complete a degree.

From Oil Changes to Influence

David Beumer

University of Louisville

Finishing my degree was so much bigger than just a piece of paper or a stroll across a stage for me. Coming back to finish what I started was an internal battle for me: I had to prove to myself that I was more than what I was told growing up. I had so many teachers tell me it was okay that I wasn't "college material," and for a very long time I believed it. I was convinced that because I didn't test well that I couldn't be successful in college. After all, only my grandfather, who passed away when my father was eight, had ever attended college. He was in one of the first graduating classes of the University of Louisville Law School. It wasn't until I owned my own business and had to learn many new skills and learn them very quickly on my own that I realized I was by no means "slow"; I was different. I learned differently than most other students. I learned that I could not only learn but learn a lot and very quickly. I was not destined to be in a blue-collar role my entire life if I didn't choose to be. Not only was I capable, I was actually very good at learning and implementing.

After selling my first business, I was looking for my next opportunity. A close friend had mentioned the program at the University of Louisville that allowed adults to use life experience and time in business to complete a degree. I found that very interesting and attended an information session put on by the university about the degree program referred to as organizational development and leadership. Well, leadership interested me a lot, and I wasn't sure what organizational development even meant. I could relate to many of the experiences that were mentioned as helpful toward the degree—things like being in a leadership role regardless of your profession, raising your children, and just working hard in an industry. It was the first time I was introduced to the idea of experiential learning. This is the idea that you can reference things you have done and learn how to extract the lessons from those experiences. This idea excited me; it resonated with me; it was how I thought about problem solving and how I viewed things. It wasn't a test, and it wasn't a preset outcome. It was real life application on how you learn from the things going on around you. It was about past, present, and future that you could not just relate to but own. It was the ability to learn as fast as you wanted to. You could literally create your outcomes. You could go into an experience knowing that what you really wanted was to understand the steps along the way not just be concerned with the outcome. This develops the ability to extract the lesson and apply it faster the next time. Act, fail, document, learn, do it again. I literally have turned so many facets of my life into a big experiment. The things that held me back in the "normal" learning environment of being "taught to" have become my biggest assets. I consider myself an application guy, not a theory guy. I like to make things, break things, learn, and then build again. This program set me free to understand the impact of that and not judge it.

My degree holds a significant value in my life. This program has been a complete course change in my life. I believe that the pursuit of this degree may mean as much as the degree itself. Like many people in this program and programs like it, I am an adult. I have a family and a full-time job. I have been promoted several times during this journey, and my responsibilities have grown and so has my influence. The pursuit of this degree has allowed me to be an example to my four daughters. I have the opportunities to not just tell them school is important but to show them that it is. More importantly, to show them *why* school is important and why figuring out how you learn as an individual is important. I've shown them that learning differently usually means you likely have a very highly developed skill; you just must be committed to figuring out what that is. This will lead you to how you learn and how you best take in and deliver content and information as well as experiences. This later path has allowed me to gain influence in the workplace as individuals see my commitment level. The content in the program allowed me the opportunity to demonstrate how quickly I can learn content or a new idea then apply it. I believe this to be the key to success: One must learn and act, whether it be from failure, a book, a podcast, a blog, or a conversation. Extract the information, find the applicable lesson, apply it, and act. In my experience it really is that simple; if you're willing to try it, you are likely going to grow in depth of knowledge.

This lesson is what really caught me off guard. Once I figured out the magic formula, not only was I college material, but I was actually really talented and gifted in my skill sets. I had believed others' stories about me for so long that I almost missed out on what I was truly capable of in life. All of us are different; we have our own stories, lessons, and experiences that make us who we are. Through our lens on life, and by applying the structures taught in this program, I discovered the pathway to realize that while many of these stories are similar, they have different meaning when told through a different perspective. This has allowed me to question my perspective on so many things in life. It sounds absolutely crazy, but the mindset of questioning how I learned gave me the skill set to question my biases, judgments that were not my own, and beliefs that I was told to believe. I didn't expect for my major to completely change how I operate in relationships and how I communicate. I have discovered that how you communicate and the mindset you bring into a conversation and relationship have an impact on every aspect of your life.

I can't believe, sometimes, that I am a college graduate. I was the young man who was told I should drop out of high school and get my GED so I could go change oil for a living. Now, I hold a high-level leadership role in one of the most influential companies in Kentucky. I am building a successful consulting practice and have the opportunity to influence hundreds of lives a year. Most of all, this degree has allowed me the confidence to lead my work colleagues and my family, and to teach my children through experience, relationships, and challenges. This opportunity has not just impacted our financial future, it has changed the direction of my family's legacy.

I am grateful for this program, its instructors, and most of all for Dr. Matt Bergman for inspiring so many people to believe they can make it, and instilling the confidence to know they will finish and finish strong!

Grandma Goes to College

Jeanine Smith

Tennessee Technological University

My name is Jeanine Smith. I was an older student, returning to school after my children were grown. I have been married for 32 years to my husband, Walter. We have two beautiful daughters, Elizabeth and Rebecca, ages 31 and 27. We now have two grandsons, Isaac and Ian from our oldest daughter, and we are expecting another grandchild this fall from our youngest daughter. I returned to school after I was laid off from a position I held for 17 years as a purchase agent in 2013. It was extremely difficult to find a position making the same income, and I knew I needed to earn a degree. My husband is not able to work due to several medical issues, and a suitable income was mandatory. After working several full-time jobs trying to earn a decent wage, I enrolled at Roane State in Crossville in 2014 to earn my Associate of Science degree. I graduated magna cum laude in May 2016. Later that year, I enrolled at Tennessee Technological University (TTU) in the fall, and I recently graduated with a Bachelor of Science in Interdisciplinary Studies. Ironically, last year, I was asked to return to my former place of employment as I finished my degree. I am not sure what the future holds, but I have been thinking about obtaining my master's degree in psychology. It has not been an easy journey to work full-time and attend school full-time, but it has been extremely rewarding and I would not change this experience for anything.

I returned to school not only to earn a degree for a better income but to prove to myself that I could do it. Even with working full time and attending school full time, it was easier than I thought. My fears were bigger than my strengths. I would advise anyone to take the chance in life, to better themselves, to prove it to themselves. Going back to school instilled confidence, the ability to "look outside the box." I look at situations completely differently now; I see many solutions and disregard any form of negativity.

Just as Glorious 50 Years Later

Ronald Tiller

Tennessee Technological University

My name is Ronald Todd Tiller, the eldest of five boys born into a low-income, blue-collar family who resided in and around Memphis, Tennessee during my adolescence. With these thoughts in mind, education was not a priority within our household. My mother graduated from high school while my father did not complete junior high. Although my mom exhibited an appreciation for academics, my dad's mission for us was work, work, and more work.

During my early teen years, I was busy in and around a dairy barn or on a milk truck making home deliveries before I was off to school. Getting up at 2:30 a.m. and completing such chores made school attendance difficult—so much so that I graduated from high school as a 20-year-old. Graduating from high school at 20 years old was probably a good thing for me in that I was mature enough to appreciate all the encouragement from my principal, teachers, coaches, clergy, employer, and friends who pushed me into thinking about advanced education.

It was evident that I had no means to attend college, so I made the decision to enter the armed forces with intentions to utilize the G.I. Bill. That is exactly the path I followed. I listened very carefully to five close army acquaintances who had dropped out of college in order to fulfill their draft obligations and more so, as they clearly identified what they wanted to do with their lives beyond the military and returning to college. It is rewarding to acknowledge that two of the five became college PhD professors, one a dentist and the other two who were in fact dropouts from the college of my choice (Tennessee Tech University) also proved to be successful; one a CPA and the other a protestant minister. The last two and I reunited on the campus of Tennessee Tech and roomed together.

I am proud to say that this background afforded me the opportunity to attend college, and yet I departed the campus some four years later lacking 17 hours in order to graduate. I don't think my excuses for dropping out are as meaningful today as I thought they were at that time (no money, no job, too old, lack of study habits). My college agricultural background was very instrumental in my signing on with a major agricultural firm where I was employed for 30 successful years followed by an additional 15 productive years with a smaller firm.

During the 50-year span, the thought of not having a college degree was a very troublesome decision that amplified with time. There were many times when I had dreams and visions that would someway somehow lead me to a path for graduation and the uncanny opportunity did happen. Several factors made it possible for me to return to campus and bring the unfinished business to fruition May 8, 2010. First and foremost, I made up my mind to do it. The fact that I did not have a degree was always in the back of my mind and the bewilderment of the same over 50 years was a constant burden. The opportunity of being able to complete something I had started but failed to finish in 1957 was exciting, but not without anxiety. There is one more very important fact that helped finalize my final decision. Plain and simple I did not want to go to my grave without being a college graduate. I explained to my spouse that I wanted my obituary to state I did graduate from college. The terms "studied at" or "attended college" are disturbing to me because my belief is that a person did or did not graduate. Again, the term "studied at" implies a false sense of accomplishment or other ambiguous motives. This is not conjecture, because I used the terms over the years to satisfy a desire to let people know that I had been to college but the emptiness of not having a degree was humiliating.

My decision to return to college after 50 years was due to a gnawing consciousness that haunted me throughout my working career. It became a serious matter to me in the workforce as ownership of a degree was highly recognized in the advancement process. There was only one way to overcome the lack of a degree in the workplace and that was to outperform your peers in a tedious, positive, and heads-up attitude in the selection process. That was my approach and frame of mind that afforded me the opportunity to reach and enjoy several management positions throughout my working career that represented 45 years. Once I made up my mind to accept the challenge of returning to college and improving my GPA substantially, I had no fear of failing. To prove matters, my GPA for the final 17 hours in order to graduate was 3.98, versus the 2.0 I left behind in 1961.

Without question, my degree ranks very high right behind family and religion. Although I was able to reach a very respectable status of success without a degree, it was always a distinct void in my lifetime ambitions. After graduating from the College of Interdisciplinary Studies at TTU in Cookeville, Tennessee on May 8, 2010, I immediately became a different person in the areas of fulfillment, pride, and self-assurance. I was fortunate to manage and lead many employees with various degrees, include master's degrees, all the while feeling a lack of value. All and any such thoughts suddenly disappeared after graduation. It would be difficult to express these feelings had I not experienced the very facts as stated. Thus, these comments are with humility and honesty. During my working years, I always thought it would be an honor to return to the campus and express my views on how a young person might enter the workplace and progress within a corporation. After a couple of suggestions, my offers were never accepted. However, after my graduation, it was gratifying to acknowledge the amount of interest and invitations received to lecture several groups and present my route to graduation. The recognition was appreciated, but more importantly, I was honored to be able to give back to such a great institution. Another great honor was being selected as part of a committee in pursuit of hiring the first dean of the College of Interdisciplinary Studies at TTU. An outstanding experience! Another great honor bestowed on my behalf was being selected as 2011 TTU Outstanding Alumnus at Tennessee Tech University by TTU's College of Interdisciplinary Studies.

I know for a fact that if individuals really want to complete the commitment, it can be done. For a person to have to overcome the obstacles that I experienced from a dysfunctional background, I would be hard pressed to think it cannot be done. Beyond that, it should be done. In closing, I would like to say it took living the life of a nongraduate in order to really appreciate the features of a degree, and they are numerous. I steadfastly agree that without the college experience, my choices for survival and success in life would go wanting.

Internationally Acclaimed Musician to College Graduate

Nappy Roots
Brian B. K. "Buffalo Stille" Scott
University of Louisville

It had been more than 15 years since I turned in a homework assignment. I was going to another university studying for a degree in business when my college career was cut short due to the mounting obligations of another career, this one being music. My talent for writing songs and my passion for music earned me a record deal at age 18 during my second semester in college.

Recording and touring became more frequent, and I just did not have the time to do both. So, I elected to follow my dreams and forfeited my initial attempt at getting my college degree. Seven albums, thousands of tour dates, millions of record sales, and countless accolades—including two Grammy nominations—and a holiday named after my group in my hometown, I decided that I wanted to finish school. Going back to get my degree was a frightening notion for a while until my wife told me about this degree program at the University of Louisville called organizational leadership. As I did more and more research on this major, I felt it was a perfect fit for me as I am beginning to run my own company right now. I talked with a student advisor, and we were able to transfer 60 hours from my previous stint in college, and I only needed to take one cultural diversity class at Louisville before I was eligible to start major courses.

Once I got into the major courses, I was hooked and received crystal clear confirmation that organizational leadership was right for me. I've learned a great deal about myself through the self-assignments in the textbooks and through working with fellow classmates as well. We all challenge each other when it comes to the assignments, and the support is second to none among students and staff alike.

There are three things that drive me to be a successful adult learner. The first comes from a promise I made to my mother over a decade and a half ago, which she so conveniently reminded me of after I expressed an interest in going back to school. When I left the first time to pursue music, I always told her that one day I would go back and finish. The second motivating factor was my student advisor at Louisville. She advised against me taking four classes, 16 hours, my first semester back after 15 years and said most adults like to ease their way back into college. I registered for the classes anyway and ended up with a 3.75 GPA to kick off my journey in adult learning. No disrespect to my advisor, but I'm not most adults. The final factor that keeps me focused is something a professor said, which was to visualize myself walking across that stage as a University of Louisville graduate and to always approach each class with that vision in mind.

Earning a college degree allowed me to check off this box that has been empty for so many years. I feel it has helped me take that next leap and give me the credibility I need in order to achieve the success I want in life. I've built a platform that allows me to reach many people, and I have also created a network of powerful and influential individuals in the process. My degree in the field of leadership will continue to unlock all the potential and possibilities that are found within my strengths.

It is hard to believe, but I took classes while on tour, ran a clothing business, consulted for two other companies, and kept raising my family. I would have to say that the most unexpected thing that has happened to me was being asked to write a compelling narrative for this book by one of my professors. I did not see this coming, so I hope this compels any reader who may be on the fence about returning to college after some time off to make the decision to go for it. I wish someone would have offered this major years ago. Just believe me when I say that if I can do it, you can too!

This VP Finished What He Started in 1987

Norris Hamilton

University of Louisville

My name is Norris Hamilton, and I am the youngest of seven children and grew up in a single-parent home. We did not have much, but I never wanted for anything. I graduated high school in June of 1987. I knew I wanted to attend college and knew I would be a first-generation college attendee for my family. I started college in August of 1987 and did well and was on track to finish my bachelor's degree in the winter of 1991 or spring of 1992. However, in 1990 life happened, and I was faced with needing to work full time and could not balance college and full-time work. Fast forward 20 years later, fall of 2010, I enrolled at the University of Louisville. Here it is: I am now 41 years old and going back to school because I was bound and determined to complete that bachelor's degree I started some 23 years earlier.

Having to quit school in 1990 left me devastated, but I knew it would be my lifelong goal to finish what I started. The reason this was so important to me was because I wanted to defy all the stereotypes about poor Black kids not being college material or not being able to graduate if they did start. Don't get me wrong, there were many days along my journey when I thought, "This is too much!" The faculty and staff in the College of Education were very supportive and encouraging. I had a great career. I had been with the same company for 10 years and had reached the level of vice president. I earned this success without a degree, so why was I so determined to finish? I had not been treated less than because I didn't have a degree; I was not told I needed my degree to continue my career. However, it always bothered me. It was this personal bother and determination that fueled me to complete my degree.

I graduated with honors in 2014, and I received the Malcolm S. Knowles Award for my work as an adult learner. I was 45 years old when I finally walked across a stage to receive my college degree. The value and importance of having my degree is priceless; no one can ever take it away from me. The blood, sweat, and tears I put into this personal achievement means more to me than anything else I have ever done in my now 48 years on this great planet. I have a sense of completion. It gives me confidence when I sit around the table with my colleagues knowing what I accomplished and the journey I had to take to get it done.

When I reflect today, I am still amazed by the support I received from family and friends, but more importantly the support from my boss and my work family. Working full-time in a senior leadership role, taking evening classes as well as online classes, and being the best leader and student I could be was the highlight of this journey. I cannot say enough about my college degree journey. If I had to do it all over again, I would certainly do so. Earning your degree should be about you and only you. Don't let anyone tell you what you can or cannot do. Make a promise to yourself that if you want your degree, you can and will get it!

What Happens to a Dream Deferred?

Jo Ann Herron

Rockhurst University

I'll start by paraphrasing the Langston Hughes poem: "What happens to a dream deferred? Does it dry up, like a raisin in the sun? Or fester like a sore and then run, maybe it just sags like a heavy load. Or does it explode?" Just a year ago, I had no idea that I would be returning to Rockhurst University, the college of my choice. A dream deferred but one that did explode. My story begins with one ordinary day while working at Thomas Roque YMCA Headstart Program in Kansas City, Missouri. I spotted a brochure that stated, "If you are an adult and have at least twenty-one (21) credit hours of college you could apply for a KC Scholars Scholarship." I immediately looked through all of the schools listed, and when I saw Rockhurst University, I thought, "Oh my God, is it possible that I could return to Rockhurst?" The desire to obtain my college degree was buried deep within my heart, but I could instantly feel it coming alive and whispering a soft yes, then a louder yes, you can do it!

I had previously attended Rockhurst while working at AT&T in the Engineering Department in the early 1980s. I was experiencing problems understanding telecommunications circuit provisioning design, which is an electrical engineering discipline. My background in math was limited. We had training class after training class, and I still didn't fully understand the transmit and receive levels required in provisioning a circuit. I didn't understand if an echo suppressor, amplifier, or other equipment should be added. So, I decided to take several philosophy courses at Rockhurst. I don't know why I chose philosophy, but those classes helped me to think at a deeper level, and I began to understand circuit design. I was later promoted to management and relocated to AT&T Engineering Headquarters in Bedminster, New Jersey. In Bedminster, I was responsible for writing AT&T Provisioning Methods and Procedures for the United States, Virgin Islands, and Puerto Rico. As a manager, my title was process engineer. I interfaced with all regional managers in Atlanta, Chicago, Pleasanton (California), Walnut Creek (California), and Cincinnati. While working in Bedminster, I was introduced to statistical thinking, Six Sigma, Lean Quality Process Management, project management, and later process flow chart design. After all the experience of traveling, coordinating across the country end-to-end circuit design, and working with diverse groups of people on all levels including mathematicians and scientists from Bell Laboratories in Holmdel and Cherry Hill (New Jersey), I returned to Kansas City and worked in Operations, followed by another relocation from AT&T to Atlanta. I decided to retire from AT&T in Atlanta and returned to Kansas City. I then went to work as a process engineering specialist II at Sprint utilizing the same skills applied at AT&T until 2009 when I was laid off, but I was fortunate to receive retirement after working there 10 years.

I contribute all of my technology experiences mentioned above to the philosophy classes that I took at Rockhurst years ago. And now at this time in my life, thanks to KC Scholars and partners KC Degrees, I have the opportunity to return to Rockhurst and complete my degree in religious studies and theology. Many years ago I had read the story of Ignatius Loyola, founder of the Jesuit Order, whose motto was to "Find God in Everything." I believe that's exactly what I have tried to do all my life—in my work, in my education, volunteering in corrections, social justice activity with the Johnson County NAACP, and in the community mission work of Palestine Missionary Baptist Church.

One might ask the question, "Why was it worth it to return and finish your degree?" My answer would be that it was a dream deferred, and it was hidden in my heart since 1960. I was number two out of 365 graduating seniors in my class but after high school graduation, I got married and had a family. I could not go to college at that time, so it was delayed in my heart but never forgotten. When I saw that KC Scholars brochure, 57 years later, I knew I still wanted to get my degree. While working at AT&T, I took as many college classes as I could, but it was not easy working a technical job and going to school. After being promoted to management and traveling, I felt college was over for me. Finishing college was a goal set long ago in my life, and I always knew if opportunity presented itself, I would gladly jump on it. I was raised to go to college; I had so many mentors who had a great impact in my life at an early age. Those people were not forgotten and nor was my dream of obtaining a degree.

I always felt that I could get a college degree because I wanted it so bad. It was something I had missed at an early age, and I knew if given the opportunity I would make it happen. I have an excellent work ethic and always believe that if you work hard you can accomplish your goal. Yes, I was nervous about applying for the scholarship but my KC Scholar/KC degree counselor walked me through each step and informed me of everything I needed to know. We met at different libraries on Saturday to discuss next step plans. After I enrolled in school, there have been times I said this is too hard being isolated from my friends or giving up a weekend trip to the lake. But I have discovered that the desire in my heart to complete my education was greater than any of these things that would hinder me. I talked to my KC Scholar/KC degree counselor about my feelings: When it came to taking tests, I felt like I could not retain what I had read. He recommended that I speak with a Rockhurst counselor. I did, and this was my turning point. She shared with me a learning pyramid and it had three levels. She explained the bottom level was confidence, the next level was application, and the top was learning. I was at the bottom; my confidence was weak. But I had a desire to reach the top. These levels helped me to understand the Ralph Waldo Emerson quote: "That which we persist in doing becomes easier to do. Not that the nature of the thing has changed but that our power to do has increased."

I will be a junior next semester and looking forward to becoming a senior, all because of KC Scholars and their commitment to education. The education I am receiving at Rockhurst would not be financially possible for me without KC Scholars support. My goal is to major in religious studies and theology. I will use my education to continue reaching out to those incarcerated and other 501(c)(3) programs that help the poor and uneducated. The value that this degree will hold in my life is one that is more precious than gold or silver or any other earthly treasure. The reason is that it comes straight from the heart and that is love. Love for knowledge and understanding, and wisdom to use it as God has intended for me, is priceless. There is a Nigerian word *Iyanu-Oluwa* which means "Miracle of God." The Hebrew word is *Nah-Sha*, meaning "Miracle of God." The Arabic is *Iyanu* translated as "Miracle of the Lord." KC Scholars is a "Miracle of

God" to me, and I am so grateful to be a recipient. I am attaining my heart's desire, and so many others like me would not be able to attend college, if it were not for their support. They are dream catchers; they caught mine, let them catch your dream.

Showing Myself and Others It Can Be Done

Althea Jackson

University of Louisville

For as long as I can remember, I wanted to pursue my college degree. Although I attended the University of Louisville straight out of high school, life happened, and I did not complete the program. However, that yearning to get a degree never left. My "a-ha" moment happened about 10 years ago. I was on a job that I loved, but I understood that not having a college degree would make it hard for me to replace my job if I ever lost it. Additionally, I was attending a church where my pastor at the time had long encouraged the congregation to make higher education a priority. This reminded me that education is not just about my own career security. It is also a way that I can sharpen my talents to benefit my church, community, and world around me. As a person of faith, it was important for me to live a life pleasing to God and to do everything within my control to better myself. So, after much prayer, and talking with family and friends who had returned to school, and my very supportive supervisor, I made the decision to go back to college.

The prospect of returning to school after 28 years, at age 45, was very terrifying for me; but I did it. That little bit of fear was a wake-up call for me. I spent 2 years at Jefferson Community Technical College before transferring to the University of Louisville's organizational leadership and learning (OLL) program where I earned my bachelor of science. I knew it was not going to be easy to head to class at the end of a busy work day and to devote my weekends to my studies. Although sometimes I struggled a little and weekends became a time to double-down on schoolwork to make sure I kept up, I did it!

Did I say it wasn't easy? I was determined to finish! And while my job offered a tuition reimbursement program, it didn't cover all the costs. Therefore, while attending community college, as well as the University of Louisville, I worked a full-time day job as well as a part-time evening job to make sure I did not graduate with school debt. During this time, I also took time to serve as a volunteer at an elementary school where I interacted with children who may also, someday, face struggles in finishing their education.

My goal was to be an example of why they should stick with it—and what you can do when you put your mind to it.

Finishing the OLL program was a dream come true for me. It was an opportunity for me to actually complete something that I started. Although, I retired 3 months after obtaining my BS degree, I have now returned to the workforce as a director and am able to pull from the lessons learned that I received as an adult learner.

Initially, my focus for all this was job security and career advancement. Although my studies made me a smarter, more talented employee, I realized that my focus on graduating became less about my career and more about setting an ambitious goal and achieving that goal and showing others that it can be done. The networking opportunities with other adult learners and the support from faculty and staff at the university were immeasurable; the time and energy spent to accomplish my goals were all valuable. Additionally, my family, friends, church, and employer—and the support I received from them—were all part of a college-going culture that I have experienced in Louisville, Kentucky.

Pursuit of higher education is not easy, but it is definitely worth it.

Turning Nagging Regret into Triumph

Melissa B. McGarry

University of Louisville

I can honestly say that graduating from the University of Louisville, walking across that stage with my family as witness, was one of the happiest days of my life. Yes, I got married and had a family, and those were good days too. But, not earning a bachelor's degree was a huge regret that I seized the opportunity to make right. You don't always get that chance in life. I, along with every adult student I met along the way, had circumstances that were a barrier to finishing their degree. For me, it was financial, along with the lack of support. When I was young, I did not really understand the purpose or benefits of having a degree. I grew up with blue-collar parents in a blue-collar neighborhood. To them, landing a good paying factory job ensured your financial security.

Everyone has a story full of what were, for them, very real obstacles at that time. One girl I met quit school and came home because she didn't get along with her roommate. Whatever the reasons, those reasons were in the past, and the missed or unavailable opportunities were very much a real part of my present. Over the years, not finishing was a nagging issue. I would periodically investigate returning to college. But, I needed so many classes, and with a life full of responsibilities, a degree just felt unattainable. Then I discovered that there were programs that awarded credit for experiential learning. Although I still needed many general education classes, this brought the timeframe into something I felt was more manageable.

When I first started back, I was very nervous. I questioned whether I could even do it. I decided to tackle my list of general requirements first before I began the major classes. Big mistake. I ended up in on-campus lecture halls with freshman and was older than all the students and sometimes the teacher. But, I was committed, and as I tackled each project or test, my confidence grew. I was not the best student when I was young, but I believe adults learn easier. Our thoughts are more organized, and we have life experience to attach to theories and concepts.

General education requirements finished, I finally walked into the intro class of the OLL program. My first thought was, "Well, here are my people." I was so happy to have made it that far and more importantly, to be around others like me. It was these fellow adult learners, or "comebackers," that would become my project partners, supporters, and friends. I witnessed first-hand that older generations have a huge advantage over millennials. Growing up without technology, we know how to network and carry on conversations. Adult students are more likely to support each other and share information. If I were doing it over, I would certainly seek out "my people" much sooner and team up with some of them to tackle those early classes.

Since earning a degree, several things have changed in my life. I do not have that nagging regret of not finishing or that something was missing. Also, after graduation, I secured a job as an associate publisher for a business magazine. While I had the experience for this position, having a degree gives me the confidence to work in an environment where everyone is college educated. Although it may have been a non-issue for my colleagues, in my mind, it would have been a huge issue.

Also, having a degree opens doors to career paths that would have not been possible before. Although there are many positions that I could have certainly done prior to having a degree, if the job description requires one and you do not have it, then you do not have the minimum qualifications to even apply. For these jobs, a degree is the minimum threshold of knowledge and proves that you can complete a goal. It's the first level of separation in job applicants. There are thousands of jobs out there like that—jobs that I hadn't even considered. For instance, I saw a posting for a job coach for the Mayor's Summer Works program here in Louisville. This is a program that employs teenagers for the summer and oversees their experience. It was a position that I was extremely excited to apply for, and because I had a degree, I was able to. In the end, I worked with at-risk youth over that summer and enjoyed every minute of it.

It took me 4 years of taking classes part time, both seated and online, to finish. Along the way, my confidence grew, and I gained knowledge in a variety of areas that I use today. I made friends and connections and broadened my career opportunities in ways that I could not have foreseen. Although, admittedly there were certainly times when I'd ask, "Why did I get myself into this?" there were many more times when I'd think, "Wow, this is finally going to happen!"

Our lives are in a constant state of change. Everything in life is either improving or deteriorating (depending on your actions), but things are unquestionably not staying the same. This can be applied personally to relationships, health, abilities, or career. The way I see it, those 4 years would have passed whether I was taking classes part time or not. In the end, I am glad I acted to improve, and I do not have a single regret. I used to hate the dreaded question of "Where did you go to college?" Although, once you get older you don't really get that as often, but when I do I am proud to say, "The University of Louisville." And, I always add "Class of 2015" to that answer. I am not embarrassed that it took me so long, but I am proud that I went back as an adult and finished what I started.

Dropping the Emotional Baggage and Building Self Confidence

Cindy Wentworth

University of Louisville

For most people the traditional way of getting a degree is to graduate from high school and attend college. A new freshman will take advantage of the college life to learn about themselves and establish what they want to be when they finally get a degree. However, many people do not follow this traditional path. By getting my degree so late in life, my educational experience was anything but traditional. I am a 60-year-old woman who just received her college degree. Although I wish I had received my degree sooner, life had different plans for me.

When I graduated from high school, I was a teenage bride and a new mother. My husband worked for my father who was self-employed as a contractor. It was essential for me to go to work to help pay the bills and put food on the table. We were a young struggling family. Without having any work experience and only a high school education, my career options were limited. My mother worked at the University of Louisville, so having a reference from someone that had been at the university for many years was definitely a plus. I was fortunate as I was offered a position with the university.

My first job at the university was a file clerk, but I knew very soon that I wanted to do more. The university offered a tuition remission program for employees so I signed up to take a night class. My husband and I only had one car, so he would have to pick up our daughter from day care and then pick me up after class. I really enjoyed going back to school and experiencing a part of college life. It was not long after I started back into school that my husband was hired as a police officer. This was a great career opportunity for him but a major adjustment for our family. A police officer's schedule is not a routine 8:00 a.m. to 5:00 p.m. schedule, so it prevented me from continuing my education. I was the primary parent with transportation and care for our daughter. School came to a halt.

In my heart, I knew I would someday get back to school. Working in an educational institution and not having a degree was difficult, because I always felt a bit inferior to my colleagues who had degrees. This held me back. Not only did it prevent me from being promoted, it caused low self-esteem and confidence for not accomplishing a goal that I had set for myself. This only made me work harder and push myself to fulfill my dream of getting my degree. Throughout the years, I continued taking general education courses when I could fit them in my schedule. In 2014, I was given an opportunity of a lifetime. I was offered a position that I would never have perceived to be in my future. This opportunity pushed me to return to school and make it a priority. I enrolled in the Workforce Leadership Program at the University of Louisville. I was able to take my years of work experience and use it to earn credit hours. This program offered many of the classes online, which provided me the opportunity to do class work at home.

The scariest part of going back to school was making the decision to do it. Once I did that, I knew I was going to go all the way. I have been asked if it was worth it to return and finish my degree especially so late in my life. My answer is, "Absolutely." To overcome a fear of failure and to build self-confidence is huge in any circumstances. Carrying this emotional baggage for so long is something I am glad is finally gone. I could not have done this without the support from my family and colleagues. My mother was so proud of me for going back to school, as I was a first-generation graduate. It was her dream for me to get my degree. I received my degree just weeks before her passing. Seeing the look on her face when I had my cap and gown on was worth it all. No one should ever underestimate the value of a degree.

It is life changing, and it has personal effects on a person in so many ways that only that individual can understand and appreciate. As I look back, I reflect on why I waited so long and wondering what would have been different. However, in the end all that matters is that I did it, and I know that getting my degree was one of the best things I ever did for myself.

Finding a Lost Treasure

Steve Shaw

Boy Scouts of America
University of Louisville

I have always wanted to go back to school to finish my degree, but life got in the way. My freshman year, more than 30 years ago, my grades were not the greatest. One thing that I was not told before attending college was the obstacles of college life, and as a young man would I have listened anyway? When you're not in college, you need to go to work. Then came marriage and children, and I never found my way back until 30 years later. After working minimal jobs and getting turned down for promotions one after another, I found myself realizing that I had to do something different. It was worth it to return and finish my degree, because it afforded me more opportunities and a chance to have a career instead of a job.

One of the reasons it was worth it to return to college to finish my degree was it made me feel confident about the next stages in my life based on my experiences and education that I have obtained during my journey. My aspirations in life required a college degree for me to be able to advance within certain areas of a company. Whenever I applied for a lucrative position, the description required that I have a degree; often when you go on a job interview, one of the first questions that is asked, if it's not already on your resume, is what schooling have you had or do you plan to continue your education.

I told myself over the years that I wanted to complete my college degree and finish what I started. For me it's personal, because now I can say I was able to reach a goal that I have wanted to accomplish all my adult life. I learned so much about myself. I learned that I was an extrovert and that I feed off others. I would be so excited about the interactions with my classmates and my teachers. I learned what time of the day I retained the most information. I learned how to manage my time and started keeping a planner to keep track of everything I had to do in a day. Having my degree gives me the confidence to go out and be competitive with others that have a degree. It's a game changer. I felt I could do it because of my lifelong learning experiences, the support that I had from family and friends, and the burning desire to be able to say, "I'm a college graduate" means the world to me. I also wanted to be the first in my family to receive a bachelor's degree. I wanted to increase my income and lifestyle as well as provide for my family. I thought I could do it because I believe in myself and my capabilities. There were times when I was at work and thought, "There has to be something better than this. One day, I will get my degree and will improve my financial situation." Once I went back to school, I started to have doubt, but with the support of my wife I began to visualize myself walking to the stage to get my diploma. That was the breakthrough for me.

There is no dollar amount that I could give that would explain the value my degree holds for me. I can't put a price on it, but it is more valuable than money. It gave me the confidence to pursue my goals. It was an eye opener for learning. It's like finding a lost treasure: Now that I have found it, I can conquer the world. I feel more knowledgeable about a variety of subjects from psychology to astronomy and everything in between. I feel that if I had received it 30 years ago, it would not have meant as much as it does now. I understand what having the degree can do for the betterment of my lifestyle and my family. I can live comfortably without working several jobs. After receiving my degree, I can have a career instead of just having a job to make ends meet.

By getting a degree this late in life, I hold it in high esteem, as one of the most important things that I have received, next to God and family. It's something that no one can take away from me. If I can say anything about my teachers at the University of Louisville, they gave me the tools, motivation, and direction to succeed. I didn't expect the long nights, the summer school, and the online classes. I have learned more in a four-year period than I have learned in my whole life. I did not expect the mental strength that it provided me or the man that I have become. I didn't exactly expect my family to be as excited for me as they are and the pride that they feel from my achievement. I had never taken an online class, and I feared the unknown. I felt I did better in a classroom setting. I found that online classes were not as difficult as I thought they would be. It gave me the opportunity to overcome my fear. Taking online classes allowed me to be in other places and be able to prepare assignments when I had time and not be in a certain location, at a certain time, on a certain day of the week.

I realized that I needed time for studying for quizzes, homework assignments, which included reading and writing as well as any special projects that were assigned. This took more than a couple of hours a day; there were times when I stayed up all night to complete a project or study for a quiz or test. I developed better study habits. I learned that for me to retain the information, I did better at night. At that time of the day, I didn't have as many distractions. It took me a couple of times reading the material to ensure that I retained it. I also took notes as I read to help with retention.

I didn't expect how difficult it would be to balance work, school, and personal life. It affected my work because when I was at work, I was thinking about what I needed to do for school or that I had to leave work on time to get to class. It affected my personal life because I was not able to have date nights or go on trips with my family. When I had online classes instead of enjoying my vacation, I was studying or preparing an assignment for summer school. I did not expect school to be fun. My instructors from the University of Louisville were engaging; they wanted me to learn and make sure that I was successful. It wasn't just me that they made feel that way; they were engaging with all their students. They were always willing to go the extra mile to help their students to pass the class. If I can say anything about my teachers at the University of Louisville, they gave me the tools, motivation, and direction to succeed.

By me contacting my teachers before the class started, to let them know my expectations for their class and to find out as much as I could about what they expected of me, they realized I was taking the initiative and was taking control of my learning experience. Since my classes encouraged the group/team work, I was able to develop team-building skills and understand diversity and inclusion. We assisted each other with assignments and I bonded with my classmates. I gained relationships that I will have for a lifetime. I could call them at any time and get assistance.

Now that school is over, I never thought that I would miss it. However, I can say that I have missed my fellow classmates, my teachers, and being in a learning environment. This is something I thought I would never say while I was going through the process. I expected to graduate, but I did not expect to graduate with a 3.9 GPA or to be a member of an honor society and be recognized for my accomplishment.

Fulfilling the Promise

Amy Lear

University of Louisville

Many years ago, I made a promise to myself that I would achieve my goal of graduating from college with my bachelor's degree, but life happened and all did not go exactly as I had planned. I grew up in your classic 1970s family. My dad graduated high school, being the first to graduate from high school in his family. After high school he left for the army and married my sweet momma once he returned home. He began his career sweeping the floors of a factory. He worked hard and moved from floor sweeper to management and instilled a strong work ethic in our family home. My mom was also the first to achieve a high school diploma in her family; she graduated from high school and a few months later married dad. Two years later they started their family giving birth to a baby girl, my older sister and only sibling.

We grew up in what I thought I was your typical family household, a working middle-class family with rules and expectations. My sister followed the pattern of graduating from high school, then went on to college and finished her degree. I, on the other hand, didn't follow the pattern. I fell in love with my high school sweetheart. We were engaged my senior year of high school. I graduated May of 1989, at the same time my fiancée was leaving for the Navy. We planned to get married after he completed his 3-year commitment, and I would work on my college degree while he was away.

Being in love and serving in the Navy was not always the easiest on the heart! After high school graduation, I registered for classes at the University of Louisville. My goal was to obtain my teaching degree. My goal was not always my top priority, however. I traveled to see my fiancé in California, South Carolina, and West Virginia, whenever possible, while he wasn't at sea. My schoolwork was never a priority at this point in my life, and I just got by in college.

We married in December of 1990 and my husband left for another tour at sea, when our country was in the middle of the Desert Storm War. As one can imagine, there was a lot of unease during this time. I was not focused on my classwork and did not put forth the effort to succeed in college at this time. I continued to take courses and took a full-time job to prepare for my husband's coming home and starting our life together. He returned home, and at the time we made the decision to focus on him returning to school, which would allow us financial help with the G.I. Bill. Eventually, I did not register for any classes and just focused on working and starting our family. In 1994, we welcomed our first child, Kevin, and in 2002 we completed our family with our youngest, Kelsey.

Fast forward to 2008. We were attending our son's high school open house, and during the open house, I had the realization hit me that in four quick years, I was going to expect my son to register for college and pursue his college degree, and I had not completed the same myself. My husband had; we worked hard to ensure he completed his degree but never really visited the subject of me going back to school to complete my degree. I was working at a wonderful company and had a job that I loved, so the thought of going back was never pressing until that evening. After we returned home, I had a discussion with my husband about my thoughts and desires to go back to school to complete the degree that I had always promised myself would happen. As always, he was fully supportive and within the week I had made the phone call to setup an advisement appointment.

My thought was to go back to obtain a language degree. My employee offered tuition reimbursement, so obtaining a language degree seemed logical, since I supported the west coast and had several interactions where English was not the most common spoken language. I met with the advisor, explained where I was in my career and my goal of obtaining my degree and obtaining it for me—not necessarily for changing my career but obtaining my degree to help me advance with my current employer. After our brief discussion, the advisor thought she had a better opportunity for me with a different degree program. She walked me over to Dr. Bergman's office and explained my situation to him. Approximately 30 minutes later I was enrolled in my first College of Education and Human Development course.

This course helped me build a portfolio to obtain additional college credits based on my work history. These were college credits I would not have to pay for, and I would have a whole semester to help me build my portfolio to obtain the additional credits. I was amazed by the program and how the program was geared toward adults like me with a family, with a work history, with prior college courses to help me utilize all of this experience to obtain my promise to myself of completing my degree. I was also amazed at the convenience of going back to school in 2009 compared to the 1990s. I was able to attend classes online, and each Saturday while my daughter attended her 4-hour gymnastics class I was able to go to the library and complete my weekly college class work.

In May of 2014, I had one of my best days, walking across the stage and receiving my Bachelor of Science degree from the College of Education and Human Development. While walking across the stage, the best gift of all was hearing my daughter yell, "Go Momma." I had set the example for her and for my son, not only the importance of obtaining an education but setting the example that it is never too late. It is never too late to obtain your goal, and it was not too late to accomplish the promise I had made for myself. When I reflect back, obtaining my degree is one of my proudest accomplishments. I could not have accomplished it without the help of my amazing family, who supported me along the way and cheered me on each step of the way, and the amazing program geared towards someone like me. I feel confident that walking into Dr. Bergman's office that afternoon helped me complete my goal and helped me keep my promise to myself.

48, and Not Too Late

Chad Jones
Bethel University

> *Life should not be a journey to the grave with the intention of arriving safely in a*
> *pretty and well-preserved body, but to skid in broadside, in a cloud of smoke, thor-*
> *oughly used up, totally worn out, and loudly proclaiming, "Wow! What a Ride!"*
> —Hunter S. Thompson (1997)

As my life-clock ticks steadily towards the bells of 48 chimes, it is with fondness that I reflect on my path of unexpected twists and turns, which has been paved into a cerebral rolodex of experiential treasures and oddities that I can flip through at a moment's notice. A substantial component of my education came from O.T.S. University (On the Street University), my first real alma mater, from which I earned my first, and only PhD. While it would be rewarding to gaze upon my official gold leaf-embossed parchment, O.T.S. University is not currently bestowing awards for the Poor, Hungry, and Driven ("PhD"). And yet, to me, the value of a quality education has never meant more than it does today.

My name is Chad Jones, of the small, Midwestern, "Anywhere, U.S.A." Joneses, hailing from the quaint and modest Cooksville, Illinois. Recognizable as a small dot on any map, the village population of approximately 200 was primarily known for good, common sense folk with a flair for farming. I grew up on the corner of Lincoln and Walnut streets, in a town so small, house numbers were unnecessary. I inhaled my share of fall corn dust from the annual harvest, as it processed in the local grain company's grain dryers.

Throughout my youth, and because of modeling from my maternal grandfather, I sponged up the demonstrative skill of selling. A natural conversationalist, I never once witnessed a dull moment when he wielded the eloquence of a smooth sales pitch. Like a young King Arthur attempting to draw Excalibur from the stone, I tested my newfound skill regularly as I engaged in various sales efforts. Not one to miss an entrepreneurial opportunity, I developed a knack for door-to-door selling. Walnuts gathered and carted in a Radio Flyer classic red wagon, customized stationery, and even little league baseball sponsorship stickers—the sky was the limit for a budding sales professional willing to knock on the door of a welcoming neighbor. Once, I even amassed a sizeable collection of nightcrawlers (a.k.a. earthworms) to package and sell by the dozen. "No at this door? Not to worry, let's try the next." After all, it was merely a matter of numbers. *And persistence.*

Midway through my childhood, with two younger sisters in tow, I found myself challenged with the concept of a family breaking apart at the seams. A 10-year-old boy laid sprawled across his bed in a red-shag carpeted room with gray and black paneling. Crying atop his Star Wars comforter, he wondered why his father must leave. Little did he know then, but would certainly learn later in life, of the relational intricacies that challenge many adults.

It is inconceivable that a town so small would maintain its own education system. Hence, Cooksville, Colfax, and Anchor, Illinois collaborated to operate the Octavia grade, middle and high school. Following in the footsteps of my mother and her four younger siblings, I absorbed a quality education from even higher-quality teachers. Operating within the walls of one contiguous building, Octavia School District provided the groundwork for my life to come. To this day, I can rattle off the names of every primary and secondary teacher. Some are remembered with fondness, others with reservation; yet, with clarity, I acknowledge learning something important from each of them. Perhaps two of the most memorable, Mary McCarter and Pam Rathke, left indelible marks on my long-term memory. McCarter, an English and grammar professor, taught me the power of words, while Rathke, specializing in fine art, inspired me in my quest to learn darkroom photography. The latter would later help me call forth my inner artist. Strange as it may sound, I traversed the line of education, from Kindergarten to graduation, with nearly the same 18 students. Sure, occasionally a family moved away, or a new face popped in, but by the sixth grade, the remaining chips on the table were the same. A small class, yes indeed; however, the curriculum was challenging, and the lessons were wrought with staying power.

I watched my mother fight to support our family unit, broken apart from the wrath of divorce. In my teen years, while she worked at Illinois State University, she enrolled in college to earn an education. I sometimes wonder, though, if the end didn't define the means. You see, from her vantage point, she was able to leverage the system, so to speak, by taking on a part-time working role and enrolling in school full time in her final year of school. A divorced, single mother of three, feeding her children with financial aid, food stamps, and sheer determination, virtually maxed out the education grant, scholarship, and student loan opportunities as they presented themselves. As a youth, I didn't really understand the concept of low-income living, until, at Christmas time, I was forced to choose between purchasing a $.99 coloring book or a loaf of bread. As my mother worked her way through the curricula at Illinois State University, I met Dr. Marcia Hickrod, director of adult education, who I would come to know as another significant influence in my life.

Like spawning salmon fighting their way up Alaska's Indian River, post-graduation I navigated the path of what I believed was expected, by enrolling in a communication program at Illinois State University. With a short break between high school graduation and freshman orientation, I worked over the summer leading up to the first day of class. My first two semesters fared perhaps slightly better than average. Focusing on communication and graphic design, I fell into a groove of working, studying, and commuting 20 miles back home, to do the same the next day. The allure of music, friends, ping-pong, and billiards drew my focus away from the necessary work at hand. As Dr. Hickrod can surely attest (I do believe, being an academic and capable of viewing my grades, thus also reporting them to my mother!), I began a downward spiral of lost focus, leading me to the imminent point of no return, called academic suspension.

For the next 23 years, from age 19 to 42, I traversed the world of gainful employment. Parallel to my lack of focus in higher education, I allowed the sails of my life to direct my rudderless ship to the ports of least resistance. A safe place to dock, I could make a few bucks and a couple friends before being siphoned back out to sea for a new adventure. Seven years in Chicago, working on the railroad. A short one-year jaunt to South Carolina. And back to Illinois, to work in manufacturing, then television advertising sales. And a valuable lesson in how to not be married.

By the mid-2000s, and in marriage number two, my entrepreneurial spirit continued to beckon. With camera in hand, I boldly set up a side hustle as a self-proclaimed professional photographer. I crafted my skill parallel to my primary employment, and became an accomplished wedding photographer. From 2007 to 2010, I concurrently taught darkroom and digital photography as an adjunct professor of fine arts at Eureka College, alma mater of our 40th president, Ronald Reagan. In 2009, being granted a great and rare privilege, I met and photographed Mikhail Gorbachev, former president of the Soviet Union. On a trip to pay homage for the 20th anniversary of the fall of the Berlin Wall, Gorbachev spent the afternoon touring Eureka College while paying respects to his political colleague.

Eventually though, as the toughest of any seafaring sailors will attest, storms arise, and often without warning. During my marriage/photography/selling/teaching path, America was dealt the card called the Great Financial Crisis of 2007–2008. Under the stress of falling property values, derailed consumer confidence, and the failure of marriage number two, my ship set sail for Dallas, Texas and then 2 years later, Nashville, Tennessee. A circuit of performance venues to make any music star envious! And a full book of experiences, no doubt, to recount from each port.

Is it unfavorable to float aimlessly, to embrace the unknown with excitement and awe? I think not! In the words of one of my favorite authors, Theodor Seuss Geisel: "So be sure when you step, step with care and great tact. And remember that Life's A Great Balancing Act. And will you succeed? Yes! You will, indeed! (98 and 3/4 percent guaranteed). Kid, you'll move mountains" (Dr. Seuss, *Oh the Places You'll Go!*). Finding myself in a new city, outside Nashville, and for the first time in my life, without gainful employment, my rudderless ship encircled the world's waters aimlessly. At the urging of my younger (and middle) sister, I took a J-O-B in 2013 as a furniture salesperson. And with that, I felt my ego crushed like an aluminum can under the stomping boot of the juggernaut called life. In that moment, I had an epiphany. I asked myself, "How many people do you know who set out in life to become furniture salespeople?" It can certainly be leveraged as an honorable career, but I can't say it is where I thought I'd see myself at age 42. And with that, I made the decision to install a rudder. I enrolled as a transfer student with Bethel University, a small Christian school in McKenzie, Tennessee. Participating in an accelerated, online format, I transferred in with 32 credits and simultaneously worked on my education while also becoming a million-dollar furniture salesperson. If I were to be in this role, after all, might I not choose to simply be the best I could be?

Three promotions and three stores bracketed in between, I was transferred to manage the organization's flagship location in Louisville, Kentucky. Who would have thought that Cupid would have appeared yet again? Out of arrows, and as if to say "Don't mess this up!" Cupid smacked me upside the head with a two by four. My first date with my new flame (who winked at me on Match.com first, for the record), and I knew my new rudder had brought me to my final harbor. A year and a half in, we were married. One day, just 4 short months after graduation, and 2 months after exchanging nuptials on the beach of St. Lucia, I was helping a budding salesperson close a sizeable sale for a gentleman wearing a blue oxford shirt with a Papa John's Pizza logo. Pleasantries aside, we began a conversational volley back and forth over a newly created leadership development position and his interest in my qualifications. A few short weeks and three interviews later, I was offered a position as head coach of Training & Development at Papa John's corporate headquarters in Louisville, Kentucky. In my role, I use the experience and knowledge I gained from my work in Organizational Leadership to hone professional facilitation skills. I can interact with multiple levels of the organization and impact the lives of others by helping enhance their leadership paths. Perhaps one of my greatest accomplishments in my role has been to create a series of educational alliances between Papa John's

Pizza and institutes of higher learning, wherein corporate team members can earn a company-paid college degree at no cost to them.

As I look back at a life chock full of interesting experiences, and at age 48 working on my master's degree in human resources and organizational development at The University of Louisville, I ponder whether a more focused and intentional career path could have led to this point sooner. But, hey... Dr. Seuss did predict my arrival with "98 and 3⁄4 percent" accuracy.

In closing, I can confirm that a life well lived is sometimes disproportionately laden with both joys and sorrows. I've loved. I've lost. And some days I just managed to survive. Yet I've lived to tell about it. There were indeed days I might have been badly bent, but I can say with absolute certainty, that because of an incredible network of caring family, and my wife, Adrienne, who loves me more than life itself, I have never been completely busted. I'll gratuitously reflect on my final thought, with your permission, and self-indulge with a nod to the late, great Frank Zappa: "If you end up with a boring, miserable life because you listened to your mom, your dad, your teacher, your priest, or some guy on television telling you how to do your shit, then you deserve it."

4

Pursuing Career Advancement

Previous generations of the American workforce were able to secure a wide array of jobs with a high school diploma. The average American worker took a job and stayed with that employer for the entirety of their career. However, in today's job market, workers are changing jobs more than 10 times during their career. In this nation's ever-changing economy, a bachelor's degree is a virtual necessity for most jobs in the workforce. Cabrera, Burkum, and LaNasa (2005) took this point one step further: "A bachelor's degree is no longer considered a potential stepping-stone to a better life; it is fully acknowledged as the gatekeeper to a myriad of social and individual benefits" (p. 2). The narratives presented in this chapter demonstrate that a college degree can open doors the graduate had not even considered existed. These adults present a clear case that barriers that once existed have been moved to create a pathway to long-term success.

If You Have a Pulse, You Have Purpose

Troy Marables

University of Louisville

I grew up in Louisville's West End. My father, Charles Robert Marables, was born in 1918 and passed away in 1983 when I was just 13. After hearing stories of how my family had progressed from slavery and survived the Great Depression and the civil rights movement, I was determined to try to create a better life for my own family some day. Although neither of my parents had obtained a college degree, they had always taught me that education could open doors, and so they did everything they could to prepare me to attend college after graduating from high school. I graduated from Louisville Male Traditional High School in 1989 and received a 4-year, full Army ROTC Scholarship to attend Florida A&M University in Tallahassee, Florida. In college, I enrolled in the School of Business and Industry at Florida A&M. During my junior year, I became further ahead in my ROTC courses than I was in my academic courses, so I became ineligible for my scholarship to renew until I caught up in my academic courses on my own. Unfortunately, it was also during my junior year that my mother, Frances Marables, passed away, so I was forced to drop out of school and return home. In 1992, I came home, married my high school sweetheart, and began working at Citizen's Bank.

From the time I returned to Louisville until December of 1997, I worked in the customer service department for Citizen's Fidelity Bank in the mortgage banking area. My expertise in serving clients resulted in numerous recognitions and a promotion to team leader in the call center. After Citizen's Mortgage was acquired by PNC Mortgage, the mortgage customer service department was merged with the collections department, and thus the dynamics of the calls we handled changed. Instead of merely assisting clients with basic mortgage questions, we were now required to make collection calls on delinquent loans and make referrals to the foreclosure department. After realizing that my personal skill sets were more aligned with assisting clients and creating a positive experience on each call, I decided it was time to move on and find a more rewarding career path.

In December of 1997, I was hired at the Presbyterian Foundation. Although I began my role with the company as a client services representative, I demonstrated that I had knowledge, skills, and abilities that aligned me with managerial opportunities within the organization. Soon after my arrival and after the departure of a long-time employee, I was promoted to manager of Client Services, and I served in this role until January of 2018.

In 2016, I was also hired to concurrently work as a trust officer for the New Covenant Trust Company. I re-enrolled in college to transition from working a job to having a career. I love the company that I work for, and I wanted to find a way to advance my career development. I knew that obtaining my degree would play a critical role in achieving my goals.

Completing my degree was the fulfillment of a goal that I set for myself decades ago when I graduated from high school. I realize that numerous sacrifices were made for me to have the opportunity to attend college and earn a degree, and I also wanted to teach my own children the importance of obtaining a degree. I knew that obtaining my degree would play a role in my own career development opportunities; however, I never expected that it would have such an immediate and profound impact. After obtaining my BS in organizational leadership and learning, I was promoted to vice president director of Human Resources for my current employer.

A Lifelong College Journey

Kathleen Sailings

Indiana University Southeast

As I reflect upon my journey through college, it has definitely proven to be a lifelong endeavor. I am so grateful for my experience at Indiana University Southeast (IUS) and fully appreciate how I have grown and shaped into the person I am today. I have had many great moments of influence throughout my nontraditional journey that have positively contributed to my growth and development both personally and professionally.

I was determined from a very young age to be successful and to prioritize my education. I always made good grades throughout grade school, then on to middle school and graduated with honors and as a member of the National Honor Society in high school. After high school, I did what was expected and what I planned; I went right into my first year of college. The following year, I transferred to another university where I knew, from the moment I walked into my first class, it was not the right fit for me. What happened next was never part of my plan.

Real life took over and prompted a break from the college world for a bit. I became a wife and a mother, and I had a very successful career. However, I always felt something was missing. Going back to school was something I needed to do for myself and to set an example for my children, so I re-enrolled, completed my associate degree in general studies, and continued on as a successful career woman.

All was going well in my world until the day I realized the impact of not having a 4-year degree. It hit me right smack in the face! I had applied for a promotion at work, a place I worked for 18 years, and was turned away because of the lack of a bachelor's degree. With 18 years of results-driven experience, I thought nothing would hold me back from advancing my career; boy, was I wrong.

This rejection was hard for me to accept, and I knew at that moment I must further my education and finally finish that 4-year degree, even at the age of 40. I made an appointment with the advisor of the general studies program to review where I had left off. Lo and behold, I discovered I was only 12 credit hours from a bachelor's in general studies. I enrolled the day after that. With a lot of effort, time management, and personal sacrifices, I finally graduated with the long-awaited 4-year degree that held me back from a promotion.

During college, you come across many people who impact you along the way. Two of my professors stand out as that inspiration as they had a distinct impact on me both personally and professionally. The first is Rebecca Ford, professor for the Women's Health classes, who really inspired me to approach life in a way that encouraged a healthy work–life balance. She taught me that saying "no" when my plate was full is perfectly acceptable. The second is JoEllen McCollough, my professor for the General Studies Capstone, who contributed to my growth and confidence. Coming back to campus after a 10-year hiatus was intimidating and overwhelming. Hearing her personal story and having her continued support throughout the semester was refreshing!

As you can see, I did not have a traditional college experience; it was broken up over many years. I surely did things out of order and not as planned. I started college, experienced several different universities, took a break from school for several years where I got married, started a family, and had a successful career. I then returned to school where I was fortunate enough to find a great fit with IUS to finish my associate degree in general studies in 2007. At the time, I had a great career and was raising two wonderful children. Continuing my education did not seem possible, so I stopped there and things were smooth sailing for 10 years.

After the blow to the gut when I was rejected for that promotion for the lack of a 4-year degree coupled with influencing my high school age daughter to think about college, I decided I needed to see what it would take to get it done. Meeting with my advisor at IUS was one of the best days of my life this year, where I learned I only had 12 credit hours necessary to graduate. Looking at the number of years it has taken me to get to this close to graduating with my bachelor's degree, it feels like an eternity; however, I know I would not be the person I am today without the challenges I have faced personally and professionally. There was a time I thought a 4-year degree was not possible, but with perseverance, the support from my family, and the amazing faculty and staff at IUS, I am proudly able to list a four-year degree on my resume.

18 Months and 89 Credits

William P. Dugan, III

University of Louisville

As a successful 48-year-old business professional without a college degree, I did not recognize the value of a college degree. Throughout my life, education was never important to me. From an early age, I was only interested in being a professional baseball player, and my parents never emphasized or held me accountable for achieving educational success. I attended college with the sole purpose to play baseball and with dreams to one day play professionally. In school, I was doing the bare minimum to stay eligible. Two years in, I realized my dream was not a reality. Without baseball, I was not motivated to keep my grades up and school fell to the wayside. After leaving college, I was determined to find a career to be successful in. With that said, I was fortunate that someone took a chance on me. At the age of 24, I was offered my first professional opportunity as a sales rep in the sporting goods industry. I have always enjoyed people and building meaningful relationships; it didn't take much for me to enjoy selling.

Being a professional without a college degree, I always felt that I was under the microscope. There was this additional pressure on me; knowing I had to outperform my counterparts meant out-servicing, out-selling, and being more responsive to leadership. Furthermore, this additional internal stress drove me to consistently outperform my colleagues with MBAs. As a result of my drive and success, I was fortunate to experience the culture of companies such as Reebok, Nike, Stryker, Biomet, NuVasive, and my current company, Medtronic.

Having attained that success, I have since reached a new challenging position. Due to my lack of a degree, I knew I could not advance my career into management with a blue-chip company. Here is where my new chapter and outlook on education begins. A regional vice president of Medtronic recruited me via LinkedIn. After a few meetings with Medtronic leadership, I accepted a position. Medtronic proceeded to perform a background check like previous companies; this showed that I did not have a college degree. In the meetings, we had never discussed education; now, for the first time my lack of a degree presented itself as a major issue. I was no longer qualified for the position according to company policy. Stress came over me; I had already resigned from my previous job, had money down on a new home, and was in a fight for my career with the HR director to save my incredible opportunity! After multiple phone calls, the HR director agreed to go forth with hiring with one stipulation: I had to earn my college degree within 18 months.

As stated previously, I was never interested in school and felt so far from achieving this precious degree document. I vigorously started researching every potential institution in search of a program that fit my timeline. With limited credit hours earned previously, it was crucial that the school accepted them. In my search, I came across the University of Louisville (U of L) organizational leadership and learning (OLL) program. After a few conversations with the U of L staff, I knew this was the program for me and the path to accomplish my goal. While enrolled in the U of L OLL program online, I had to take some online classes through Kentucky Technical Community College to finish up my general education requirements. On top of that, I was still working a full-time job and traveling the region.

Some people have asked me, "At this stage of your life why is it worth it to return and finish your degree?" Mainly, it's worth it in order to continue with my new job, but further, it is crucial for me going forward as future leadership opportunities present themselves. I am very grateful that my current employer demanded that I obtain my degree; this will erase my insecurity I have had over the years of being held back by my lack of a degree.

The U of L OLL program has allowed me to utilize all the knowledge and skills that I have acquired through my business experience. In addition, the courses have extended my bandwidth to flourish in the future. As a father of two daughters, one who has already earned her college degree and the other only two semesters away from hers, I want to continue to be a respected role model to them. It is extremely important for me to lead by example and show them anything is possible through hard work.

Before starting my first class, I must tell you I was scared that I was going to fail. My prior educational background caused me unease; I was nervous and unsure I was able to earn this degree. After my first few classes, I became confident that I could do this. It helped that the material is project based, and the courses added tremendous insight to what I was striving to accomplish in my professional career. My timeline to achieve my goal still felt distant, but I overcame my fear and took the first step in the right direction. Failure was not an option if I wanted to retain my job. Earning my degree has allowed me to confidently pursue sought-after positions that I previously did not. I thought it was just a piece of paper with a stamp on it, a so-called check the box at this stage in my career. In retrospect, I was completely wrong! Even though I had a formidable amount of work and life experience, I have grown exponentially since starting classes; I was able to learn new concepts and terminology, and I apply them in my daily professional and personal life.

I cannot thank my employer enough for stressing that I obtain this degree. In addition, I am very appreciative that the University of Louisville has a program in place to allow adult learners like myself to finish their degree. This program has provided me with a new foundation to excel in my professional life. Along the way, I was enlightened in other ways. First, there were a lot of adult learners in my age demographic enrolled in the program. Second, I actually enjoyed the classes, and I am able to apply what I learned to daily life. Third, the professors have a great appreciation for adult learners and are there to help you succeed. Fourth, I can take on more than I realized. Lastly, I can achieve any goal when fully committed.

I graduated in the summer of 2018 from the University of Louisville with a Bachelor of Science in organizational leadership and learning. (Wow that sounds so gratifying to say.) I started off in the program with 36 accepted credits from my previous institutions. I completed 19 general education credits from On Demand Courses at KCTCS, 34 PLAID (prior learning assessment) credits from the University of Louisville, and 35 program credits from the University of Louisville, which equals 124 credits and a college degree. In 18 months, I completed 89 credits to earn my degree and keep my job. This was not easy to accomplish in such a short time but with dedication, focus, and time management it was possible. If I can do it, I am confident that you can do it! Don't allow your fears to hold you back; having a college degree is very important for your growth and development, and earning the degree will present a plethora of opportunities.

Finally, I would like to thank the University of Louisville for this program, all the OLL professors, Medtronic for demanding this of me, my regional vice president and my direct report for all their support, and most importantly, Amy, my loving wife of more than 23 years, and my daughters Ali and Emily for all their support and encouragement during this 18-month journey.

The Chief of Police Recommends a Return to School

Jamie Land

University of Louisville

After graduating high school, I signed up for an evening college English class. I made it one night before deciding to quit. I felt that it was more important to make money at 18 years old versus obtaining an education. After a couple of years working as a cabinet maker, I decided I wanted to do something more with my life. I participated in a ride along with a police officer. After the ride along, I decided that serving my community was what I wanted to do. I tried getting hired at several police departments only to find that I needed a college education or some kind of experience in order to be hired. This was the first barrier I encountered, because I did not have a college education. I decided it would be easier for me to join the Marine Corps and obtain the training I needed to help me obtain a job in law enforcement. Fast forward 20 years. I was a deputy chief with a municipal police department in Kentucky. My career was stagnant. I could not advance my career without a college education. This was the second time in my life that the lack of a college degree created a barrier for me. I regularly attended trainings that were all police related. I would learn things while attending each training, but I felt something was missing. Through encouragement from my wife and my supervisor, I decided to start taking college classes. I intended to pursue a degree in criminal justice. I called and spoke with an advisor in the Criminal Justice Department who told me I would be wasting my time by trying to obtain a degree in criminal justice. She referred me to the organizational leadership and learning program. Unbeknownst to me at the time, she did me a huge favor.

I began taking classes in the fall of 2012. I decided to take two classes. I was scared to death because I didn't know what I was getting myself into. I had been out of school for 21 years at that point. I took a program class and a history class. It was very challenging at first. I had never worked with Blackboard Learning Management System before so it took a while to learn how to maneuver through the program. My work schedule at the time was very busy, so I struggled with time management and finding time to work on my classes. After the first few weeks, I was able to get settled into a routine. The instructor for my program class, Elizabeth Krauss, was phenomenal. She was very helpful and encouraging, and she made my first experience in a college class go very well. Through my degree program, I have met countless other adults who are in the same situation as me, working full time and trying to obtain their degree.

My experience in taking college classes has been wonderful. I have learned so much. It has opened my eyes to things that I previously had no interest in learning. I feel as though I am able to make better decisions because of the experiences I have had through taking classes. Currently, I am the chief of police of a municipal agency in Kentucky. I would not have been able to achieve this goal had it not been for my college education. I would encourage anyone considering going back to school to do it. You won't be sorry you did.

Shasta for the Win!

Tamra Switzer

Shasta College

My journey to the Accelerated College Education (ACE) program really began about 21 years ago. I am a Shasta county local, raised here and graduated from West Valley in 1995. My plan was to take some classes at Shasta College to save money before transferring to a university. In reality, I did not take school seriously; I found a decent paying job and then dropped out and worked full time. I moved around, always working full time, but by 22 or 23, I was realizing that without a college education I was not ever going to make the kind of money you actually need as an adult. I started at a technical school in Sacramento but did not qualify for financial aid. Since I couldn't quit my job, after five months I quit school. I tried online classes a few times, but a whole semester, with minimal human interaction, was too much for me to manage. So, I quit.

I got married in 2004 and had my first daughter nine months later. My husband was in the military, so we moved all over. As a military wife it is very hard to find work without a degree in something, so I stayed home for 7 years and took care of my two girls. When my husband, at the time, got out of the military he took advantage of his G.I. Bill and went to school. He started at Butte and then finished at Chico State. It made me envious that he was able to accomplish that, but it seemed out of reach for me. We didn't have time or money for me to go back to school.

I found a job with the county in 2013 and thought all was going well— until I realized it is nearly impossible to be promoted to any of the higher-paying jobs without a college degree. I got divorced in early 2014, and I had to reevaluate life and what I wanted out of it. I looked into Simpson's Aspire program, thinking the night classes and fast pace would be ideal for me. Unfortunately, I still needed about 24 units just to start the program and about 50+ to complete my undergrad. That would take four or five years of night school, on a traditional schedule, just to *start* the Aspire program. I gave up on that idea and resigned myself to not finishing school.

In July of 2016, a friend was signing up for classes to complete their nursing degree. I decided to check on the Simpson thing again and talked to a counselor at Shasta first to see what units would transfer. I was so shocked when she mentioned the new accelerated ACE program! I signed up that day, before I left campus. I was so excited to hear that the classes would be geared toward nontraditional students, in the evenings and sometimes online. It was like they designed it for me! There is no way I could have finished the units I needed without Shasta College and the ACE program. Only a year and a half after I started the ACE program I will have completed 47 units and earned not one, but two associate degrees! I am now on the doorstep of completing my bachelor's degree, I have taken a little time off to spend with my teenage daughters, but I will return in January 2019 to finish later this year. I had thought there was no chance of earning my college degree. I look forward to my girls watching me graduate from college!

Securing the Future

Andrew English

U.S. Marine
University of Louisville

Having made a halfhearted effort to attend college right after high school, failure was immediate and as such, I was looking for any other course of action to help me move forward. I am a 2002 high school graduate, and like many in my generation, the military seemed like a reasonable enough location to figure out life. Before the age of 25, I had been married, gotten divorced, had two kids, and been deployed twice (Iraq and Afghanistan). Somehow in the chaos of this I still managed to secure a decent IT career with Humana and finish my associate degree. However, one day I realized I was working three jobs (Humana, military reserves, and waiting tables) just to get by in life. This work–life balance to me was insanity and something needed to change. Having obtained my G.I. Bill, I knew I could cut out job number three and still yield a similar income by going back to school full time, so I made the leap and committed to my education wholeheartedly. In light of my new-found commitment to my education and life goals, I realized I needed to do one more thing before jumping into this journey. Step one was to cancel my cable, because I knew the limits of my willpower, and cable managed to suck me in with HGTV goodness.

The transition throughout the next 3 years was unbelievable, and I even saw cascading effects on my children. Having two little boys—the youngest who didn't like to read—this newfound promotion of education was very important. I started reading in front of them and as such noticed an attitude shift in their educational persistence as well. This alone, to me, was worth every long night of homework and weekend filled with writing research papers. Having emerged on the other side of my undergrad program as magna cum laude, I was incredibly motivated and honored because my children and my family were proud of me. In a number of classes, fellow students asked how I was able to manage a full course load with two jobs and two children. I was able to show my classmates that not only did I enjoy the research projects and topics personally, but the underlying motivation behind my dedication was how proud my kids were and how much it also changed their outlook on their own education (my youngest started reading more and more!).

There were days I honestly do not know how I managed full-time school in conjunction with the family and work–life I already had established, but because of various training programs and deployments I had conducted in the Marine Corps, I knew it was possible. After finishing my undergrad degree, I kept going. I pushed and persevered through a lot of less than ideal circumstances, and I am happy to report I finished the master's program in the College of Education and Human Development. Having continued to work in the military and at Humana throughout my schooling, my degree has opened doors previously not available to me. Within 6 months of finishing my undergrad program, I applied for a job internally with Humana and was hired. Having been a young 25-year-old with two babies of my own, I am humbled by the work each teacher and professor invested into my education throughout the process. I also reflect on my military service and see odd similarities now that I didn't see before. Similar to long durations and deployments with fellow military service members, I became friends and comrades with these individuals in my classes. Then just as we found ourselves getting comfortable with the new friendships and relationships that formed, we'd find ourselves with a fresh batch of teachers and students the next semester. I know that having my degree gets my resume into a different "stack" for hiring managers now; however, the learning process and perseverance will be a valuable lesson I share with my children for the rest of their lives. Sadly, I had very little coaching and conversations related to college while growing up, so I have had to figure it out along the way. Unfortunately, that is not the best approach when considering a massive financial and time commitment. I do not wish that type of "figure it out" life on anyone knowing the type of financial hardship that could come with poor decisions during and after college.

Now, 5½ years after the start of my journey back to school, this education has helped me in ways I didn't see going into this work. I am currently on my second deployment to Central America as a foreign security forces advisor, and I am excited to put my degree to good use in years to come. Having had a robust educational program focused on organizational leadership, learning, and development, I have a unique perspective among my peer group and host nation of Belize. My perspective will be effective and useful to partner and develop a cohesive group dynamic, as well as to deliver robust training programs to their military forces. Beyond that, the skills of professional writing, clear communication, and general professionalism I learned in the classroom now enable me to work in my corporate career and military endeavors. Those skills have also added an additional approach to the mentoring of my children. I can say there is a time and place for education in everyone's life, but for me it was when I simply had reached my limit and had enough of simply getting by. I wanted something in my life that I was proud of accomplishing, and I wanted to use that accomplishment as a jumping-off platform for the rest of my professional career. I am pleased with the work accomplished and continue to look for new learning opportunities to enhance the life and well-being of my family as a whole.

Fulfilling the Dream to Become a Teacher

LaKeesha Turner

University of Louisville

Have you ever read the perfect job description and thought, "This must have been created just for me?" But when you get to the bottom of the page you see the infamous words *bachelor's degree required.* Many times, I wanted the opportunity to say, "I would be perfect for this job, I have the experience you are looking for, this is a dream come true for me, you should hire *me* because...." But those opportunities never came. Many jobs opportunities and promotions would come my way, but without that degree, those opportunities would always go to someone with a degree. I remember making it to the final round for a job that I was perfect for. I had wowed the panel and then had the opportunity to meet the director. I was told it was down to me and one other candidate. I left the last interview with an unofficial offer. Later on, in the afternoon, I get a call from Human Resources confirming that I had a bachelor's degree. I had 90 credit hours but no completed degree. The company stated that a four-year degree was required for that position and offered the job to the other candidate.

As a senior in high school, my plan was to attend a 4-year college, get a degree in engineering, co-op, and then work my way up as a computer engineer in a Fortune 500 company. I enrolled at the University of Louisville (U of L) in the fall of 2000, was accepted into the Speed School of Engineering, and hated it! I was not good at science, and I wasn't enjoying any of my classes. So, guess what, I failed all of my engineering classes my freshman year. I transferred over to the School of Business the following semester as a business management major. I was in the business magnet in high school, aced all of my classes and graduated high school with honors, so how much harder could business classes in college be? Same material right? I was successful in the School of Business but not successful enough to raise my GPA high enough to keep my scholarship. Without the scholarship, I could no longer afford to attend school at U of L. I then transferred to Indiana University Southeast the following year. Over the next couple of years life happened. I married my amazing husband Eric, we had three beautiful children, and finishing my degree sat on the back burner of my list of priorities. After working with the public school system for 7 years as a facilitator of a life skills program, I finally realized that I wanted to become a school teacher. Before I could make my dream happen, I needed to finish school and earn that bachelor's degree!

I was a busy wife, a mother of three active children, and I worked full time. Why did I ever think I could go back to school? After I got over the initial shock, it was time to make a game plan. First, my husband was my biggest supporter. He told me about the organization leadership and learning (OLL) program at U of L. Words could never express how blessed I am to have my husband in my corner. Secondly, my awesome advisor, Tammy Albers, was so amazing! She was so incredibly patient and encouraging from the very beginning. As an adult learner, I was coming back to school with a different mind-set than I had when I enrolled at 18 years old. I was no longer afraid to ask questions. Tammy helped me every step of the way and always made time for me and my questions! Lastly, each of my instructors and professors in the program were absolutely remarkable. They all understood that we have families and careers outside of school. Their support and flexibility really helped me throughout this educational journey.

Getting my degree is one of the most important achievements in my life. My parents always encouraged my sisters and me to go to school to further our education. As I walked across that stage in December 2016, I felt like my life literally changed. My dream had become a reality. I stood a little taller and held my head a little higher. I had finally made it!

Every day it seems like I'm telling someone about the OLL program at U of L. I tell any and everyone about this marvelous program and what it means to me. With my dream of becoming a school teacher, my bachelor's degree helped me get there. I am now in the Jefferson County Public Schools Alternative Certification Program (ACES). With my bachelor's degree, I applied and interviewed and was officially accepted into the ACES program. I am currently teaching second grade and I love it!!!

Plans change. Those two words represent the story of my life and how I was able to go back to school to finish a degree 16 years after graduating high school.

Gain a Competitive Edge

Nancy Williams

Columbia College

In 2008, I felt extremely accomplished, coming from a physical laboring, low-paying job at a factory to working for Louisville Metro Government (LMG). I was able to move from receptionist to housing program assistant in just 2 short years. Not bad for a person without much education past a high school diploma, but I knew I had much more to offer LMG and the Louisville community. However, I was not qualified for those positions without that degree. The job market was getting tough and I needed to be marketable, even if it wasn't at LMG, and my manager and mentor Anna Shobe-Wallace encouraged me to embrace getting that degree. I spoke with my sister and my parents; my sister had recently obtained her BSBA from Columbia College, going online. I decided in March of 2009 to go back and try it with just one class, but because of my busy life, and my family dynamics, going to a class really isn't what would work for me. The online option was worth trying: one class, 8 weeks—let's try it and see what happens. I could be home with my family in the evenings and could even do some of my studies during lunch, since online allowed me to study anywhere on the go. One class at a time, 8-week sessions is the same as part time, two classes a semester, so it is eligible for financial aid. Columbia College Online accepted many of my credits that were 20 years old that many universities would have made me retake; that was a huge plus to choosing this institution. By going online, I was able to continue my education even as I had a few surgeries, including back surgery. I was able to schedule my classes around my surgery schedule and able to work from the bed. Going to a traditional education classroom would have meant dropping out for the semester. Life happens, and it is great to have a system that flexes with you.

If it wasn't for the flexibility of the online classes, the tuition reimbursement, and the true support of my family and manager/mentor, I would probably still be answering phones. My degree isn't just my path to a better career, but I am proud that at the age of 37, I was able to go back to school and get an education. It may have taken me longer than most, but I was able to keep my GPA up and not be so overwhelmed. I am delighted that I had the persistence to chip away at it one class at a time. I would rather see someone go slow and succeed than to try to take on too much too fast and feel like a failure.

I worked very hard, and before I knew it, I had more than enough for my associate degree. In 2012, I declared and obtained my associate degree in general studies, and this made me feel great. It was my first college accomplishment, and I was far from done. I looked at my daughter and my granddaughter and told them both it is never too late. My daughter is very proud of my accomplishments. The Associate degree allowed me a promotion to housing program specialist. Since I was still working toward my bachelor's degree, my manager began grooming me to take over the Lead Hazard Control Grant in late 2012. I finally obtained my Bachelor of Science in Business Administration majoring in management in December 2014. My degree situated me to be promoted to the lead program coordinator.

My degree means I do not have to settle for a job; I can enjoy a career. The job market is tough and competitive, and my BSBA permits me to be competitive and marketable if I choose to change career paths. I look periodically to see if there is an opportunity out there both internal with LMG as well as outside LMG, and I am qualified for so many positions in a wide variety of professions. Knowing those opportunities are out there in case I need or want them allows me to rest easy, because as a college graduate with a solid employment record, I will not likely be unemployed long.

I like sharing my story with my coworkers, clients, and friends. I believe anyone can try just one class; once they get through one and realize how good it feels to accomplish that in just 8 weeks, they are ready to take on another. I loved concentrating on one subject, because I wanted to do one thing and do that one thing very well. It allowed me to keep my active lifestyle, get my education, and maintain a high GPA.

A 29-Year Journey to Graduation

Dawn Hall

McKendree University

My college journey began the fall after my high school graduation in 1987. Everything was on track for a solid college education at Bellarmine

College, a private school in my hometown of Louisville, Kentucky. My confidence was soon shaken by my first semester grades. They were less than stellar, and I was having a difficult time adjusting to the rigors of higher education.

I married my high school sweetheart at the end of my first year of college. He was a sailor and would be stationed in Norfolk, Virginia. Acting as the dutiful wife, I packed up and moved to Virginia. Finding a good job was a high priority, since we wouldn't be living on base. Rent was high, and we were new to the area. One job turned into two jobs, and school kept falling lower on the priority list. I landed a decent job at a local hospital as a clinical laboratory secretary. This job required taking a class in medical terminology, which was enough to get my college career restarted. That terminology class turned into becoming a part-time student at Old Dominion University. Again, the stress of a job, a relocation, and a new lifestyle proved to be overwhelming, and I dropped out after just one semester. Sadly, a miscarriage and a divorce were my next life hurdles. The recovery time seemed to stretch on forever.

At the age of 26, I was back at home in my mother's house, and I had secured a very good job that offered tuition reimbursement. Here was my chance for another restart. I took three more classes during the fall and spring semesters at McKendree University. They offered 1-month courses, and those fit my schedule well. Then life happened again. I married for the second time in April of 1996. By May of that same year, I was expecting my first child. My husband and I bought our first home and then welcomed our first baby in February of 1997. Again, school fell down the priority list.

I didn't return to school until the Spring semester of 2006. Kentucky was desperately looking for substitute teachers, and by this time I was only a few credits shy of the 60 credits needed to apply. I took three more classes and qualified, and I was subsequently hired to be a substitute teacher for Jefferson County Public Schools. It didn't take long for me to realize that teaching was not the profession for me. I returned to a sales position that I had earlier left to be a stay-at-home mother. I was asked back to the industry by a very welcoming employer.

In March of 2013, my mother died unexpectedly at the age of 61. This was a profound time of reflection for me as I did some true soul searching. I had been able to put off my college education because my husband was our breadwinner. He had a terrific job that took care of all of our needs. But the death of my mother brought out some true concerns. What if something unexpected happened to my husband? Sure, I would be able to get a decent job, but not one that would replace his income. I felt like I needed a degree to make me a more desirable employee. I returned to school in 2013 and was able to continue at a somewhat regular pace until I graduated in December of 2016 with a Bachelors of Arts in business administration with a concentration in human resource management.

My 29-year journey was full of ups and downs, sideways and rest stops. Nothing I experienced is really much different than what most people handle. I loved being a stay-at-home mother. I stayed home with my three children until my youngest started kindergarten. By the time I returned to school in 2013 my children were 15, 13, and 11. I served on the school PTA, chaperoned field trips, and even served as a troop leader for two Girl Scout troops and treasurer for a Cub Scout pack and Boy Scout troop. Actually, I'm still a Girl Scout leader, and I'm still treasurer for the Boy Scout troop. I'm grateful for the experiences, and things have turned out well for me.

I'm certain that the degree I earned will help me in advancing my career. In today's atmosphere, a degree is such a necessity. I now qualify for supervisory positions within my field, and I have considered several. Should the right job opportunity come along, I'm so much better prepared for it than I was just a couple of years ago. I would not want to be an example of how it should be done, but I wouldn't mind being a voice saying that it can be done, no matter how long it takes—just keep going.

Private Commencement Ceremonies Are the Best

Lawren A. Just

CEO Persimmon Ridge
University of Louisville

Goals. As adults we've heard this word for years, decades, maybe some of us even half a century! As children the goals were simple—keep a clean room, make good grades in school, make the volleyball or basketball team. Often, reaching these goals was rewarded in the form of allowance or recognition. As young adults, the goals became greater—go to college, get a good job, marry the person of our dreams. These too were met with rewards for doing so in the form of a degree, a good paycheck, a life partner.

But what if the goal of earning that degree was put on hold? That was certainly my case more times than once. I started my journey at Bellarmine College in 1972 and loved it. I was making decent grades and playing basketball for the women's team, which was created as a result of Title IX! After my freshman year, a disagreement with my father meant I had to move out of his house and pay my own tuition. I worked two jobs to do so, while still trying to play basketball and do the work college required. Realizing

I couldn't do this on my own, after completing my sophomore year I quit and took classes at a local community college. I hated every minute of it and missed my friends, missed basketball, and missed everything about Bellarmine. I married my high school sweetheart and moved to Colorado where we started a family.

But I had a goal to get a college degree, so after my second child was born, I took a couple classes at the University of Colorado—Colorado Springs. It was interesting and exciting to work hard for As, but after one semester I found we were moving back to Kentucky in the spring.

Once back home, my world drastically changed when my marriage ended in divorce. This meant life was taking a new turn, with working full time to support my children and pay our bills. Earning a degree was the last thing on my mind.

In 1983, I married a wonderful man and our blended family totaled five. We added two more to the fold and worked together to create two businesses. When these were successfully underway, I decided to once again make an effort to get that long sought-after degree. I returned to U of L and took two classes in the Fall of 2000. But when a business opportunity arose for us, I put the spring classes on hold, expecting to continue in the summer. On April 23, 2001, my world crashed when I lost my husband to a massive heart attack. He was 53 years old, our youngest children were just in high school, and there were four businesses that were now my full responsibility.

As difficult as life is and with all the challenges it presents, there is something about a personal goal that continues to eat at you. In 2015, I was a successful businesswoman in the community, a mother of five, grandmother of 14 and moving to the point in my businesses that retirement looked to be a possibility in the near future. I had remarried, and my husband was a wonderful man. I enjoyed life and everything God had blessed me with. But something was missing in my life that I had sought many times for years. I decided to once again pursue it.

In a book I recently read, called *Perfectly Yourself* (Kelly, 2017), the author shares that happiness is an inside job and has very little to do with substances, money, possessions, pleasure, or circumstances. I knew I could never be totally fulfilled in my life until I had a degree in my hand. So, I called U of L.

Having worked my entire adult life, I was able to use that experience toward earning my Bachelor of Science in organizational leadership and learning. The OLL program was a perfect fit for me. The classes I took in 2015–2017 would have been extremely helpful while I was more active in my businesses, but I also found they were helpful as I work to transition toward retirement, helpful with the social aspects of my life, and helpful with my personal life, including discussions with my husband, kids, and grandkids.

In the Fall of 2017, I took my last two classes toward earning my degree. I was excited about graduating in front of my kids and grandkids, and excited to learn the date of commencement. It was announced to be Friday evening, December 15, the same day my five sisters and our husbands and kids and grandkids were to celebrate Christmas—at my house. Eighty-seven people who scheduled a year in advance to be together this one day of the year, and it happened to be the day I would finally graduate from college—45 years and 4 months after starting the journey.

I was heartbroken. I couldn't cancel Christmas for our large family, and I wanted that cap and gown and ceremony. My two daughters were the only ones who even knew I had returned to school, and they didn't know I was finishing in the Fall of 2017. I told them the situation, and they insisted I go to commencement. I told them it wouldn't be the same without the kids and grandkids there. I wanted to show the grandkids that if you have a goal in your heart, it is never too late to pursue it. So, my younger daughter came up with a plan.

At 32 years of age, her husband is one of the younger professors at U of L, having earned his PhD from there 5 years ago. They had just moved home from Florida where he taught for 4 years and started as a professor of physiology and anatomy at U of L in the Summer of 2017. She suggested I have my own private graduation at my house with my son-in-law presiding, in front of not only my husband, kids and grandkids, but also my sisters, brothers-in-law, nieces, nephews, and my dad.

It was an awesome idea that my daughters made happen. At 9:30 p.m. that evening, my son-in-law walked upstairs with me. He put on his robes and cords and walked back downstairs. Everyone applauded, thinking they were welcoming him back home and congratulating him for his position at U of L. Then he quieted them and said he wanted to introduce the newest graduate of the University of Louisville. I came down the steps in my cap and gown, to tears from everyone from myself to my kids to my father. I had finally achieved that lifelong goal.

At nearly 64 years of age, I didn't need the degree for my business life or for business growth. I needed the degree for me. I felt so good inside when my picture was taken in that cap and gown. Friends said I was crazy for spending the money and time to go back to school at my age. They didn't understand how important that piece of paper was for me.

So now that I've earned my degree, what will I do with it? Smile. A goal has been reached that was sought after for years. It's a lesson the grandkids will remember their entire lives, because I will remind them, and when I'm gone, their parents will remind them. Having earned that degree filled a void and brought happiness. I will cherish it forever.

My Educational Journey: Third Time is a Charm!

Raylene Pollio

University of Louisville

There were not many resources available to me growing up, as I was born to teenage parents and raised in my grandparents' home as a youngster. College was rarely a topic of discussion in our family and the majority of my role models worked in blue-collar jobs. I wasn't a good high school student, and I never knew exactly what I wanted to be when I grew up, but I did have dreams of working in an office and carrying a briefcase each day. My first attempt at continuing education came at age 26 when I enrolled in a local community college and flamed out after a year. I was not ready. A few years later I tried again (while also working two jobs) at the University of Louisville, and again, dropped out after only a few courses.

Years passed, I married, raised children, and worked for one of the top companies in my city surrounded by highly educated professionals, many of whom had attended Ivy League schools. Although smart and capable, my lack of education held me back, and I often felt inadequate. In 2009, the company experienced the largest reduction in workforce in its history and my job was eliminated. Fortunately, I was reassigned to another position in the Diversity and Inclusion office where I felt like a fish out of water—I knew nothing of this topic. Hurt and scared, I was also grateful to have a job. And then I met him ... my new boss, who also became my advocate and mentor. The first sit-down meeting went something like this: "The way I see it, you have two choices; return to college and finish your degree or get your diversity practitioner's certification. Otherwise, I'm not sure how you can continue to compete professionally and also build credibility in this space."

It occurred to me that I may be fighting for my entire career, as everyone around me had a minimum of a bachelor's degree, and many had their master's degrees. That feeling of inadequacy and vulnerability was once again very high. My boss was extremely supportive, expressed an interest in developing me, and agreed to invest in my education. While completing the diversity practitioner's certification, I became more confident with each course, realizing for the first time how much I enjoyed learning. Finally, I was ready!

In 2011, at age 50, I enrolled at the University of Louisville in the organizational leadership and learning program in the School for Human

Development. The program was perfect for me as an adult learner because they recognized (and gave credits for) professional experience, seminars, previous college courses, and other learnings from my career. The classrooms were full of people just like me, adults who had a desire to complete their educational aspirations. This time, I excelled as a student and my confidence continued to build. My boss pushed me too, stating that if I were going to do it, I needed to do it well. Ultimately, I received an academic award, graduating at the top of my class after attending full time in the evenings for about 18 months. The third time is a charm, right?! My persistence paid off.

The sense of accomplishment was so rewarding that I was inspired to pursue my master's degree, which I completed in about nine months. This time, I was one of the oldest people in my class, but the other students welcomed me with open arms. Again, I received an academic award, graduating at the top of my class. It's almost euphoric as I think about how I felt receiving my Masters in Business Administration degree. The sense of accomplishment is rewarding enough, but the confidence in knowing that I can do anything I set my mind to is incredibly empowering.

Upon reflection, it's easy to realize now that fear of failure held me back for a long time. When my boss encouraged me to go back to school, he was brave enough to have a candid conversation with me about my goals, aspirations, and dreams for my career. He took an interest in me, believed in my abilities, and challenged me to extract the most from the experience.

Today, I'm a successful diversity and inclusion manager at one of the top companies in the world, and the education I persistently earned contributed to my personal and professional development in many ways, as I became more focused and committed to growing myself each and every day. I'm now a lifelong learner and curious about a broader spectrum of interests. I'll have to say that I'm also proud of myself, which is quite remarkable after the feelings of inadequacy that plagued me for so many years. I feel more confident about my independence and ability to compete in the modern world and my skill set has expanded in numerous ways. My gratitude is abundant for those who supported me along the way. What a rewarding journey!

Advancing to Become the Police Chief

Jim Ferraris

George Fox University

In 2010 at 53 years old, I had about 95 hours of college under my belt and no degree. I decided to go back to school—you will read why in a bit. So, I enrolled in an adult learning program at George Fox University (GFU), seeking a Bachelor of Arts in management and organizational leadership (MGOL). My experience at GFU was outstanding! The GFU motto is "Be Known." That was so true—I was known at GFU. I have a busy life, both professionally and personally. Staff and faculty did everything they could to make furthering my education workable within the demands on my life.

Several professors and instructors stand out. Frank Barsotti taught human resources. He was a perfect fit. He has years of experience working for Hewlett-Packard as a global HR director, responsible for more than 30,000 employees. I learned a lot from him that I am able to apply in my professional life. Carol Hutchinson was another fabulous instructor. From a spirituality perspective, she helped me grow as an individual. Dr. George Byrtek was another great professor. He shepherded us through the MGOL program, was always available to us, and pushed us to be better. I had to work hard during the time I was in school. I was often the oldest student in the class and often had the most diverse career and life experiences when compared to other students. During the 2½ years I was in school, I worked as a precinct commander for the Portland Police Bureau, retired from Portland, and went to work for the Salem Police Department as a deputy police chief. I juggled a very demanding career that often included work weeks of 50–60 hours, then tackling my school studies, which took up almost all of my free time.

Clearly, I have changed as a result of returning to school. I have grown exponentially since completing my degree at GFU, both professionally and personally. I think the turning point was when it hit me that I was finally done. The 26 months I had invested were complete, and I had a diploma to prove it! My satisfaction with GFU was contagious to the point that my 30-year-old son enrolled in the same program at GFU that I did and he graduated in May 2015. One of my closest policing colleagues needed to return to school to finish his degree. After talking positively about my experiences at GFU, he enrolled in the same program I had and he graduated from GFU in 2017.

I continue to mentor those in my profession, and I push those lacking formal education to get back to school and finish that degree just like many people did with me. One person stands out. My colleague, now retired Portland Police Commander Dave Benson, constantly talked with me about the value of a formal education. Dave, who teaches part time at a community college and holds a master's degree, explained to me the utility of finishing a degree program and helped me see how I could get back to school while working full time. I owe Dave a debt of gratitude for pushing me in that direction and not giving up on me. So in return, when I hear people talk about barriers to going back to school, or just the words "I don't have time to do that," I use myself as an example. I explain that if I was able to work full-time, be a husband and father, and seek and achieve a new position of employment, all while juggling a full class load and graduating with a 3.963 GPA, then there is really little reason that another person can't give it a try! I'm now nearly 62 years old and I'm in my 41st year of policing—and I continue to learn each and every day. Much of that has been reinforced by finishing my formal education.

Going back to school has had a positive impact on my career. I work in a world of folks who are educated professionals from a variety of disciplines. While I am very experienced in my field and enjoy a great reputation, both locally and nationally, my confidence always lacked because I did not have a formal degree. Now that I have finished school, I am more confident in my day-to-day work, when dealing with people and groups and when speaking publicly. One of my career goals was to serve as a chief of a police organization. I had the experience and necessary boxes checked for that goal, except having a 4-year undergraduate degree. Not having that degree was always a barrier to further advancement or to achieving that career goal of being a police chief. Once I graduated from GFU, I was very marketable having earned a bachelor's degree. In 2015, I reached my career goal and was appointed chief of police for the City of Woodburn, a position I currently hold. Later in 2015, I enrolled in the Center for Homeland Defense and Security's Executive Leaders Program at the Naval Postgraduate School in Monterey, California. I finished the NPS/CHDS program's postgraduate studies at the end of 2016, an accomplishment I would have not been able to attain had I not received a bachelor's degree from an accredited university.

5

Overcoming Barriers and Beating the Odds

Significant life events are ever present in most people's lives. Beating cancer, escaping poverty, managing care for a sick parent or child, or fighting personal demons and winning the battle—these victories over significant life events provide some of the most compelling stories in higher education. There is no doubt that students from lower socioeconomic statuses are more likely to experience barriers to completion. Efforts in higher education to address affordability and assimilation for those who are first generation can go a long way in addressing retention. However, there is no way to avoid all challenges that life presents to students. Given the wide range of ages, life situations, and backgrounds, the variability of significant life events an adult student may encounter is impossible to easily categorize. Consequently, these events are likely to occur, and it is critical to establish flexible and adaptable policies that enable adult students to finish their coursework and overall degree. Creating this sort of "solidarity movement" in which faculty, staff, and students bond together to lift one another up in times of challenge and crisis may help usher students through the problems and help adult learners push

Unfinished Business, pages 79–119

through to the finish line. Overcoming the odds and reaching a higher quality of life is evident in each story in this chapter.

The Thousand Mile Journey to a Better Life

Philip Young Alier

University of Louisville

I left my hometown of Bor, in South Sudan, when I was about nine years old. It was during the Second Sudanese Civil War, and Bor was destroyed. The civilians were forced to run to the surrounding villages, but the government kept chasing and shelling us, so we had to keep running. Eventually, guerrilla leader Dr. John Garang gathered us up and took us to Ethiopia. That's when I was separated from my parents.

I was in Ethiopia for 4 years, and it was the worst time. There were around 46,000 of us gathered there in a refugee camp that also served as a military camp because it was the base of our guerrilla movement. Some of the older children were taken away for military training, and many children died—approximately 16,000—due to a measles outbreak and other diseases brought on by malnourishment. There was nothing to eat, and we were there for almost nine months before the United Nations and the Red Aban (an affiliate of the Red Cross) was able to bring us food supplies.

When the Ethiopian government under Mengistu Haile Mariam was overthrown, we had to leave. So, we ran back to South Sudan to a town called Kapoeta. By that time many of us had become teens, so we now understood what was happening, and we were tired of running. We wanted to join the army, but they would only take you if you were old enough—around 17 or 18—or if you were muscular. If you were too young or too skinny, they would turn you away, but many of us younger kids would just put on camouflage and sneak in anyway. I was around 12 when I joined the Red Army.

After joining the army, we were trained and deployed. They tried to keep us away from the front lines by assigning us to logistics roles where we would just transport food and ammunition to the fighters, but most of us would sneak to the front lines anyway. After a couple of years, when I was around 13 or 14, the town we were staying in was recaptured by the Sudanese government. At that time Dr. Garang insisted that we be taken to safety, so, with the help of the United Nations, the Red Army was mobilized to the border of Kenya where we were disarmed and taken to Kakuma refugee camp. We were the first refugees at Kakuma, and other refugee communities would be brought there later.

It was there, in Kenya, that I became interested in concentrating on my education. I had received a little bit of schooling before that. During my 4 years in Ethiopia I learned some basic English and Arabic, and I also went to class in South Sudan while I was in the Red Army, but it was class in the bush, "under trees" (outdoors). It wasn't like class here in America. You would go and sit in class with your gun, and they would teach you, and you would keep going!

I finished high school in Kenya, and because of that I was admitted into a program where they train you for 9 consecutive months to be a nurse, similar to an LPN program here in the United States. I spent the rest of my 9 years in Kenya working in the hospital at the Kakuma refugee camp.

My communication skills improved during that time, because I got used to meeting international people at the hospital, and I made a lot of friends. There were Malaysians that came to the hospital, along with Australians, British people, and even an American. I got used to talking with them and learning the different patterns of English through their accents. Though this was very helpful in preparing me for life in the United States, it was still a challenge to transition from British English to American English. I quickly learned that wouldn't be the only challenge I would face in America.

Coming to the United States wasn't easy for me. I arrived here on July 17, 2001, and when I got off the plane I did not know who would receive me at the airport, where I would go to sleep, or where I would eat. That kind of experience really makes you do a lot of thinking; you're not sure what will happen next or who you can trust. It can make you feel very insecure! Getting settled in and overcoming culture shock was also a huge challenge. It was like going from "the bush to the town." It was a nightmare. I didn't know how to do simple things like flush a toilet or warm up food in a microwave. I felt like I was going to die here because I didn't have the proper experience. It was like being from another world!

That is why I am still so thankful for the generosity and support I was shown when I arrived here. I came here under the sponsorship of the Hurstbourne Baptist Church via the Kentucky Refugee Ministry, and the church members who signed up to sponsor me were the ones who received me at the airport. When I got off the plane they had a bulletin board that said "Philip Young Alier, Welcome to America." When I saw that, it really blew my mind!

They covered the rent and utilities to furnish me with an apartment for 2 months and helped me to get settled in. From there I started working as a mental health worker at Our Lady of Peace, and went on to earn my GED. After that, I enrolled at Jefferson Community and Technical College where

I earned 90 credits before transferring to the organizational leadership and learning program at the University of Louisville (U of L). I earned my bachelor's degree in 2012, which paved the way for my promotion from mental health worker to risk manager at my job, and gained me acceptance into graduate school. I am now awaiting the results for my application to a PhD program in epidemiology from the highest-ranked university in the region.

I am the first person in my family to earn a higher education, and I believe that education is the key to liberty. My wife has also earned her GED, and I have helped her enroll in college too. We've had two children together since we arrived here.

When I arrived here it was very difficult for me to allow myself to trust strangers who were not like me, in a place where everything was so different. But I had already suffered so much up to that point that I decided to put my trust in God that whoever would receive me that day would not harm me, but instead they would help me and be like my best friend. The way I see it, even though we are not all born the same—some of us are Black and some are White; some of us are short and some are tall—we are all from the same mother, and we all have the same blood. That mindset allowed me to reach out and establish a relationship with whoever I would encounter. I believe that God has a plan for all of us, and He sends people to you who have opportunities. You have to open your heart when those opportunities knock.

That's how I was able to persevere through the challenges of coming to the United States, and that's how I met my mentor, Dr. Matt (Bergman). Mentors like Dr. Matt are important because they are like the headlights on your car that illuminate the path in front of you; without them you do not know what you might hit. They allow you to see the holes in your path so you can avoid them before falling in. They also provide support. They are the ones who say, "Hey, I know you can do it." Without that support, it is easy to fall behind. Once you have it, you will keep going in order to make proud the ones who have given it to you. You persevere because you don't want to let them down.

From Gangster to Graduate: The Untold Story of My Pursuit of a Dream

Orman E. Morton, III

Oregon State University

Three things occurred to me at a very young age. First, the situation I had gotten myself into was the product of my own and my parents' decisions and naïve faith in people. Second, I needed to get out of the situation. Third, the only way out was a good education.

I grew up in a high-crime, drug-infested, suburban neighborhood outside of Baltimore, Maryland. I was recruited into a street gang at the age of eight. My father was a recovering alcoholic. My mother was poor. They were divorced. To escape this world of depression and chaos, I decided I must achieve a college degree. However, neither one of my parents were in a financial position to assist me in this endeavor. I would have to earn it.

My plan started out fine. In elementary school, I received the William H. Heller award given to the student with the highest GPA. In middle school, I routinely made the honor roll and was placed in the highest-level class for each grade. My GPA in middle school combined with my community service through the Boy Scouts helped me to get acceptance in the only blue-ribbon high school in Baltimore County. High school brought more honor roll and my academic letter. And then I started my senior year.

In my senior year of high school two events would occur that would set me back 20 years. The first was my protest of the inadequate computer equipment our high school was using to teach computer programming. My brother was a year behind me. I knew I couldn't change the system to accommodate me. I was already aware of the budget cuts that had limited my school's ability to keep up with the constant change of technology. However, I wanted the change for my brother. A simple request and a "no" became a sit-in and a reprimand. I refused to budge, and they refused to let me stay in class. I would report to the principal's office for the three computer programming classes as a result of my refusal to partake in the class. Three "E"s and a tarnished GPA resulted (although my brother's class had a brand new computer lab the next year). The second event was my inability to control the warrior/gangster I had become. A rumor had circulated around school that a person who had been bullying me for the past 6 years was planning on removing me from my own home and humiliating me by beating me down in front of my family and friends. Although my gang affiliations were well-known throughout the neighborhood, this young man did not live in my neighborhood and thus was unaware of what I had become. Six years was enough, and it was time to end the harassment. I inflicted a beating upon him so severe that he could not walk. I had damaged his eye and concussed him. The result was a suspension with the intent to expel for a Category II assault and battery. The story was a lie. These two events ended my chances for a scholarship.

With no other options available to continue my education, I completed a FAFSA (Free Application for Federal Student Aid) and hoped for the best. I received the letter acknowledging my receipt of funds for continuing my education and quickly realized that I would only be able to afford the local community college. The funds would pay for one year with the help of in-state tuition. After reviewing my options, I decided to pursue an Associate of Applied Science in business management. I struggled with the first two semesters, but eventually hit my stride and ended on the Dean's Highest Honors list in the third semester. I reapplied for FAFSA knowing my funds were running out. I was denied. I needed to solve two problems: the gangs and college funding.

My gang affiliation had networked to three gangs. The introduction of the Bloods and Crips had changed the Baltimore gang landscape, and guns ruled the day. My life was in danger. My search for a way out provided only one suitable option. I would join the local police department. The police department had just announced that they would be hiring 45 recruits. This would provide me a way out of the gangs and funding to continue my education. After a grueling physical fitness test, background check, and psychological exam, I was notified of my acceptance into the next recruitment class. I immediately applied for funding and received a Baltimore County grant for an additional year of college with the requirement that I complete additional courses in Criminal Science. I was back on track. I picked up where I left off and made the Dean's Highest Honors List in the fourth and fifth semesters.

I contemplated the sixth semester knowing that I would only need to maintain my GPA to qualify for the transfer program to a 4-year institution. As a recruit, I was required to complete patrol hours in which I would assist a police officer during their shift. The hours required amounted to a part-time job. This requirement caused me concern. I did not want to put myself into a position of becoming overburdened by college and the police department in a way which would negatively affect my GPA. I felt there was no other choice than to reduce my credits at college. Being a part-time student would cause me a delay in meeting the requirements for my transfer to university, but it would allow me to fulfill the requirements of my funding organization. I would only take six credits in my sixth semester.

It was a balmy September evening. My partner and I were enjoying a rather quiet evening on shift patrolling the area where I had grown up. I had just been reassigned from Precinct 9 to Precinct 11 to help them with their officer shortage due to retirements and injuries. A call from dispatch broke the silence of the radio. A local bowling alley was having problems with a gang of teenagers loitering in front of the entrance into the establishment. Upon arriving on the scene, I quickly left the patrol car to approach the individuals. As I approached, I recognized one of them. He was the leader of a local gang who I had several previous encounters with as a gang member. He immediately recognized me. A rant ensued in which he listed every street crime he knew I had been involved in and all three gangs with which I had affiliation. I threatened the group with arrest if they did not leave the area, and they eventually left. Following the incident, my partner began asking me questions in relation to the comments made by the young man. I told him it was someone merely lying to seek revenge. He dropped the conversation. A week later I was notified by my commanding officer that my presence was requested at headquarters. Upon arriving at headquarters, I was greeted by an Internal Affairs officer and taken to a room that contained a desk and chair sitting in front of five other officers from the Internal Affairs unit. I was told to open the folder on the desk and read the contents. I opened the folder and started to read every crime I had committed as a member of the street gangs. I closed the folder. An officer explained that I had the option to turn in my badge with no further consequence. I took off my badge and placed it on the folder. I was told that I was no longer a member of the police department. I walked out of head-quarters with the realization that my college funds had just been canceled.

Around this time, I met a young lady. A courtship ensued and mar-riage quickly followed. We were young and enjoying the moment. Again, I found myself in the position of needing funding to continue my education. I decided to work two jobs and use the extra income to pursue six more credits in the next semester. I applied for a job at a local electronics store and started working there the next week. I started attending college again the following month. About halfway through the semester, my wife got sick. The sickness occurred nearly every morning. Her mother suggested she buy a pregnancy test. It was positive. I was going to become a father. I fin-ished the semester, but it would be my last.

The daunting financial burden of a child caused me to panic. I needed to support my family and my current income wouldn't suffice. I asked my boss for a promotion. Based on my college credits in business management, the company promoted me to regional logistics manager. With the pay in-crease, came more hours and responsibility. I would hold the position and its burden for 6 years. My son was born with several health issues includ-ing jaundice, asthma, anaphylaxis due to severe food allergies, and acid reflux. I would need more pay. The company continued to provide me with raises, but they weren't enough to help offset medical bills and the increas-ing debt. I applied for a position with a local steel mill. After a month of interviews and testing I was notified that I had received a position in man-agement. I asked to be placed within the union. The company balked at my request. I explained the situation with my son and my need for good health benefits. They reluctantly agreed with the notification that I would eventually become management. I agreed.

After one year as a union grunt, I was promoted to a quasi-management position where I was the shift foreman but maintained my union status. I held this position for 2 years. In total, I would work for 10 years at the steel mill holding 13 different positions. During this time, I would divorce, remarry, and have another child. In 2010, it became apparent that business was starting to slow down. The import of cheaper steel from India and China was crippling the domestic steel industry. I started to worry about my future within the steel industry. The union decided to hold a meeting. They notified us of an impending layoff. The union had invited various agencies to set up tables and provide information on funding available for union workers in the event of a layoff. One of the tables was being manned by representatives from the community college where I had taken classes 14 years prior. I asked if it was possible for me to acquire my AAS in business management. The representative explained that there was a legacy program for adults that had not had the opportunity to complete their 2-year degree, but it expired after 15 years. I had one year left to complete the required courses. The next day I visited the college to inquire about my status. I was notified that I would have to satisfy the requirements under the current curriculum. After reviewing my records, the dean determined that I needed to complete four classes to achieve my AAS in business management. He also notified me that my union had a college tuition program that would pay for college courses based on the number of years of service. I visited my union office at the steel mill the next day and was told that I qualified for funding for 36 credits. I only needed 12. I was back. I graduated in August of 2011 with my AAS in business management. I was so ashamed of taking so long to achieve the degree that I decided not to attend graduation. Besides, a 2-year AAS degree had not been the goal. I still longed for the 4-year degree.

The next 2 years would bring a pattern of 6 months of work followed by a layoff with each subsequent layoff lasting longer than the previous one. It was obvious now that the end was near. I decided to use the remaining funds to start my pursuit of my dream degree—environmental science. As a Native American, a member of the Penobscot tribe in Maine, I was born with a respect for our natural world. Ancient teachings from elders had taught me the ways of our people and our respect for our brothers and sisters of the land, water, and air. I had long been an environmental activist and wanted nothing more than to be able to have a positive influence on the environment. I needed to decide on a college that would enable me to pursue my environmental science degree. After phone calls, websites, and brochures, I made my decision. I would pursue my degree at Oregon State University through the Ecampus program. The Ecampus program provides out-of-state students the ability to pursue a degree online while paying in-state tuition. Oregon State has an active native student union with its own dedicated long house, Eena Haws. It was a win-win-win situation. Furthermore, the Environmental Science program offered a wide range of classes covering multiple disciplines in the Environmental Sciences and was the most demanding requiring 180 credits to graduate.

Upon contacting Oregon State, I was put in touch with an academic advisor who would assist me in applying for the College of Earth, Ocean, and Atmospheric Sciences. There would be one factor that would need to be addressed. My classes for transfer had been attended at the Community College of Baltimore County (CCBC). Oregon State University had never had a student transfer from this institution. Every class would have to be individually reviewed for merit to the Oregon State curriculum. The next step was to coordinate the completion of science lab courses in physics, chemistry, and biology. The decision was made to complete these courses at CCBC under the direction of the Oregon State advisor. In other words, the Oregon State advisor was choosing my classes at CCBC based on Oregon State curriculum requirements. This helped to assure the full acceptance of my transfer credits. I utilized my remaining funds to begin baccalaureate core classes that I had not previously taken.

On August 31, 2012, just 2 weeks after the birth of my third child, I received a letter in the mail from my union. It stated that my company, RG Steel, had filed for bankruptcy terminating our jobs effective immediately. Gone were my job, health benefits, and college funds. Once again, I had received another setback in the pursuit of my dream. The union made the decision to petition the U.S. Congress for assistance under the failure to place tariffs on imported steel in order to protect our jobs. Congress agreed to provide assistance on an individual basis. Two months later, I received a call from a government agent who explained that since I had previous college credits, I qualified for a work reintroduction program. This program would fund my pursuit of a 4-year degree as long as I pursued a degree within a field in which I could acquire employment at a pay level within 65% of my steel mill salary. After some diligent research, I was able to prove that a degree in environmental science would provide me such an opportunity. I was placed into the work reintroduction program the following month. Things did not start out well. When I expressed my desire to attend the Oregon State University Ecampus program, the director of the work reintroduction program denied my request on the grounds that the program was only approved to pay in-state tuition. I provided documentation which showed that the tuition for the Ecampus program was actually lower than the in-state tuition at the University of Maryland. The director reluctantly approved my request to attend classes at Oregon State.

It had been 9 months since my last contact with Oregon State. I called to set up a phone call with my advisor, but she had been promoted to a new position. I was connected to a new advisor who immediately accessed the file and picked up where the other advisor had left off. I was once again directed to complete classes in physics, chemistry, and biology. Upon completion of these credits, the advisor assisted me in my application to the College of Earth, Ocean, and Atmospheric Sciences. I waited impatiently, running to the mailbox every day to check for the acceptance letter. Finally, I received a letter from the university. I was so nervous and worried about its contents that I simply stared at the envelope for minutes. Finally, I gathered the courage to open it. I had been accepted. I sat on the curb for about 10 minutes and cried. It was one of the defining moments of my life; it was the opportunity to have what I always wanted, which had been nothing more than a dream for so long. I raced into the house and immediately logged onto the internet to access the Oregon State website. I walked through the defined steps, and there it was: my name listed as an Oregon State student.

As part of the initiation into the university system, I was assigned an academic advisor. This advisor would assist me in course selection, check my progress, and make recommendations based on my success with my curriculum. However, her first assignment would be to assist me in the transfer of my community college credits to Oregon State. This required a review of each class for merit and compatibility to the Oregon State course requirements. The review process concluded with the removal of six classes due to insufficient information on curriculum. My advisor notified me of the decision and gave me direction on how to proceed with acquiring acceptance for the six classes. I followed her directions and was successful at getting all six classes reinstated. The remaining credits required for graduation would require an additional 1½ years of study and determination. I was ready to complete my journey.

I started my Oregon State journey in the Fall of 2014. The next year and a half would be filled with awe, sleep deprivation, wonderment, challenges, and contemplation. At times it was one of the greatest moments in my life, and in other moments it tested my full resolve. There were just as many moments of pride as there were of soul searching. My spirituality became reinforced, as I relied heavily on it for strength. During the course of my pursuit and subsequent push to the finish line, I was diagnosed with Lyme disease and ventricular tachycardia. On December 22, 2014, I suffered a heart attack which left me clinically dead (I had no pulse). Through it all I continued my pursuit. In the end, I persevered and achieved my ultimate goal. I completed my final class in the Spring of 2016 and was notified that I met my requirements for graduation.

The notification provided me with a moment of contemplation. I had decided to forego my graduation from the Community College of Baltimore County out of shame for achieving something that took most people 2 years to complete yet took me 20. Again, I was in the same position. Should I attend my graduation from Oregon State University? Would I be out of place amongst a plethora of 20-somethings? A gray-haired old man who would stand to be ridiculed. I changed my decision daily. My mother begged me to attend. She explained that it would be her proudest moment. She would be able to watch her oldest son graduate from college; a feat that had never been accomplished on either side of my family. She explained that it would justify all the sacrifices she had made. Upon hearing this, there was no doubt that I would attend and my mother would be my guest.

I graduated from Oregon State University on June 11, 2016. The graduation ceremony was nothing short of spectacular. The morning began with a free breakfast sponsored by the Ecampus program. My academic advisor, professor, and classmates were in attendance. For the first time, we met face-to-face to talk of our journeys and celebrate together. My friend from San Diego, California surprised me with his attendance. We quickly embraced upon seeing each other. He was about the same age as me, which comforted me, since I feared I would be the only "old man" in attendance. Obviously, this was an unrealistic thought as people fulfill their dreams all through life. We were the 147th graduating class from Oregon State University totaling 6,406 graduates from young to old. At the breakfast, we were asked individually in a video documentary to express what graduating from Oregon State University meant to us. When it was my turn to speak, I started strong but soon the power of the moment hit me. I remembered the thoughts that I would never achieve my dream, the constant setbacks, the struggle, the determination, the fight to continue, and the words of my mother. I broke down. The crew stopped recording. I regained my composure and the filming continued. When I finished I was embraced by my new friends, my mother, my academic advisor, and my professor. It was one of the greatest moments of my life, and it all became real.

Following the breakfast, we gathered outside at the designated area for the students from the College of Earth, Ocean, and Atmospheric Sciences. Here I would meet for the first time face-to-face another classmate from Seattle. The two of us would enjoy the rest of the festivities together. We marched across campus, 6,000-plus strong, led by our mascot, Benny the Beaver, and bagpipes. We marched into Reser Stadium to stands full of families and friends. Somewhere in the crowd was my mother—alone, but proud. Upon reaching our seats on the football field, we all took out our cell phones to help locate our loved ones. My mother waved so I could see her. I waved back. Tears started filling my eyes. We sat through the ceremony discussing our lives and laughing at the remarks of the speakers. Finally, we were asked to rise and proceed to the stage to receive our diplomas. I have never been prouder of myself as an individual. I had persevered and never given up even when the odds were against me. I had achieved my dream.

Two weeks after graduating I received a job interview with a company called Brightwater, Inc. The owner, Jim Gracie, had decided in his 40s to pursue his dream of owning a company that would provide him the opportunity to restore the waters of the Chesapeake Bay. He asked me a series of questions including questions related to water quality. Oregon State had provided me all the correct answers. I started working for Mr. Gracie 2 weeks later. It has been more than a year and a half since and I have become certified in wetland delineations and received training in the Rosgen stream classification system based on river geomorphology. Along the way, I have relied on my Oregon State education and the mentorship of Mr. Gracie to maintain my success. I currently hold the position of Environmental Scientist with the experience of almost 100 wetland delineations, an active role in four stream restoration projects, and the continued monitoring of four streams for erosion and water quality.

In the path to my success, many people have contributed their time and effort to make my dream a reality. I would like to thank Angela Harkness, Dana Williams, and Tondi Correll of the Baltimore County Workforce Development team for encouraging me to fight for my dream and fighting for me when it was necessary. I would like to thank Kathy Baker-Brosh, Chris Snow, Kriste Garman, and the staff at the Anita C. Leight Estuary Center for introducing me to the demands and rigors of environmental science. I would like to thank Theresa Harper and Dawn Marie Gaid from the Oregon State University student support team for their work on my behalf, their coaching, encouragement, and work as a free psychiatrist. I would like to thank Dr. Kaplan Yalcin, Oregon State University professor, for demanding my best effort and providing a higher level of education to prepare me for my future position. I would like to thank Mr. Jim Gracie, president of Brightwater, Inc., for taking a chance on a washed-up steel worker just hoping to pursue his dream. I would like to thank my mother, brother, and sister-in-law, Ishrat Siddique, for providing free childcare and encouragement through some of my darkest moments in this journey. I would like to thank my children for being my inspiration. Finally, I would like to thank

Beaver Nation, the staff and students at Oregon State University, for the memories, friendships, and reality of fulfilling my dreams.

Passion for Learning at Any Age

Deborah Kay Prather

University of Louisville

I was born in Louisville, Kentucky in 1960 and have lived in Louisville my entire life, but I enjoy traveling the world. The desire to be a medical doctor was apparent at a young age. I wanted to help discover the root causes of illnesses and disease. Hence, medical research was my desired field of study. While in junior high school, I campaigned to allow younger students to take Latin classes. I wanted to learn Latin to support my future career. I successfully got this passed and took Latin in eighth grade of school. Also, in high school I took vocational classes to become a medical assistant. As a result, during the last 2 years of high school I worked part time in an OB/GYN office. Six of my closest friends had nicknames for each other, based on the seven dwarves. My nickname was Doc. Again, I lived knowing I would be a doctor, so this was a very appropriate nickname.

As planned, I began my college years at the University of Kentucky, planning to continue my studies to be a medical doctor. However, I was sidetracked due to missing my boyfriend and went back to Louisville to marry my high school sweetheart in 1980. We had two children together and remained married until his death in 1997 due to cancer. College was put on hold, so I could work full time and take care of my family.

I began working at Kentucky Fried Chicken (KFC) Corporation in 1982, the year my first child was born. I ended up working in the Computer and Information Systems (CIS) department. In 1984, the year my second child was born, I returned to school but changed my focus to be in CIS and Management, to support my current career. In 1987, I received an associate degree in CIS. I had an extremely successful career in CIS at KFC and spent most of my 16 years in various technology management positions. After the death of my husband in 1997, I took a leave of absence to spend more time with my children as I began the life of a single parent.

During and after the death of my husband, I delved back into reading medical journals and doing my own medical research. Fortunately, the doctors assisting my husband were open to detailed communication. Subsequently, many late-night discussions regarding medical research occurred. The doctors encouraged me to return to college and become a medical doctor. As a result, one of the doctors set me up with the University of

Louisville (U of L) to discuss a new program that was being developed in Bioinformatics. He believed I would be the perfect candidate to join the program and assist in the development due to my technology background and strong medical interest and knowledge. Unfortunately, with the recent death of my husband and having children to raise, I did not take advantage of this opportunity.

In October 1999, I remarried, and I began working with my current husband in the training industry. On my 49th birthday, I returned to college (U of L) to complete a bachelor's degree. I completed a Bachelor of Science in workforce leadership and workplace performance in May 2010. I continued school to get a Master of Science in human resource education over the next couple of years. My first corporate job after receiving my master's degree was at Kindred Healthcare Corporation in Louisville, beginning in April of 2012. This again piqued my interest in returning to work in the medical community.

While at Kindred Healthcare Corporation, my friend and manager introduced me to the International Quantum University of Integrative Medicine. My friend recognized my love of helping others and love for medical knowledge, especially in more non-allopathic ways, focusing more on holistic medicine. This university sounded perfect, so I enrolled in August 2015. I have earned a Bachelor of Science in holistic health and a Master of Science in natural medicine. I will have my PhD in natural medicine with International Quantum University of Integrative Medicine, once I complete my dissertation.

I strongly believe in continuous improvement and growth. I have completed many other training programs and certified with various organizations. Among these are certification as a Reiki Master in Usui Reiki, Myers-Briggs Type Indicator® (MBTI®) Certified, a certified Mini Me Yoga Ambassador, a Holistic Healer Practitioner, a Life Activation Practitioner, Ritual Master, Celtic Shaman, and a teacher of eight courses (Sacred Geometry, Max Meditation, Astral Travel, Sanctuary Meditation, Awaken Thyself, Spiritual Intuition, Stress Rescue, and the Seven Mystery Schools) with an international Mystery School based on the lineage of King Solomon teachings.

I am a master of e-Learning training development, which has been used by many large corporations internationally. I plan to continue using these skills to create e-Learning to support my work in the health and spirituality fields. A lot has happened in the last 10 years since I returned to college at the ripe young age of 49. However, there is still more business that needs to be finished. In Fall 2019, I will be the co-publisher and editor for a new magazine; *E.P.I.C. Magazine: Bluegrass Edition*. All the education and life experiences that began when I returned to college 10 years ago have joined together to perfectly align with this magazine. Producing and editing a magazine requires specialized tools and skills. Due to the training in the instructional design and development program, I have these tools and skills. Also, the magazine's focus on spirituality, health, and sustainability is a great fit with my educational and career evolution. This combination allows me to continue to support my love for helping others grow in these areas.

Overcoming the Odds

Rachel Hensley

Oregon State University

I grew up in a household best described as working-poor. My stepdad did janitorial work, and until her drug addiction spiraled out of control, my mom worked as a CNA. Drugs took over my mother's life—and by extension, mine—around the time I was in middle school. Whenever my mom would go on a drug binge and come home, fighting would ensue with her husband, which almost always culminated in her picking me up in the middle of the school day, with the car packed full and the intention of moving away. I was bounced around to different schools several times a year, usually a few weeks at a time.

Her drug habit became so severe that she would often wait until my stepdad got paid and take all the money. Living in the dark, existing without heat in the winter, and subsisting on whatever was available at local food pantries became the norm. Difficulties at home paired with an inability to relate to my peers made school less important, and I started skipping a lot. Eventually, my mom was gone more than she was home. As a young teen with no supervision or guidance, it was easy to fall in with the "wrong" crowd. I started smoking, drinking, dabbling in drugs, and spending most of my time with older boys. My house became the designated place to party and hang out, with my mom's rule being that you could only have drugs or alcohol in the house if you were willing to share with her, if she was there at all.

Shortly before my 15th birthday, I got pregnant. I already felt out of place at school, and the embarrassment and shame I felt from being pregnant was the tipping point for dropping out halfway through my freshman year. That summer, I gave birth to my son and moved in with my aunt's family across town. In the fall, I enrolled in the area high school. Despite having a more stable home life, school was harder than ever. A typical day started with staying up most of the night with an infant, struggling through classes, feeling more out of place than ever, and after my 16th birthday, working in the evening. By the time spring came around, I couldn't keep it up any longer, and I dropped out of my second freshman year, this time for good. Coming from a family with several dropouts or a maximum of a high school diploma, it wasn't a big deal and no one made a fuss. A few months later, I got my GED.

After a year or so of living with various people in different places, I became homeless, and my son went to live with a family member. The next few years were a struggle. I managed to get a receptionist job at an office by a stroke of luck when I was 19, and when I was 21 I had worked my way up at a different company to a better office position and could finally support myself and have a place of my own.

Now that I had my feet on the ground and I wasn't merely trying to get through each day, I spent more time reading and started doing volunteer work. I had always been an exceptional student (when I was at school, anyway), and I had a strong love for learning. In time, I started to get bored with my work and wanted to do something more with my life. Growing up, college was never seriously talked about, let alone taken into consideration as something "someone like me" could do. I didn't know anyone who had gone to college, and I didn't have a clue where to begin. After a lot of time on Google, I thought, "What do I have to lose?" I enrolled at the local community college that fall. I didn't have much of a plan besides learning and hopefully getting a degree I could use as a ticket to a better life for me and for my son. At the time, I had no idea how hard it would be or how long it would take, I just knew I needed to do it. Looking back, it's probably best I didn't know how difficult the road ahead would be. I probably would have doubted my ability to make it through my associate degree and then my bachelor's, because like they often do, things happened, and they happened a lot.

During the 5½ years it took for me to finish both degrees, I ran into countless obstacles, though admittedly some were self-inflicted. The first was a toxic relationship that almost ended my academic career near the very beginning. I was in a deep depression and self-medicated with drugs. Thankfully I realized my life was starting to point back toward where I started, and I got clean. Soon after, I ended that relationship.

Within a year, I was dating again. Not having a frame of reference for what a healthy relationship looked like, I didn't recognize, or in some cases I ignored, a lot of red flags. After a few months, I became pregnant with my second child in the fall. Being pregnant, I felt trapped in the relationship, so I stayed. I graduated with my associate degree the following May, and that summer had my second boy. At that point, I knew I wanted to transfer my credits and start working on a bachelor's degree, but the choice was not an easy one. I think what kept me going was knowing that my oldest son, now eight, was watching, and after telling him countless times that I was going to get a 4-year degree, I had to follow through.

That fall, I enrolled in an online bachelor's program through Oregon State University. The first term wasn't so bad, because my baby was still young and slept a lot, giving me time to get my classwork done. Before long, it became harder and more stressful, trying to manage a baby who was now mobile, parent a 9-year-old, and live with the growing depression stemming from a bad marriage. There were a few times when I had to drop classes or take terms off. There were many times when I wanted to give up completely because it was so hard. But my son was still watching, and I felt like I had come so far already, so I had to keep going.

I somehow managed to get through most of my classes and could almost see the finish line. My kids turned 10 and 2 during the summer, and I intended to take a full-time load in the fall to finish my degree. Before I could get there, though, my relationship imploded. My then-husband was always mentally and emotionally abusive, but at this time it escalated to a level where I began to fear for my safety. When that happened, I knew I had to leave. Our terms were about 10 weeks long, and when I left I was about four weeks in. Initially we went to a women's shelter, but we were fortunate to have some friends offer to let us stay in their home. My ex closed our bank account, refused to pay any of our bills, and threatened to take our son and never let me see him again if he found us. School was on my mind frequently, but it was impossible to focus with the chaos going on around me. I tried to struggle through, but ultimately, I ended up failing half my classes and taking an incomplete in the other half. Because I had dropped classes several times before, due to the challenge of managing a family while trying to study, I was on the verge of failing to meet the policy regarding satisfactory academic progress and losing my financial aid—something I depended on greatly. It seemed like I was closer than ever, but that I still wasn't going to make it. I can't describe how defeated I felt.

After a few months the divorce proceedings began, and the children and I moved back into our home. At the recommendation of the instructor who had failed me, I filed a late drop petition in the hopes of having the classes removed due to extenuating circumstances, so I would be eligible for financial aid. With her support and the support of my academic advisor, my request was granted.

I took the spring term off to try to get my life together as best I could, and I got a part-time job at a nonprofit organization. As I was trying to find a way to complete my few remaining classes, I was offered a full-time position at my job and felt like I had an impossible choice. I had been struggling to support my family during my separation, and a full-time job offered security. I had no way to know when I would have another opportunity for full-time work, making it even harder. I had so few credits left and had come so far, but I doubted my ability to manage my kids, work full time, deal with the stress of the ongoing divorce, and successfully pass classes.

I spent a lot of time reflecting on everything I had been through, not just during my academic career, but through my whole life. It was so unlikely a person from my background would have started college at all, let alone make it to graduation. I realized then that I was stronger than I was giving myself credit for, and that if I could make it that far, I could make it to the end. I signed up part-time in the summer term, and then again in the fall term. Those few months were hard. I felt guilty about the amount of time I wasn't spending with my kids, as well as how much pizza we were eating when I didn't have time to cook (which was frequently). I had to pick and choose which assignments I had time to do and which ones I would have to take a zero on. My grades those two terms weren't great, but I passed. I took my last exam in the first week of December 2016, and a few weeks later I received a letter in the mail notifying me that I had completed all the requirements to be awarded a bachelor's degree. It didn't seem real.

I opted to have my diploma mailed to me, and in January it arrived. I cried when I opened it and still couldn't believe I had done it. That afternoon as I sat on the couch trying to soak it in, my oldest son, now nearing 12, came home from school and saw me holding my diploma case. When he realized what it was, he smiled wide and gave me a huge hug. I'll never forget the look of excitement on his face when he said, "Wow, mom, you finally graduated. That's so awesome, I'm really proud of you!" In that moment, I knew it had all been worth it.

Because You're Never Too Old

Amanda Skaggs

University of Louisville

I graduated from high school in 1978. Two days after graduation, I started a full-time job. I worked there for 30 years, until I retired in 2008. In 1979, I started my school career; taking classes at the University of Louisville (U of L) using the tuition reimbursement program at my company. My objective was to get a degree so I could get a promotion at work and make more money. Although it was a long day, to go to school at night after working all day, I really enjoyed learning and meeting new people. I tried to take one class per semester.

Well, in the early 1980s, most of the large companies started downsizing, and my company was one of them. They started at the top, with lots of layoffs. So, not only were there no promotions, I was dangling by a thread to hang on to my job! My school objective changed: Now I was trying to get a degree so I could get another job if I got laid off. I changed schools a couple of times during the mid-1980s, but ended up back at U of L in the late 1980s through the early 1990s. Everything was on track and going well until one morning in 1994. I had something very unexpected happen. It derailed not only my school plans, but my life plans. I woke up on February 15th to total darkness. Thought the electricity was out, but finally determined that it was just *my* "lights" that were out. Overnight, I had lost my sight to complete and total darkness. My husband immediately took me to the doctor. I was diagnosed with optic neuritis and told I would never see again. There had been a neurological event that damaged the optic nerve in both eyes. My doctor said it was the worst case of optic neuritis he had ever treated. He added that I would need to learn Braille and take classes to learn to adjust to my new situation. Life, as I knew it, seemed to be over. I couldn't work, or go to school, or have any kind of "normal."

Several months later, I started seeing images and shadows in my left eye. The doctor said to not get my hopes up, because the damage was so severe that it could not get any better. Well, it did get better! My right eye did not improve, but over time, my left eye returned to almost normal. I was eventually able to return to work. Under the Americans with Disability Act, my company was required to accommodate my condition with a special computer that enabled me to work. It had a screen with reversed contrast (dark background and large white letters). I had to enlarge the text until the words were about two inches tall. I couldn't do the job that I had before I left, but I was able to work again. My vision in my left eye continued to improve. Eventually, I was able to return to my former position and finish my career.

After I retired, school was still on my mind. I was just a few classes away from completing my degree. I had been away from U of L for about 14 years. If I returned, I would probably be the oldest student in the class. This seemed very intimidating to me, even daunting. I had convinced myself that I would lose a lot of my credit hours because I had been gone so long, so I would be retaking classes that I had already taken. It also seemed silly to go back to school since I wasn't planning to reenter the job market. But, the idea kept coming back to me.

A few months after I retired, I had lunch with one of my favorite high school friends, Deb. During lunch, we happened to talk about future life goals. I told her that I kept having thoughts about returning to school, but I just couldn't justify the expense, since I no longer had a tuition reimbursement plan to pay for it. She then shared with me that she had recently returned to U of L, and she assured me I would not be the oldest student in class, since she is 7 days older than me! Deb gave me Matt Bergman's phone number and I set up an appointment the next week. All my classes from the 1970s, 1980s, 1990s, and the classes that I had taken at other colleges all counted! I didn't lose any credit hours, as I had thought that I would. I started taking classes the next semester and graduated in December of 2011.

As an older adult, the learning experience was deeply meaningful, on many levels. I learned so much from the interactions with others, both the instructors and my classmates. My perspective of humanity has been broadened. It has enriched my life in a way that nothing else that I have experienced has. Although I don't have a traditional job, I am in leadership roles in my volunteer work. I often apply the knowledge that I learned in class to help me plan events and activities for my retirees' group. I also use skills that I learned to put together extensive walking location schedules for my weekly walking group.

School, to me, has been like building a brick structure. I created the foundation and started on the walls when I was in school before, when I was young. The foundation and the beginning rows were sound, so it remained strong in the years that it was left standing and unfinished. When I returned to school, I just had to go back and complete the remaining rows, and add a roof. Now I can enjoy the completed structure for the rest of my life. I am so glad that I returned to school!

An Amazing Journey

Maria Esperanza Vazquez

Middle Tennessee State University

I was born in 1972 in a rural area of Mexico. I lived there until I was 7 years old. It was then, for the first time, I attended school. I made it to the sixth grade of primary school, and then my parents moved to a city where the neighborhood was home to various gangs. I am the third child of 12, but I am the oldest daughter. I remember that my parents always struggled to make a living for their big family. By the age of 12, I started working as a house cleaner to help support my family. In my culture and by tradition, the oldest girl has to help and support her mother with caring for the rest of the children. I was 12 years old when my father decided to immigrate to the United States. He took my two older brothers with him, while my mother and I were taking care of the other children. By that time, the level of crime in the neighborhood was out of control. For example, vandals got into my house when my mom and I were inside and stole whatever had value. That was the worst time of my adolescence.

After 3 years my father returned home to plan the way to immigrate the rest of the family to the United States. I was smuggled into the United States by a coyote (human smuggler) who was hired by my father. This coyote led the group around for two nights to avoid the border patrol checkpoint. He failed twice, and the authorities sent us back to Mexico. At 15, I arrived in the United States by using the identity of another person. I wasn't legal, and I was scared.

Immediately, I started my life as an official worker in the United States. Official means that I started working full time at the age of 15 using false documents that claimed I was 18 years old. I spent 25 years of my life working at factories, restaurants, and cleaning homes. Sometimes I had to work two jobs in order to make a living. At the age of 38, after confronting domestic violence for 17 years of marriage, I decided to file for divorce.

Then, I decided to have a different life, and I started taking GED classes. It took me 2 years to finish and get my diploma; that was my first personal accomplishment. At the same time, I was studying to become a U.S. citizen. Then, I started to think about college. At first, the idea looked scary, but I always enjoyed learning. My first year at college was extremely hard, and I wanted to quit every day. I didn't quit, because I was aware that if I did quit I would stay in the same cycle and would not make any life progress. An example of a challenge I experienced is having to take a timed exam when English isn't my native language. I expressed my concern and anxiety to my professor, and she referred me to disability services. I was frustrated and crying, saying to myself, "I'm not disabled. I'm just a slow reader with the English language."

Essentially nothing was changed even when I went to that office. If I was going to succeed, it would have to be through my desire to succeed and hard work rather than intervention from an office that provided support, and the professor did not even acknowledge the accommodations. Moreover, I decided to quit my warehouse job to prioritize school more, so I began working as a house cleaner. Slowly, I started to gain confidence because I was gaining knowledge at school.

The lack of education and a poor background sometimes makes me feel that I was treated unfairly in my past. I could have chosen to go to school before I got married or chosen to marry someone else. But looking back on my hard life is a waste of time. Instead of dwelling on the past, I use that wisdom from those difficult times to make better choices in my life.

Then, the situation at my work took a good direction. I began to run my own small cleaning business. The knowledge I gained helped to grow my confidence, not just as a small business owner but also as a minority woman owning a business with a GED. I did not start my business with a business plan. I was not prepared to write, plan, or think about a strategy in which a certain level of education is required. I started this business right after I was accepted into a community college. Since then, I have made progress and success in my business with the knowledge I have acquired in school. I wanted economic freedom, and I needed time to go to school.

Referring to my professional career, I plan to connect my school training and apply it to training my employees. I want to create a workplace that can provide women with skills and training to become confident so that they can use these skills to gain independence in life. Making this business an organization that supports other women in any way is something I have always wanted to pursue. This will be a main goal for the future.

I spent the first 30 years of my life in this country thinking that I was different than the majority of people living in the United States. This was because I came from another country, and I have different characteristics and culture. I was wrong; now I know that I was intimidated by the host culture, and I realize that I was wrong about it. Certainly, I know that maybe a few look at me differently, but every other anxiety was something that I mistakenly assumed.

As a member of the Latino community in the United States, I still think in my native language, Spanish, and that makes it difficult for me to understand the communication around me. I had to overcome the language barrier that was affecting me as a student who speaks a language other than English. Understanding the language is very important for a person who is in college, but more important is to overcome that barrier and do all the work as many times as necessary to understand the content of the classes. This double work that I have to do complicates my life as a student and as an individual for the reason that I do not have time to do other things that are also important in life. I am an immigrant, a woman who has been facing challenges with determination for a better life for many years, so getting this degree is more than a piece of paper for me and worth overcoming all of these struggles.

Happy Tears

Rachael Black

Western Governors University–Texas

I had never cried happy tears. I remember thinking to myself when watching people cry of happiness, that I just didn't get it; I didn't understand. How could someone be so happy that they could physically cry?

Arlington, Texas in the 1990s was not the best place to raise children— at least in my part of town. School was my escape, and to get there, I had to walk two miles in the city every day with my siblings carrying a book bag full of the things I loved—books. Every summer, I would ask my teachers for all of their leftover worksheet copies and I would use them to teach my siblings or to better my own skills. I knew eventually that I would be a teacher; I wanted to give other kids a way to escape their own lives, and at the same time better them.

Time flies by so very quickly and before I knew it, I was 17 and in love. Being the oldest of six children, I was working at the local Pizza Hut to help support the family. My mother and father were violent to each other, and my father was in and out of prison for drugs, alcohol-related offenses, and family violence. My paycheck would go to my mother, who was not working but instead was collecting federal assistance. I was doing okay though; I was taking college courses at the local community college as a high school student, making straight As, and I had great friends. I was going to be different than my mother and father—neither of them had graduated high school, much less ever attended a college.

My boyfriend at the time was soon to be deployed to Iraq. He had heard from fellow comrades that if he got married, he could qualify for more benefits from the Army; soon, we were married. I was 17, lived at home, and was still in high school and college. After my husband left for Iraq, my mother decided I should no longer live at home. I moved in with my in-laws, finished high school, and although I was accepted to Baylor (my dream college), I enrolled at the community college, which was a more financially attainable option.

A few months into my second semester I discovered I was pregnant. I knew my dreams of finishing college were over. It is difficult to write it down on this page but it's the truth: I was devastated. It sounds selfish, but truly it's the complete opposite. I wanted my children to have at least one educated parent, so that they would have a better foundation than I did. I wanted to be able to provide for them things I was not privileged to have when I was young. I wanted them to be more successful than I was. This was the end of the college road for me. I knew that I had to be an amazing mother, and that it would now take two immediate incomes to support our small family.

In an effort to better our lives, my husband and I decided to move to Arizona so that he could go to trade school to become a motorcycle mechanic. While he went to school at night, I worked at a local retail store during the day. This was great because we didn't have to pay for childcare. However, it wasn't long before he met his current wife, and it wasn't me. I know now that it was because we were so young and we had just grown apart as any two humans do over a 7 year time from the ages of 17 to 24.

Here I sat, back in Texas; soon to be divorced, a single mom of a 3-year-old, and working two jobs to make ends meet. When my son was four, I realized that two basic incomes still were not enough to adequately support a small family, but more so, I missed learning. My best friend at the time was excited to be going back to school at an online college and wanted us to commit to being educated together. I researched the college and had a few reservations, but I wanted to get my degree so badly that I enrolled and began classes. I soon realized I was in over my head. The demands of even an online school were too difficult for a single mom working two jobs. Would I ever finish my degree?

It wasn't long after that I met a man who ultimately would give me the two best gifts a woman could ask for. A beautiful son and a college degree. As he worked, I went to school and worked when I could. I began my third attempt at college as a pregnant mother nearing the end of her second trimester. I was dedicated. I knew at this point in my life there would never be another obstacle that would prevent me from achieving this goal.

There were challenges and so many trials, but I was determined. My boyfriend would work out of town two or three weeks of each month; this left me alone with the boys for most of the time. I made it a point to stay up each night working and studying until sometimes two or three o'clock in the morning. Luckily, the college I attended had a mentor program where each student was assigned a mentor to help them both academically and emotionally with the struggles of school. My mentor was Caroline, and she was absolutely amazing. She would cry with me, laugh with me, and sometimes just listen. For this chapter in my life, she was quite literally the mother I never had.

Three and a half years later, I experienced that which I previously could not explain—I cried happy tears. When I realized that I had met all graduation requirements, I was home alone, the boys asleep in their beds, and the man who helped me get there was out of town on work. I had done what

I always knew I could, but had never set my mind to. I cried those happy tears, with every bit of joy my body could express.

This was such a big accomplishment that I had to celebrate. So, I decided to apply for a speaker opportunity at my WGU Texas commencement—and I got the part! I couldn't believe that I was going to show those that were watching that a prisoner's daughter, a mother of two, a college dropout twice over, an Army veteran, and a drug addict's daughter was graduating with a bachelor's degree in education. All of the odds were against me, but I knew in the back of my head that the goal was always to cry happy tears—and so I did.

The Hope Messenger

O. L. Kelley, II

Belhaven University (BA)
Ashworth University (AS)

I was born in Pine Bluff, Arkansas, to an unwed mother who raised me to the best of her ability. My mom was from the south, but we migrated north and settled in Michigan. As a single parent, my mother had to work a lot to support us, which later included a younger brother. This left my brother and me alone in a city where the attraction to belong led us both to the wrong crowds. As a youth, I did not attend church much, except when I would visit my paternal grandmother during school breaks, like summers and holidays. My grandmother was Seventh-day Adventist but attended other churches and took me with her. She helped me overcome my feelings of rejection and worked hard let me know that I was loved. Throughout the years, she never gave up on me, and she prayed consistently for me. In spite of her interactions with me, I still chose to live a life counter to how I was raised.

My first experience with God came when I became a teenager and moved to Houston, Texas, to live with my Dad. I had gotten into trouble and my mom said I was too much for her to handle. Before moving to Houston, I became active in gangs and drugs, and I was on the wrong track for abundant life. Eventually my dad and I had a disagreement that led to him kicking me out of the house, and I stayed with a family friend who mentored me. After I dropped out of high school, I moved back to Michigan and fell back into my old ways. Despite my inability to get things right or to do the right things, God still found it easy to protect me from myself and to not give the enemy permission "to steal, kill, or destroy" me (John 10:10).

Unfortunately for me, my life took a serious turn and I got into serious trouble which led to me being sentenced to 30 years in prison. Early on in my incarceration, God began to deal with me. I knew who He was and what He can do; however, I did not know who I was or what I could be. Even in the midst of my current situation at the time with no freedom and the courts saying that I would be past 50 years old before I could be released without parole, I still had hope.

While I was incarcerated, the Department of Corrections moved to take out all the glass mirrors in the prison facilities, to ensure the safety of both Corrections staff and inmates. They replaced these mirrors with long sheets of aluminum-coated metal that they bolted to the wall to serve as a mirror, so that we could see our appearance while brushing our teeth, combing our hair, and so on. The problem was that the aluminum coating was a very soft metal, and once it came into contact with the abrasive multi-purpose cleaner we used to clean with, the aluminum coating smeared and became warped, fuzzy, or blurred. It left those who looked at themselves in the mirror with a distorted image. Can you imagine living your life 1, 2, 5, 10, or 20 years without actually knowing what you look like (because your reflection was smeared)? That was the problem I found myself in every time I looked at myself: I could not see what God saw, I only saw a warped image of who I truly was.

I remember as if it were yesterday, sitting in that cold cell alone waiting for the guard to do mail call. Prayerfully, he would bring me a card, a note, a letter, magazine, or anything that was connected to the outside world. It was Wednesday, and unfortunately for me Monday and Tuesday proved to be days where the mailman passed by. On this day when I heard the "Mail Call" cry, I didn't get up to go to the window to see if I would get anything. This time I sat on my bunk staring off into the distance, daydreaming of a better day.

Hope came to my cell that day. I heard "Kelley!" and noticed two pieces of parcels sliding underneath the door on to the floor right in front of me. It was two letters addressed to me, a letter from the Parole Board and a letter from my grandmother. I opened my grandmother's letter first and read the words, "When you pass this test, I want you to go back to school. God see fit you can be Dr. Kelley." I pondered her words for a moment, and I said to myself, "If God sees fit, I can be Dr. Kelley." Education was important to my family. It was always emphasized, but the examples of those who went on to get their education were few and far between. I grew up in the western part of Michigan on the rough side of a small city surrounded by many lakes. I can remember when I was a little boy, people would ask me, "What do you want to be when you grow up?" I would always answer "a doctor" not really knowing what type of doctor I would be; my response was almost robotic. All I knew was a doctor was a big deal in my family. So even though I was a smart kid and school came easy for me, I lost interest in academia and dropped out of school in the 9th grade. I knew that higher education was important, and I committed that when God prepared a way for me to pursue a degree I would do it. I opened the second piece of mail addressed to me from the Parole Board. It read amended sentence parole eligibility date modified. I went from being sentenced to 30 years in state prison to only having to serve 10. I knew then that God was not through with me yet, and that the second chance at life he offered me was to fulfill his purpose for my life, which is helping those in crisis to see that God's love does not cease. When I got out, I became a minister and started working to make changes in my community and to deliver hope.

The value my degree holds in my life cannot be estimated. I believe that my purpose and destiny are uniquely tied to me accomplishing my academic goals. I need my degree to carry out my purpose. I had to get my GED, and after I accomplished that, I enrolled into college. I enrolled into an undergraduate program with a ninth-grade education, after spending 20 years without seeing the inside of a classroom. The endeavor was daunting to say the least, but despite it all I still believed and trusted that I was supposed to be there. My grandmother said I should be there, and I believed her. She said, "If you believe you will achieve." After I enrolled in college I began to adapt and apply myself to the lectures and studies. I am proud to say that I have been on the Dean's list since I entered college and currently am as I write this. The exposure to college and the people that I met on my journey inspired me to do some things I didn't expect or plan to happen. October 20, 2017, I published and released two books. *The Tale of Two Sisters* and *Tale of Two Sisters 31 Day Workbook & Prayer Journal.*

I can honestly say that it was partly because I went to school that a lifelong dream came true. It was in college that I met someone who was able to walk me through the process of self-publishing, and it was in my collegiate English classes that I learned to write correctly and established the belief that my writing was good enough to publish. All in all, making the decision to return to school turned out be life-changing for me. In just a short period of time I was able work full time, go to school full time, be a husband, release two well-written God-inspired books, and remain on the dean's list the whole time. If you're reading this and trying to make the decision whether to go back to school or not, I encourage you to do so. Because if I can do it, then I know you can. Remember if you do what you always did, then you will be where you have always been. It's time to give ourselves a fighting chance by giving ourselves, and those who watch us, the satisfaction of earning a degree.

Changing the Trajectory of My Life

Lisa Spencer

Shasta College

When I was approached and asked to share my story, my initial reaction was "that's funny." But after consideration and some soul-searching I knew it was the right time to do a project like this. I am in my early 50s and I have made numerous good, bad, and disastrous decisions in life. Yet, all of them got me where I am today: with a degree in business administration and changing the outcome and trajectory of the rest of my life. That is the story that I want to share with you. First, I must start at the beginning.

I was born in the upper Midwest in the mid-1960s. My parents both worked outside the home. I was the youngest of four. My brother closest to me in age developed complications due to a high fever when he was about four that caused him to be in a coma for several months. He came out of the coma with diabetes and he suffered many setbacks because of this. For most of my childhood, my brother was in and out of hospitals and was sick almost all of the time. My childhood memories were mostly that my parents were financially, emotionally, and physically exhausted. Then in 1976, my father was diagnosed with renal cell (kidney) cancer. He had to have an extensive surgery to remove the tumor. I was still pretty young, and I was spared the details of the severity of his prognosis. Then in 1985 it came back, and he passed tragically just a couple years later. In the early 1980s, I started experimenting with drugs, and I used them as a way to cope with the overwhelming sadness of everyday life. In between middle school and high school, I just stopped going. My mother was so busy trying to manage paying the bills and keeping us afloat, no one really noticed. It was a different era back then, and I slipped between the cracks until what would have been tenth grade. Then it finally caught up with me. I was told my only option was taking the California High School Proficiency and getting a job. So that's what I did.

I spent the next 20 years hiding behind drugs and dysfunctional relationships. I was working entry-level jobs off and on to make ends meet. My mother died from breast cancer in 1999. Just a few years later, in 2003, my diabetic brother passed from complications (kidney and liver failure) due to his bad lifestyle choices. I was a single mother living in Tulsa, Oklahoma, with a little girl who needed me to get my life together. I had spent most of my life taking care of everybody else, and I needed to take care of me (and her). I finally had my wake-up call. I got off the drugs and got a stable job in retail, and I raised my daughter in the Midwest. I knew that I needed to go back to school, but I always told myself, "Next year." When my daughter was getting ready to graduate high school I knew it was time. I started to come up with a plan. The first step was to move back to California. The second step was to figure out what I wanted to do with my life. Here I was 50 years old and I still didn't have a clue what I wanted to do. The final and most important step was finally making that appointment with the counselor at the college. I was so scared my hands were shaking. She probably didn't notice but I was terrified.

For me personally the ACE (Associate Completion in the Evenings) program was the perfect fit. It provided me with a hybrid format, both on-line and in-person classes that fulfill the requirements for the degree that I am seeking. Returning to school at 50 years old was terrifying in many ways. I had so many misconceptions on how hard it would be. Prior to my enrollment, I had minimal exposure to computer concepts such as Word, Excel, and PowerPoint. I had a Facebook and e-mail, but my computer skills were very limited to say the least. The faculty, tutors, and classmates were all super approachable and helpful. They were there to help me be successful. At first, I was embarrassed to say I needed help. Now I celebrate the use of every tool and resource available. Finally, I was not afraid to speak up and ask for guidance.

The pride and accomplishment I got from every class I passed was the best feeling in the world. Looking back, I wish I had done this sooner but right now in my life I think I appreciate the experience more than I would have 10 years ago. It takes a lot of discipline to work all day then come home and spend another two or three hours on the computer doing homework. I have such drive and passion to be a lifelong learner now. I know that my education is going to take me places I never dreamed of, and hopefully I will never have to work in retail *ever* again. I would encourage anyone on the fence or unsure if they are ready to go back to school to talk to a counselor and see what the options are. An education changes everything. The only thing stopping you from being the best version of you is *you*.

Tenacity to Reach a Lifelong Goal

Jenny Chatman

University of Louisville

I am excited to share my experiences as a nontraditional college student and why along the journey it became so much more than just obtaining my degree. I had no prior college experience when I began my undergraduate studies in 2010 at Jefferson Community and Technical College (JCTC). None! My goal was simple when I enrolled in college—get my degree! Why? I had been turned away from so many positions I was well qualified for because I didn't have what I called "that piece of paper." So, I took the step and began my journey as an adult college student at the age of 33.

One of my first memorable college moments was English 101. Our professor often required self-reflections to complete assignments. One assignment I vividly recall was a paper titled, "Why Am I Here?" This was a difficult assignment for me because for more than half my life I felt like I had lived a double life; I was one way around other people, and I was another way at home. This behavior was a direct result of domestic violence. I didn't know people in the classroom; after all, I was nearly 10–15 years older than most of them. I recall how difficult it was to read my reflection to the class. Yet, I also don't recall a dry eye in the room, including my own. For the first time in a long time, I really felt proud of myself. I felt a sense of relief and knew anything was going to be possible. I was no longer in a difficult personal situation, and I told the truth about what happened to me. This class made me very proud to be someone who beat the odds with domestic violence.

Another class that really defined my college experience was Women and Gender Studies. This class brought depth and meaning to difficult issues women have faced such as acts of sexism, marginalization, oppression, denial of basic living rights, lack of respect, and equality. Some of these topics were beyond challenging for me because of my past personal experiences with some of them, such as living with lack of respect and equality in my own home and denial of basic living rights like being proud to have a successful career or having friends. I gained so much depth about my perspective on topics related to women and gender issues, and I was really proud to finally be pursuing one of my goals. I completed all of my general education classes at JCTC and with one class pending, college mathematics, I decided to go ahead and transfer to the University of Louisville for my core program.

My entire series of classes in the organizational leadership and learning (OLL) program were beneficial to me. I had had 12 core classes including the Exit Program. Each of my core classes in the OLL program further developed my personal and professional skill sets. After earning 48 college credit hours for prior learning experiences, I gained a sense of empowerment seeing how things I already achieved were equal to or above having a college degree. I demonstrated the ability to adapt, I could apply critical and strategic thinking skills, and I felt more confident in my leadership skills. I saw and felt growth within myself each and every semester.

The core classes in the OLL program built on each other in some capacity. I gained a better understanding on how to analyze workplace performance, develop interventions, implement and evaluate change, and how to manage and lead others more effectively. I improved my overall knowledge in core concept areas including, but not limited to, analyzing and proposing solutions, designing and implementing learning plans, collecting data, tracking and trending information, and applying practical approaches for workplace improvement and development. My improvements in these skill sets added value to my past learning experiences and are providing new opportunities in the workplace. I also developed better communication, networking, and negotiation skills, which have improved my life professionally and personally. Professionally, I feel more confident to pursue director-level positions; personally, I have learned how to create and implement change while delivering results. Communication, networking, and negotiation are necessary skill sets to adapt in various situations, and I feel more confident with technical and practical approaches in professional environments.

One of the most heart-wrenching moments was finishing all of my core classes and all but one of my general education classes. Remember, I transferred from JCTC to U of L without meeting the college math requirement. I began to study for the College Level Education Proficiency (CLEP) test to complete this general education course and graduate in December 2016. I took the test in November and missed the cut-off score by four points! I hung in there, kept studying, went to tutoring, and took the test again in April 2017 hoping to graduate in May. I missed the cut-off score by two points. I was devastated! But, I still did not give up. I was able to find an online class with JCTC that met the U of L requirement. I was approved for direct access to the class because of how close I was to passing not one but two CLEP tests on my own. I ended up finishing final requirements to graduate in June 2017.

It took me 7 years (2010–2017) to complete my degree. I cannot begin to explain the long nights going to class, later being online as a distance learning student, staying organized, juggling a full-time job, a part-time job, trying to have some kind of life in between, and in the midst of it all a relocation. At times I just wanted to say "no more," "I am done," and "I quit." But I was not a quitter, and I was determined to finish what I started.

My personal and professional experiences, general education classes at JCTC, and OLL classes at University of Louisville have given me a much broader perspective today. All of them are cohesively combined and very much intertwined to my overall growth as a confident and independent woman, as a professional, and as a member of society. Appreciating and understanding my personal experiences have helped me evolve inside and out. I continue to set goals that further challenge my personal and professional development. The concepts and learning experiences I acquired as an adult learner have provided more meaning in what is possible in my life.

It's pretty simple in the end for me: I am a high school dropout with a GED who obtained a CTBS Certification and a nice career path at a young age. I could not predict the future. I beat the odds of domestic violence, relocated, started my life over with nothing, and decided to go to school. Halfway through school, I relocated again for a career opportunity, still in school, failed two CLEP tests, and yet I was approved with all necessary degree requirements to graduate and received my Bachelor of Science in organizational leadership and learning in August 2017. Words cannot express what that means to me. It was not only worth it. It changed my life.

The Ladder of Success: One Rung at a Time

Clifford Hicks

Sullivan University

The decision to continue your education is complicated in itself; the road travelled upon making that decision is even more difficult. For me, the decision to return to college was not easy, but success doesn't come without sacrifice. Once I made the commitment to earn my degree, it began a return to a process I had begun more than 20 years ago. There were many obstacles to overcome, but the end results made it all worthwhile. I hope that sharing this experience will inspire other adults who were sidetracked like I was early in life to realize that goals may become blurred or altered, but they are never unattainable.

I was born in Cleveland, Ohio, and my mother, father, and I moved to Atlanta, Georgia 2 years later where my sister was born. Soon after, my parents parted ways, and we moved to the southeastern area of Kentucky, where my grandparents lived. Life in the country was a far cry from city life, but I learned values and morals that assisted me growing into the man I have become. My mother was a registered nurse and had to travel 50 miles a day to work at the nearest hospital in the area. Despite her work schedule, my mother was an integral part of our lives. She made it a point to be present at my athletic events to show support, and encouraged my sister and me to participate in positive extracurricular activities.

When I turned 13, my mother gave birth to my youngest sibling, and at this time we moved to Dayton, Ohio where she found more suitable employment at a larger hospital. Again, the move from the rural area back to suburban living took some time to adjust to. Being a natural introvert, making new friends and finding social activities were difficult for me. To me, the only strength I had was in sports, and through that I was able to enjoy a modest position as one of the "popular kids." My mother did her best to remain active in our academic and athletic endeavors, but her new schedule made this difficult. I was able to maintain a B average, but my study habits were minimal, at best. Because I was able to do well on tests, I gave teachers and fellow students the perception I was much more studious than I was.

My achievements in football earned me a partial scholarship to a small college. Unfortunately, my poor study habits carried over, and my GPA took a sharp drop after my first semester. Feeling that college wasn't the right fit for me, I entered the military and enlisted for a 4-year tour. While the military gave me much needed discipline and maturity, my desire for a higher education began to slowly take a back seat. I made an empty promise to my mother that I would attend college after my military commitment, but marriage and children derailed any thoughts I may have had at the time. Meanwhile, I watched my sister earn her degree in engineering and land an excellent job that made our entire family proud. I was extremely happy for my sister and proud of her success, but in the back of my mind I wondered if I had taken that route, where I would be in life.

In 2005, I gained custody of my oldest son, and I felt that a change in scenery was needed to start our new life and possibly motivate me to improve my situation. So, we moved to Louisville, Kentucky where I accepted a position with Youth Detention. While attending college became a goal in my life, mandatory overtime and raising a teenage son took precedence for several years. Then, I met the woman who would become my wife and joined our families together to establish a modest but emotionally enriching new life. This gave me a new purpose in life: To achieve a better education, be a stronger provider for my family, and show my children that determination and hard work can make any goal attainable. This is when I decided to enroll at Sullivan University and seek a degree in Public Safety and Justice Administration.

The next few years were filled with challenges and hours of study that pushed my mettle to its limits. But along the way, something happened that I didn't quite expect: I began to relish the challenge. When an assignment seemed as if it was too much or I wouldn't have time to complete it, I found the inner strength necessary to push through. Also, my family encouraged me and never let the thought of quitting even enter my mind. With this new vigor and persistence, I was able to make the Dean's list several quarters while attending Sullivan. I also began to realize my potential as a leader, as my fellow students requested that I take lead on various projects and assignments.

In 2015, the fruits of my labor came into fruition and I obtained my Bachelor of Science from Sullivan University. In a bittersweet ending to my academic journey, I missed graduating cum laude by 0.001 points!

The degree I earned has already shown great value in my life. Soon after graduating, I was chosen for a supervisor position at Youth Detention, and I recently received another promotion that has added duties and responsibilities. My family and friends are happy to see me reach heights that they knew I could achieve but I myself had trouble envisioning. But this story is far from over, and there are higher rungs I plan to climb in my professional development. I pray that my story may serve as an inspiration to others who have the desire to continue their education but may have apprehensions of taking the first step towards that goal. Success is something we can all wear, but first we must put it on. It is faith in God and a strong support system that helped along the way, but faith in *myself* was the final ingredient that made my return to college a complete success.

My 44-Year Journey to a College Degree

Debbie Webb

Indiana University Southeast

I had little support or encouragement from family (neither of my parents attended college), but knew I wanted a college degree from about age 14 when I attended a student leadership conference at Indiana University (IU)–Bloomington (sponsored by Scribner Junior High). After high school graduation in 1974, I received several scholarships and grants and enrolled at Indiana University Southeast (IUS) for the summer of 1974, and then headed to IU–Bloomington in the fall. My freshman year was debt-free, and I worked in the IU Alumni office for spending money. I had to borrow funds my sophomore year. By my junior year, the debt was mounting so I came home and started working, intending to return. I became comfortable with a weekly paycheck and put college on the back burner. I got married, bought a house, and had children, but I always regretted not finishing college and was always envious of my friends who did.

The journey to finish my bachelor's degree began in 2011 when my employer began promoting a program called "55,000 Degrees." When I checked out the website, I saw that IUS was a participating college, which excited me because I really wanted my degree to be from IU. I met with a "55,000 Degrees" counselor who told me that IUS was not as supportive of adults returning to school, and offered me several options at the University of Louisville, including online classes and the ability to test out of some credit hours in order to complete my degree quicker. This, along with the fact that my employer would reimburse a percentage of my tuition (based on my grade), appealed to me since I estimated the cost to finish to be around $18,000. As a 56-year-old widow with two boys in college, working full-time, with limited excess funds, that was a plus, but I really wanted my degree to be from IU. I started the process rolling by obtaining my transcript from IU–Bloomington.

When I received my transcript, I was surprised to see that I had flunked two classes in the spring semester of 1978. When I returned home for Christmas break in December 1977, I never returned to Bloomington. Apparently, I also never formally withdrew from those classes. I was hoping I could get those expunged to increase my GPA a tad, but I had no luck with that.

I met with a very young counselor at IUS in the fall of 2011 who was not very helpful. He printed some things that I had already printed myself online (degree requirements for a Bachelor in English and Journalism, my original focus in 1974, along with requirements for a Bachelor in General Studies) and said I needed to apply for admission first. He did not give me much encouragement for being an adult student working full time; he said my options for classes that would fit my schedule would be slim.

I applied to IUS for admission in November 2011 and received a letter stating that, because I was on academic probation when I left in 1977, I would need to complete a petition for readmission. I thought my journey had ended before it began! I mailed the Appeal for Reinstatement in December 2011 and shortly thereafter received a voice message from the IUS Academic Success Center saying I had been admitted and that I should schedule an appointment with an advisor to help me register for spring classes. I called for an appointment but there were no evening openings so I scheduled a time for December 30th at 10:00 a.m. I took off work and arrived promptly at 10:00 a.m., quite excited. I was told by someone that she had left me a voice message the day before (which I did not receive) saying I had *not* yet been admitted but that she would keep my 10:00 a.m. appointment to discuss further. After waiting until 10:30 a.m. and no sign of a counselor, I went to the Admissions Office to see what I could find out. They had no answers for me either. I expressed my frustration at getting the runaround and left. I had to return to work, having missed 2 hours of work at this point. So I left in tears, shot down again, ready to give up.

But I did not give up. The next month, I met with Saundra Gordon, director of the General Studies Program at IUS, who was eager to help. She told me the Bachelor of General Studies was the only degree where I could use *all* my credits from 1974–1976, so that was my new focus. She outlined the classes I needed to take, discussed testing out of C106 Introduction to Computers, and talked to me about online classes. I went home and started looking up classes, ready to get started. I chose a class and submitted it for approval. After more phone calls and emails, I enrolled in a freshman speech class for the first Summer Session of 2012. I received a tremendous amount of help and encouragement from my instructor (Tammy Voigt) and my classmates—more than anyone up to that point. They helped me with the technology (a huge challenge for me) and constantly encouraged me. Using Oncourse (which is now Canvas) and researching everything online was totally new to me (apparently, there are no orientation sessions for adults returning to school, which would have been extremely helpful to me). When I was last in college, we did our research at the library. I struggled along with help from my classmates and Ms. Voigt on how to research and how to cite my sources—all totally different than in the 1970s. We did not have to adhere to the various writing formats in the 1970s! I then enrolled in a freshman sociology class. Having to research journal articles was also new to me. Professor Angie Andriot helped me learn how to research journal articles online, praising my writing skills. I made it through Summer 2012 with an A in each class. Up to this point, I had not told anyone but my oldest son and the Human Resources Manager at my office about this crazy idea of returning to school at my age. Now I was ready to share my news. My confidence was back!

I experienced several negative experiences with trying to set up advising appointments after hours, and I could only schedule times on my vacation days. I was frustrated with students missing class and still being allowed to complete assignments, with students sleeping during class but getting credit for attendance (several of whom were receiving Pell grants), with students missing due dates on assignments and then being given additional time to complete them or a chance to earn extra credit to make up for missed assignments or low grades on assignments/quizzes. These types of things are extremely frustrating for those of us who are diligent about attending class and completing assignments on time. And then there are the group assignments—ugh, my worst nightmare! I usually ended up doing the bulk of the work on group assignments because most students procrastinate. Another frustration was being charged an extra $150 for online classes, when the online professors clearly do less work than those who lead live classes with lectures. Most online classes were obviously copied from the prior semester (dates were left unchanged) so little or no planning was involved. The professor does much less work for these online classes, yet the students are charged more. Another complaint is "activity fees"—most adults taking classes, especially online classes, do not use or benefit from such things. If a university must charge extra fees, they should just bundle it in the tuition!

I took a variety of classes: religion, math, geography, philosophy, several music classes (I now enjoy and appreciate classical music), several sociology classes (a newfound love), several literature and writing classes, and learned many new things in each one. I feel I have a much broader understanding and appreciation for politics, different cultures and beliefs, national and international economics, and have become more empathetic to various causes, religions, and ways of thinking.

Bottom line, universities need to cater more to nontraditional students by having orientation sessions to address some of the issues above. All in all, I am thrilled and thankful to finally say that I have a degree and that I am an IU grad! This was only a personal goal for me; I plan to retire in 4 years after working as a legal assistant for the past 33 years. I am happy I did not let the roadblocks stop me.

A Long Educational Journey

Ellen E. Elliott

University of North Carolina at Greensboro

Perhaps the most significant thing my mother ever said to me growing up was about education. She once said that, as a woman, education is the single attribute that is never lost. Men, youth, and beauty are fleeting, but an education stays with you. I'm not sure whether the value I placed on education was solely based on that statement, but I know the impact was great. Although my journey ebbed and flowed, there was always an internal voice stressing that education was the path toward survival and independence.

As a young child, I loved playing school and insisted on being the teacher. I had a heart condition that limited my physical activity, so books and learning became my greatest entertainment and the place where I stood out. As a teenager, however, the sexual abuse that became part of my story took my attention away from learning, and I began acting out rebelliously. Ultimately, my rebellion resulted in a suspension from school, and I dropped out after the tenth grade.

The value of learning led me to enter an adult diploma program, but life had become too confusing and chaotic for scheduled classes. I dropped out again and scheduled an appointment to take the GED. I scored in a high percentile and was encouraged to continue my education, but again, life was too unsettled for anything requiring structure or motivation. By

17, I was living in my car and staying stoned as much as possible. I worked a nine-month job at an ice cream factory and carried newspapers or sold cutlery in the off months. Life just wasn't working out so well and getting an education continued moving further down the priority list, or what there was of one.

That's when I met Dave. As I sat in my car rolling newspapers early on a cold winter morning, Dave staggered by. I gave him a ride and the rest is history. He threw up on my papers and said he needed me, so I married him. During our marriage, he drank, I ate, and we had a beautiful daughter. The marriage was hopeless, so I returned to school when my daughter was nine months old and left the marriage on her first birthday.

In 1990 at the age of 23, I was a single mother living in public housing, working part-time, going to school, and volunteering at a homeless shelter to obtain experience in the helping field. My life was a series of crises, but I was surviving and finding the validation I so desperately needed through school. Education became my life raft. Even so, at more than 100 pounds overweight, fear held me back from going further.

After a series of devastating events that forced me to evaluate my life and future, I lost the weight, graduated from the community college, and transferred to UNCG. After 8 years working on associate degrees, I was able to obtain my Bachelor of Social Work and a master's degree in counseling from Appalachian University within 4 years.

My life has been a unique, often chaotic, deeply gratifying journey. Intention and a love for learning has guided the process, but most often, opportunities greater than any I could have imagined have presented themselves unexpectedly. Today I am completing my PhD, a goal that was once far removed from anything I could have imagined. Even greater perhaps is that my dissertation research is being conducted in Nepal, a country I didn't know existed through much of my life. I am profoundly grateful for this journey and look forward to whatever comes next, and always aware of the impact education has had on my life.

The True Value of Perseverance

Sharmiesha Timlin

Belhaven University

Growing up in a family that did not attend college leaves it in the air as to whether or not each subsequent generation would attend. I had made up my mind early on that I would go. But life, of course, has its way of steering you in another direction. I am, however, truly glad that I made the decision to go. It was very well worth it; in spite of the doubts and unexpected events, that decision has added value to me and my life.

Returning to school to finish my degree was very worth it. It set me on the path to have more confidence in myself and to stretch me outside of my little box. I was working with a company that provided opportunity for advancement, but it was always based upon education. That was a motivator. I also noticed that most career paths that I was interested in required at least a 4-year degree. I had contemplated going to college and even attempted a few times. The first attempt was right after I graduated from high school. As much as I would like to say it sparked a fire in me, that did not happen. Mentally, I was not ready. I attempted again a few years later and at that time was not motivated. I did not even finish the classes I had paid for. As I got more grounded in life, stronger in my faith, and mentally focused, I was finally ready. I began my Bachelor of Business Administration and went through to complete my master's degree. But there were times I did not think I could do it.

At first, I did not think that I could do it. Self-doubt was my own worst enemy. Time was also a challenge, as I was working a full-time job. There were also many events that transpired over the course of attaining my degrees. First, I began my undergraduate degree with the hopes of pursuing a master's that would lead to teaching. About halfway through, the end degree I had hoped to attain was removed from the selection. I was not about to start over. There were many times that I wanted to throw in the towel as my workload and homework requirements seemed to collide. But I pushed through. Halfway through my undergraduate degree I was married, and I just knew I would have even more support. The opposite happened. I had even more distractions. I thought about taking a break as I adjusted to married life but did not want to lose my momentum. So, I pressed on. I completed my bachelor's 2 years later. I wanted a mental break so I delayed the start of my master's. But not for too long.

I began my original journey to complete my master's a few months after the completion of undergraduate degree. Toward the end of my first class, I found out that I was expecting my first child. Immediate panic mode set in. How in the world was I going to complete my master's as a newlywed, working a full-time job, *and* now expecting? I spoke with my counselor hoping she would agree to let me jump off the ledge and quit but she did not. She reminded me why I began my journey and said to try one more class. I listened and actually completed three classes before I delivered. As I began pondering my return, I was laid off from my job and a few months later my mother passed away suddenly. The desire I had to complete my degree slowly faded away and was replaced with anger and sorrow.

I was now responsible for not only my infant but also my twin brothers who were both still in school. A few months later my brother's best friend was shot and killed in front of our apartments in broad daylight. As life progressed, and after making my requests known unto the Lord, suddenly a door opened. I was hired to work for the university where I had attained my undergraduate degree. I was psyched. But 2 weeks after that, my husband left me and I was suddenly caring for three children on my own. Once acclimated to my new job, I was asked to substitute teach for one of the classes. This was the catalyst for me to finish my degree. As I began the process, I discovered I had a couple of loans go into default and the process to address this took nearly three months. I never lost hope. At this point in my life I knew that I could do it.

I had grown to accomplish what I set my mind to. But I had—and still do have—a very supportive pastor, church, and family members, as well as a network of friends that kept me motivated. I also had, and still possess, a strong prayer life. I had a Savior I could call on when times got tough. And oh boy did they!

Toward the last almost year of my master's, I found out I was expecting my second child. My husband and I had tried on many occasions to reconcile but to no avail. There I was, a single mom of technically three children, working a full-time job, and in graduate school. That was the first time in a long time that I contemplated throwing in the towel. But instead of that fueling my decision to quit, it became the fire I needed to finish. I had come too far to give up and was not going to allow circumstances to win. I was counseling students on why they should finish when they wanted to quit, and it was time to take my own advice. I pressed on.

As I came to my last two classes I was very heavily pregnant. I finished my second to last class on a Thursday evening and my second child was delivered the following Tuesday. About four weeks later I had to have emergency surgery. I was scheduled to begin my last 8-week class in 4 weeks. There I was juggling being a single mother of two small children, two adult males, recent childbirth and emergency surgery, and a full-time job. With one class to go pushing back my degree did not seem like a bad idea. After much prayer God told me to just push through. So I was obedient. I completed my master's degree while working a full-time job, caring for two biological children under four and two siblings who were young adults, all while going through a divorce. I only knew I could do it because of the wonderful Savior that I serve. Jesus strengthened me when I was weak, gave me the words to type in duress, and brought all things back to my remembrance.

Although I have credited a lot of my success on the Lord and my mind, I cannot *not* give a huge thanks to my sister, my brothers, the father of my children, and his parents. They were among the reasons I was able to succeed. The long days where I went to work then straight to school, my siblings were the ones to care for my children during the late hours. When I was physically and emotionally drained, my children's father and his parents would pick up my kids so that I could get sleep. I could not have attained my degrees without a strong support system, mental preparedness, and my faith in Jesus. All of this is why my degree holds that much more value to me.

The value my degree holds in my life is one of accomplishment! With the odds that I had stacked up against me it would have been easy, and understandable, to give up and let life take its toll. But I refused. God led me to begin my degree, and I knew He would help me finish. So, in essence, my degree is priceless and holds the value of perseverance, discipline, and love. It is a reminder that I can truly do all things through Christ who strengthens me. I am not alone, even when I feel alone and God, my family, church, and friends would and do help me through anything.

6

Reigniting the Love of Learning

Adult students are famously pragmatic in their approach to finishing degrees. In many cases, advising returning adults follows an eerily similar pattern. The interaction begins with a statement from the returning adult about finishing in as few classes as possible because of the competing responsibilities they face on a daily basis. There is a common refrain that they need to finish quickly and don't have time or finances to take anything beyond what is "exactly required" to make it to graduation. Yet, who would blame any one of these individuals for their utilitarian approach to getting to the finish line? Their experience from a past enrollment was not successful, so why would they think the process, content, or demands would be any different than the previous attempt to go to college?

Fortunately, in many cases university bureaucracy, while still daunting, has become more adult friendly in many ways. Many universities have made adults part of their core mission. Now adults can experience a vastly different and more streamlined process of enrolling and taking classes (online/evening/weekend). In addition, they now often have access to student services after normal business hours. This change is not only welcome, it is met with

Unfinished Business, pages 121–135
Copyright © 2019 by Information Age Publishing
All rights of reproduction in any form reserved.

a high level of surprise and joy. As the first conversation upon enrollment centered around getting to graduation with no extra steps, no fluff, and no busy work, the conversation at graduation ceremonies frequently centers around students' reignited love of learning and the possibility of furthering their education into graduate studies. This marked and dramatic change in tone is one of the true joys of working with returning adult students.

A Very Personal Journey

Michael S. Keibler

University of Louisville

We value or hold close to our heart those people, memories, or things in our lives that have impacted or changed us. The journey to my degree allowed me to meet and collaborate with some pretty amazing people and with those who were on the same journey. Along the way, memories and great friendships were cultivated. We value lessons learned and even the failures regardless of how difficult it was to go through at the time, which at times felt humbling. Those lessons will always be attached to my degree and the experiences it brought along the way. We value the crucibles that we faced in pursuit of a degree as those challenges often define us and strengthen us to move forward toward a higher place in life. It wasn't always easy, but I value the fact that despite those crucibles, I made it, and it felt good to win one. We value challenges as they are the things that push us out of our comfort zone and hold us accountable for how we react when faced with moments of indecision or struggle. The degree pushed me out of my comfort zone, and there were times when I struggled trying to be a dad, a provider, a family member, a friend, and somewhere in there a student. But I value the "push" as it made me realize that, yes, there is more out there and that I have more to give. In the end, the value of a degree has many meanings and can be measured in all aspects of my life. The value—it's not monetary; it's intrinsic.

I fell in love with learning. I feel like I became a whole person, finding that sense of belonging and purpose along the way, as learning moved me toward a new passion as well as direction in life. Most people go through their lives searching for what they believe to be the cornerstone of happiness and never find it. Jean Piaget proposed that the goal of education is to develop an individual into someone who is capable of doing new things and to develop someone who does not always accept everything that's presented to them. I have always been one to accept what's in front of me but through the journey of education, I didn't expect that I would become one who digs deeper for answers or presents new ideas based on a pragmatic view. I was fortunate enough to have followed the path of higher education and ultimately discovered a companion that offered me an avenue to create, discover, research, and enter a whole new world that I never knew existed.

Charles Phillips (1833) once eloquently stated, "Education is a companion which no misfortune can depress, no crime can destroy, no enemy can alienate, no despotism can enslave. It chastens vice, it guides virtue, and it gives at once grace and government to genius. Without it, what is man?" (pp. 91–92). This quote guided my pursuit of a degree and helped me understand that the value of my education goes far beyond books and classes; it defined me along the way and allowed me to achieve what I once considered impossible. In 2009, my journey toward finishing my degree began, and I soon realized that I had become an architect of change in my life. But it wasn't initially an intentional choice. I was at a point in my life where I had to refocus and prioritize what was in front of me to make sense of a senseless path I was headed down. I had just been through a divorce, changed my career, moved, quit smoking, joined the Air Force Reserves, and started a life as a single dad . . . all at ground zero. I needed an escape from reality, something that I could focus on and hold onto in order to help ease the transition of change. I needed something that would provide healing to my heart and soul and also help me find my value again along the way. This is why education became so important to me. Over the next several years—while taking classes, reading textbooks, and studying for exams—education became this outlet that encouraged and challenged me to keep moving forward. Education became my companion, guiding me toward a better, stronger future and life. I didn't expect education to have such a deep personal impact. Its value to me is not defined by curriculum but rather defined by the effort I put into it and the return on that investment that I received. I know now that returning to finish my degree was one of the best decisions in my life, and what I have learned will be something I can now share with others.

Honestly, in the beginning, I wondered if I could actually juggle an insane number of things going on in my life and still find time for school. Finishing my degree was a way for me to refocus my life and not a lifestyle . . . so I thought. But the possibility of getting that diploma in my hand was always in the back of my mind, and it actually began to become a reality as I completed one class at a time, one semester at a time, and then one year at a time toward a degree. Think of the possibilities. That's what I kept telling myself. The subjects became more and more interesting and the content began to make sense as I was able to apply the principles of what I was learning directly into my job. I began to immerse myself into my studies and over several years of school, I found that I had created a path that I could look back on and see just how much I had actually accomplished. This was a crucial point as I seemed to rarely look up or even look back.

Why did I think I could do it? I had the support of my family and kids. They were my foundation, and they believed in me even when I had my own doubts. From the first class to the last semester of my degree, I relied heavily on that support as well as the confidence that I was making a sacrifice for the greater good and that education was not only about learning but about believing in its value and in yourself. Once I understood this principle, I became intentional with my studies and discovered that what I was investing in was more than just an education . . . it was a way of life, and the return comes in the form of purpose, meaning, and understanding in life. I would be remiss if I didn't acknowledge the support of my professors and how they each took a fragmented part of my life experiences and through critical thinking or reflection, helped me make sense of what I couldn't and helped me to be able to establish order into what ultimately would be a degree. I knew deep inside that I had the disposition, the drive, the determination, and the persistence to accomplish what I set out to do but it took the support of others in this journey to help see this to the end. I will always be grateful.

The journey to finish my degree became a very personal journey, not only to finish what I started 3 decades ago, but to become a better person and to fully understand how education can make a real difference in one's life. More importantly, I saw this as an opportunity to be a role model for my children and let them know that, at any age, you can still pursue your ambitions and accomplish a goal even when the odds are stacked against you. I was a first-generation student and didn't even know what that meant until I started back to school. It meant that the odds of me completing my degree were already stacked against me—I just didn't realize it. But returning to finish my degree was a start—it was that first step and it became a reference point that I could look back on several years down the road and say, "That's where it all began."

Finishing my degree was like crossing the finish line of a marathon that consisted of classes, exams, studying, and writing. I remember my first semester taking an online course and trying to figure out how to maneuver Blackboard. Looking back, it was only preparation for what was ahead of me, and it fed into the steps needed to be able to one day walk across the platform and have a degree placed in my hand. I believe that there are two central tenets toward determining the worth of returning and finishing my degree: One is professional and the other personal. Professionally, my role in education (or elsewhere for that matter) means that I need to have the knowledge to produce results, make sound decisions, and create new paths for others to follow. Personally, in my role as a father, I need to show how much discipline, goals, persistence, and determination can make a difference in not only my life but the lives of those I influence each and every day. It was worth the late nights, the missed gatherings, the reading of homework while sitting on the bleachers for my kid's games, and just learning how to learn again. Why? Because in the end, knowledge is something that is freely given, freely shared, and can never be taken away. The degree is a reminder, not only to me, but also to others, that I took the time to learn from others, learn about myself, and learn to appreciate what education has to offer.

South End Succes Story

Gerald Kinnunen

University of Louisville

The Bachelor of Science in organizational leadership and learning (OLL) is one of the most significant accomplishments of my life. I am elated to apply for the Master of Science in human resources and organizational development (HROD) at the University of Louisville. I consider it an elevated continuation of the OLL program. I often describe the OLL undergraduate experience as a business degree, but instead of finance, our currency is people power. I imagine the HROD degree is the same, but with bigger and better tools to make an even more significant impact on organizations and their processes.

I was raised in the south end of Louisville and attended Jefferson Community College; while working at UPS, I took advantage of their tuition program. As a first-generation college student, my academic experience led me to work in corporate, private, nonprofit, and educational sectors of the workforce. I found the least bit of satisfaction in my corporate career and the most professional joy in my job as a prevention specialist in the nonprofit community. My experiences and my interactions with leadership and human resources were a mixed bag of both the positive and the negative. Sometimes there were grave indignations toward employees, and at other times organizations managed their "human capital" exceptionally well. As a professional goal, I would like to further my education and use that knowledge for organizational interventions and building better systems within a business. I felt as if I had something to prove by returning to college after my hiatus from school.

As an eager student, I can tell you all about the experience, personal benefits, and doors that have opened for my fellow peers and me because of the OLL program, but I would like to tell you how that almost didn't happen. Last year, I was living as an undiagnosed bipolar individual and almost gave up with only one class to complete before graduation. Excellent healthcare, familial support, and compassionate educators kept me out of the hospital and on track with my program. I never considered myself an academic, and then OLL molded me into a dedicated pupil. Suddenly my work experience became a catalyst that propelled me into honor societies and other accolades. I am serious when I say it has forever changed my perspective and the way I approach people and environments, both in the workplace and in my personal life. The tools that I was able to take away from the program gave me the ability to hack into the parts of life that I was previously unable to access. Organizational Leadership and Learning's theoretical models and concepts swirled in my mind, and my surroundings suddenly offered an abundance of potential and valuable opportunities.

HROD sounds like the logical continuation of OLL and offers access to a more in-depth knowledge of organizational change and performance. Honestly, when I first started back to school, I looked at all degrees as going through the institutional motions to become a product of higher education. I thought the university was a machine that chews you up and spits out a slightly altered version of your original self. I thought I would be doing a lot of rote memorization, fact regurgitation, and dumping all that information at the end of class because I would never use it after college. I was wrong. Organizational Leadership and Learning was anything but that kind of experience. The program taught me how to leverage organizational resources and utilize human capital to reach desirable outcomes. Organizational Leadership and Learning is an organized experience guided by content that has infinite applications. I am eager to understand and speak the HROD language. I gravitated toward the OLL program as a result of the camaraderie I felt with others who shared the same academic hurdles. My personal goal is to continue my education as well as advocate for others who do not consider themselves a perfect fit for the academic mold.

I thought I was capable of all this because I learned how to turn my mental illness into a superpower. I learned that in a bipolar manic state I was resilient to stress and could crush any agenda set before me. Organization and task management was never an issue. However, in a bipolar depressive state, this is not the case. I learned that two strengths of depression were empathy and connectedness. As a depressive, I would reach out to my professors and peers, and they would give me the motivation and accountability to accomplish tasks that were otherwise quickly completed in a manic state. Organizational Leadership and Learning helped me to learn that I am not my illness—I am more than my brain disorder. I am not bipolar, but I have bipolar illness.

I've suffered a lot from a traumatic childhood and witnessed several violent deaths. I have been told that I should write a book or someone could make a movie about my life. After years of therapy and medications, I found a 2-year window in my life that opened up, and that window is the era of OLL. I connected with medical service providers, the University of Louisville's Disability Resource, and a few professors who merely said, "You can do this." My medical team put me on lithium and counseled me. Disability Resource gave me access to an "audible reader" service where I can virtually recall all of my textbooks. I spent decades not understanding why I couldn't read like a neuro-normal person. In high school, I would read my text into a recorder and play it back while reading along. I had no idea why I did this, but it worked.

Most importantly, I had professors and other students recognizing my abilities and telling me that completing a degree was possible. Only one other person ever supported me like that, and she passed away in 2011. My mother was my rock, and her only wish was that I complete an undergraduate degree. I'm well on my way past my mother's wishes and hope to attain a PhD. My mother forecasting my degree was the reason I set high standards for myself. I know I could do anything now because I proved myself already with a degree in OLL. Believing I could achieve in my first OLL course would be the catalyst that propels me into becoming a post-doc student. I'm forever grateful to everyone that helped me get here. I didn't expect to attract, earn, and maintain the friendships that I have now as a result of applying to the University of Louisville to finish my academic experience. In learning how to deal with the ups and downs of the workforce, I learned how to manage myself and turn my weaknesses into strengths. I don't have anything brilliant or moving to say to students about their academic pursuits. If I had a gun to my head and had to say anything, I would say this: Take the first step. Education is a journey like anything, and it's not static. It moves and courses through your veins and daily life.

Be the Hero of Your Own Story

Christopher Reid

Company Commander, Engine 23, Louisville Fire Department
SUNY College at Old Westbury on Long Island, NY

I am answering your call to hear from people who have completed their degrees and the journey along the way. I completed my college degree back in 1997, attaining a BS in sociology from the State University of New York College at Old Westbury on Long Island. I never thought I would ever get this because I was not a very studious student in high school. I was probably a C student at best and didn't have the best study habits, but I knew I wanted to go to college. I just didn't know how.

I graduated from high school in 1989 and left for the U.S. Navy in the summer of 1990. This was a dream of mine to serve in the military and also a way for me to be able to pay for college. My family didn't have much money, and I knew there was no way for me to pay for it alone. While I was in the Navy, I was able to take a few college classes in my downtime. I credit the military for giving me discipline and creating a strong desire to succeed.

When I got out of the military, I enrolled in the local community college, mainly because I still wasn't sure if I could make it with all the studying and coursework. I eventually graduated magna cum laude with a 3.95 GPA in criminal justice. I was ecstatic and knew I could go on to a 4-year school. I attended university and graduated early with honors and a GPA of 3.98. I found that the schoolwork came easy to me, and I felt academia was my calling. I had aspirations to get my master's down the road.

Shortly after graduation I moved to Louisville, Kentucky with my fiancée and found some, let's say, small jobs with various employers. Even though I found school easy and I was successful there, I found that I didn't allow myself to apply that knowledge to the real world of finding a career. I guess I didn't know how to apply myself and was scared of challenging myself. I had become comfortable in school and wasn't prepared for the real world.

I like to think my college degree played a part in me attaining the jobs I did get, but in reality, I didn't need a degree to qualify for any of the jobs I had. Maybe in a small sense, the degree gave me an advantage during an interview or when my application was reviewed, but for the positions I looked for, I didn't need a degree.

I am a firefighter now, and I love my job. I have moved up the supervisory ladder, again not needing a degree to qualify or even to hold the positions. However, I do think having gone through college and attaining my degree helped me develop the study habits and intellect to succeed at the promotional exams. I am now trying to complete another AS degree in fire science, a little more direct to my job field. I found that getting a master's degree, though self-satisfying, would not help me in my career at this time.

In all, I am glad I completed my college degree when I did. I feel proud of the fact that I have it; that chapter of my life is complete. If nothing else, it is better to have it in case it is needed, than to find yourself facing a position were a degree is required and not have one. My college journey was a satisfying and fun one.

Thanks for letting me share my story.

A Toast to be Proud Of

Tommy Phelps

University of South Carolina

As a rule, we all want to belong to something bigger than ourselves. Having grown up in Columbia, South Carolina, I can remember as a small child, pulling and rooting for the hometown team—The University of South Carolina (USC). I recall going to sporting events such as football, baseball, and basketball, and hearing the USC alma mater sung. Never did I sing it, or if I did, I would not raise my right hand offering a toast to the school. That all changed August 29, 2013. More about the singing of the alma mater toward the end of the story.

I graduated from high school in 1983 and immediately went to work for a paper distribution company, while also starting my postsecondary education at Midlands Technical College. I graduated with an AA from Midlands Technical in 1986. After the completion of the AA degree, I started in sales with the same company and quite honestly never looked back. In fact, I am still working for the same company today!

As years went by, I recall taking leadership roles at work, church, and the community, but there was something that I felt I was missing. It wasn't until May 8, 2013, that I realized what it was. I was close to finishing my term as president for my Rotary Club, and that day the guest speaker for our club meeting was Chancellor Elkins from the newly formed online school of the University of South Carolina—appropriately called Palmetto College. That day as she spoke to the club of 56 members, I felt that she was there for one reason only and that reason was to speak to me. Chancellor Elkins planted the seed that it was time to go back to school and finish what I had started 27 years earlier.

I decided to go after a Bachelor of Organizational Leadership (BOL). Being a working professional and a parent, I thought that there would be no easy way to attain a degree from any school. I was wrong. I felt that I would be in over my head, but throughout my personal and business life, I had learned a few things that would help to get my studies going. I knew that once I got started, I would not stop until I held that degree in my hand. When I started in August of 2013, I had 81 hours to complete, and as of this writing, I have 29 hours left. I will finish Spring 2020. The support from my professors at Palmetto College, Chancellor Elkins, and my family have made all the difference in the world. Coursework generally takes a little planning for study time, but between the evenings and weekends, I feel that I have ample time to complete class requirements. Along the way, I have learned quite a bit from my studies that I incorporate into my personal and business life, and I have made some new friends with classmates and professors.

I have had many people ask me why I chose to go back to school after all of these years, and my answer was simple, I needed to. I had to prove to myself that I could do it. That degree will speak volumes on what I can accomplish, if I set and stick to my goals.

Now back to August 29, 2013. That day was the first football game of the season. South Carolina versus North Carolina. As the marching band was playing the alma mater, I was finally able to take part in the singing and raising my right hand to toast the school that I have so loved for as long as I can remember; 27 years later, I was finally a part of something that has no limits. There I was, a grown man, proud, excited, humbled, and crying. I had finally made it.

What am I Doing?

Beki Nixon Sidener

University of Missouri–Kansas City

There it was in our company's January Friday Five associate newsletter: "KC Scholars is a scholarship and college savings program designed to help low and modest-income students and adult learners finance and complete a college education. Traditional Scholarship (for current 11th graders). Adult Learner Scholarship (for adults with some college and no degree). College Savings Account/Match program (for current 9th graders). The deadline to apply is March 2, 2018. For more information and to apply for the scholarships..."

I saw myself in there—an adult with some college and no degree, forever checking the "Some College" box on various forms. It haunted me a little that I had not finished what I started, but not a whole lot. I admired other people who finished their degrees and thought that maybe someday I could take a couple of college courses here and there, contingent upon finances and a much freer schedule. But I really had no desire to complete a college education. I was fine where I was—working steadily in multiple jobs with a flexible schedule, still at a relatively low income, but pretty content.

I went to university immediately after graduating from high school in 1976 because I thought that was what one was supposed to do. I had not prepared for it, applied later than most students, and I wasn't that excited to be going, but I maintained a B average and gained 31 credit hours during my two semesters before declaring a major in Elementary Education. Then I had a plan to take a year off to work full time and return to school. I took that time off. Working at a gas station, in respiratory therapy and then as a PBX operator at a hospital, pouring coffee and making donuts, however, led me down a different path: The fulfillment of a dream I had to be in the music business, specifically, to play in bands.

It was in music that I gained an experience and knowledge that no college could ever teach. The talent of music is inherent, and this is something that has always been in me. To perform was always of my own volition. I was a natural poet, songwriter, singer, and self-taught musician from the minute I was tall enough to reach the keys of a piano. I ended up playing the finer local music circuit in Kansas City, traveled, and had the opportunity to play with some of the city's finest musicians. Therefore, I had only a low regret of not finishing my degree. I had "been there and done that," and now all I could do was work according to my previous job experience and with low-skill on-the-job training.

But all the while I was in the dregs of an eating disorder, since my pre-teen years, and it was the backdrop of my life for 30 years. It affected and overshadowed every facet of my life: school, marriage, work, and so on. More than 20 years ago, God chose to heal me of this, completely, as if it never existed. I no longer live in the prison of addiction. The thrill of victory, of overcoming, has been enough, and it is perhaps the reason why I was satisfied with where I was in life. I just felt blessed to be alive; I didn't want any challenges.

Well, let me tell you what this 60-year-old woman did with that newsletter. I saved it to look at later. I kept opening it up and reading it: "... apply..."; "... deadline...." I didn't want to, but I found myself applying and was digging my heels in with every step. I kept receiving prompts to take more steps. I took them. I wrote the two required essays in the application process. I filled out the financial form. I met the deadlines. I still didn't want to go to school, and I bet they gave the scholarship to anyone who applied. I didn't have time for this. I worked full time. I didn't want a challenge. To think of it made my head hurt. I didn't need this in my life.

On May 1, 2018, I received news that I was a scholar. I also learned that the scholarships were chosen according to the essays we had submitted. I cried. Then I thought, "Well, I guess I'd better go to school now, these people are nice enough to pay for it." I was assigned to an Adult Learner navigator who helped me through the application process. I felt like a fish out of water. Frankly, I felt like a dummy. I was lost on all the college terminology and didn't know up from down; I had been out of it for so long. But there were others who were right alongside me—those middle-aged, hardworking adults in the process of going back to college, who now had a generous scholarship to finish their degrees, and those committed to assisting in the process, who rallied behind us and told us, "You can do this." And later, "Now you have a new title. And that title is 'Student.'" I cried more.

I applied to my previous school, UMKC. When I received that acceptance letter, of course I cried again. I thought, "WHAT AM I *DOING?*" I attended more Adult Learner scholarship sessions, met with my school student advisor, picked classes, got my student ID, parking pass, and jumped in. I attended writing sessions, since I was still lost on formats and citations and the like. I was called in to meet with the UMKC strategic planner for KC Scholars recipients. We agreed that, whatever my area of concentration, it would be something that I would like to do even in retirement. I had to think about being close to retirement age, even though I still felt like a child. I had lost those 30 years in the addiction and was frozen at that preteen age whence it started. For me, it wasn't so much creating a whole new career as much as asking what do I want to learn? I have been in entertainment, business, music, dinner theater, house cleaning, sales, customer service, security, and accounts receivable; I've tutored, lifeguarded, and taught children in classes at the YMCA. I was fascinated with radio, loved studio production from my music days, was intrigued by "the interview," and have always been told that I had an excellent speaking voice.

After inadvertently meeting a station owner at a movie theater one night, I had an epiphany: radio. I was already in communications. I told my strategic planner and cried again. I now am moving forward with this. My goal in going back to school was to not get any Cs. I finished my first semester back to college with As—though I am keeping that same goal and hope to continue pleasantly surprising myself.

I prayed over every step of this path I was taking. If it was right, that doors would be opened. If it was wrong, that they would close, and I would accept it. All doors opened wide. The challenge that I thought I hated is now a welcome part of my life. My brain is being used to its full potential. I never dreamed I would love school in this way. I am deeply honored to be a scholar. I am thrilled to be a returning adult student.

The Voyage Itself is Part of the Reward

James Sauders

University of Louisville

My name is James Sauders, and I'm not unlike most nontraditional students. I went to college straight after high school, but along the way life happened. I didn't finish my degree as planned and ended up in the workforce. Over time, the decision to not finish my degree impacted my professional career. There are several reasons I ultimately decided to go back to school, and I think there are probably other people who can relate to my story. For the longest time, fear and inconvenience were my biggest deterrents, but I made the choice to come back anyway, and it's changed my life.

Growing up, I was always told how important it was to have a college education. I live in a relatively rural area of western Kentucky, and like many places, there aren't a lot of good jobs if you don't have a degree. My mother and uncle graduated from college, so I was expected to follow in their footsteps. My mother spent most of my life as a single mom and was a registered nurse when I was born. I saw her put herself through school, eventually complete her doctorate, and end up as a nurse practitioner. She set a great example for me and showed me how college could change your life. That's something I can never thank her enough for, and because of that I don't remember a time growing up that my plan was ever anything different.

I was lucky enough to earn a full ride to the University of Louisville on an academic scholarship. I had always planned to go to college and study political science, then move on to get a law degree. Moving away was hard; I had never really been separated from my family, but I was confident that I was making the right decision. I enjoyed several great years at U of L, but my path didn't end up being as straight as I thought it would be. While I learned a great deal and loved my time in college, at some point my goals changed. I was almost ready to graduate, I had more than 120 credits when I left, but I no longer wanted to go to law school and didn't know where to go from there. After 4 years of being away, I made the decision it was time to go home when my mother was diagnosed with cancer. I just didn't see the point of staying and finishing out a degree that I couldn't decide on, much less know what to do with.

So, I did what most college dropouts do, I went to work. September 11th happened a month after I entered college, and I told myself then I'd consider the military when college was over. While I wanted to go in as an officer, I was tired of waiting. This was the first time not having a degree changed my life. While I loved my time in the Air Force, it would have been very different as an officer rather than an enlisted man. Anyway, after my brief time there, I found a job I was good at, sales, and started earning money. I was back at home, being and feeling more productive, and at the time, felt like I was doing the right thing.

Over the next several years I met a girl, got married, and started a family. Unfortunately, that marriage didn't work out, and I ended up a single dad. To this day, the best thing I have ever done is become a father, and I've tried to be the best role model I can be. As you can guess, having a child makes everything in life more complicated. It restricted where I could move up in my career as I wanted to stay close to her, and so again, not having a degree limited me. Without it, I was less competitive for available jobs. Still, I worked hard and found out I was even better at sales management. I was quickly promoted at the front-line levels as I had a knack for coaching and developing others. However, while I was successful in many ways, not finishing my degree cost me better promotions over time. I didn't want my little girl to have that same disadvantage. It had always bothered me that I didn't finish my degree, and as my career stalled and she got older, I decided I was going to go back to school.

There are several reasons why this would be good for me—my daughter having a good role model, career opportunities, and so on, but the thought of having to go back into a classroom was daunting. I had tried to go back to school before but had a difficult time fitting it into my schedule. I worked retail, so I couldn't attend regular classes. On top of that, any schooling I had would interfere with my time with my daughter. While I let those reasons deter me for years, I finally decided I didn't care what the obstacles were, I was going to finish college. I was lucky enough to find the online program at U of L that offered a degree in organizational leadership and development, which perfectly fit with my career.

Let me say this, I know school is hard, lives are busy, and I understand there are important things we never seem to have time for. I know that the thought of school as a nontraditional student, as a parent, or as someone who hasn't seen a classroom for years are all scary thoughts but it is 100% worth it. There are times over my career when I felt like I just didn't have all the tools I needed. Times where I felt like even though I was the man for the job, I got passed over for promotions, and there were times that a little more business acumen would have made the difference between success and failure. The knowledge I've gotten since returning to school is what I had been missing. The courses and content I've studied would have changed my life had I had that information earlier on. Participating in this program has already been great for my career because every day I feel more capable in my duties and better qualified to do my job.

Furthermore, my outlook on life is completely different as an adult than it was as a teenage college student. The knowledge gained isn't theoretical; it's relevant to my career. I don't have to wait 4 years to use that information, I get to use it immediately. Additionally, I believe that I and my fellow nontraditional students value our experience and put more effort into our schooling than a lot of traditional-age college students. Because what we are learning is something we can relate to, it has more meaning to us, and therefore we work harder to succeed. In my first attempt at college, I squandered an opportunity and wasn't a great student. Now, I have had a 4.0 since I've returned to school while being a single dad and working a full-time job. I couldn't be prouder of myself and all the hard work I've put in to maintain my grades.

Let me give you one last reason why finishing my degree has been a life changing decision. My little girl knows that her daddy is going back to school. She knows that her father, who is "really old" from her viewpoint, decided that it is never too late to better yourself. I am showing her every day that no matter what her path, she can go back and make more of herself if she just tries. For me, going back to school isn't just about my career, it's an investment for my daughter, Emilen Brooke, and our future. I'll be 36 by the time I graduate, and I have classmates twice that old. There isn't an expiration date on bettering yourself, nor is it ever too late to inspire someone else.

I believe my favorite quote applies to my college journey: "A ship in harbor is safe, but that is not what a ship is for." While it would be very easy to just accept the status quo, not go back to school and just continue doing what I feel comfortable with, my life wouldn't change for the better. You don't get stronger without challenging yourself, and like the ship going off to sea, in many cases, the voyage itself is part of the reward. So, I say this to you: Challenge yourself and believe in your ability to do something that you know will be hard. You will find a better and stronger you on the other side. And who knows, you might inspire someone else along the way.

7

Adapting to the Changing Student Population

Colleges and universities across the United States are struggling to raise retention rates. Of the more than 145 million people currently in America's workforce (Bureau of Labor Statistics, 2018), 36 million have some college but no degree (Graduate! Network, 2019; Merisotis, 2018). Most entry-level positions and almost all mid-level occupations in the U.S. labor market currently require at least some postsecondary education. Furthermore, Carnevale, Smith, and Strohl (2017) estimated that 65% of jobs would require credentials beyond high school by 2025. They estimate that there will be a shortage of nearly 3 million college graduates to fill an available 22 million jobs requiring college degrees. There is clearly a need to better equip the nation's workforce. Consequently, colleges and universities need to better understand why so many students—both traditional-age and adult students—fail to reach graduation.

In the past, having a high school diploma was enough to qualify for many—if not most—jobs in the public sector. This has shifted, however.

Unfinished Business, pages 137–144
Copyright © 2019 by Information Age Publishing
137

High school credentials alone are no longer sufficient for many entry-level jobs and someone without any postsecondary training may find it challenging to obtain a highly skilled job (Klein-Collins, Sherman, & Soares, 2010; Kratzer, 2009). In addition, due to a phenomenon sometimes referred to as "credential creep," a baccalaureate-level education is now required for many jobs that were, historically, open for those without any postsecondary credentials (Bragg et al., 2009). College graduates earn an average of $48,800, compared to $30,800 annually for workers who do not have a degree (Kazis, Vargas, & Hoffman, 2007), which can lead to a cumulative $1 million difference over a lifetime and at least $300,000 more in federal taxes (Ewell, Kelly, & Klein-Collins, 2008). In addition, unemployment rates are lower for college graduates. In 2009, when the overall unemployment rate was 9.3%, the rate of unemployment for college graduates was 30% lower, at 5.5% (Turner & Krumenauer, 2010).

Adult Learners in U.S. Colleges and Universities

All major developed countries are recording a decline in birth rates. Therefore, active older adults are increasingly needed in the workforce. To stay current in a changing, global, knowledge-based economy necessitates ongoing training and retraining (Canja, 2002). In the United States, there are 191.9 million adults over the age of 25, 28% of whom have attained a bachelor's degree or higher (Snyder & Dillow, 2007). Although more than a third (37%) of all college and university enrollment consists of adult learners, more than 138 million adults (72% of the population) have yet to earn a bachelor's degree.

Understanding the enrollment and retention patterns of adult students necessitates defining "adult," a term rooted in cultural and historical nuances (Wlodkowski, 1999) and perhaps best thought of in terms of experience, rather than chronological age (Dinmore, 1997). After all, someone who is 30 years old who is seeking a career change after 5 years has a vastly different set of experiences to draw from—and a different set of motivations—than a 65-year-old executive who has worked for the same company for many years but is retooling for a post-retirement change in industry. Those definitions and differences, however, are challenging to quantify and test empirically, so an adult learner is generally classified as someone who is 25 and older (Horn & Berger, 2005), although some studies use the age of 24.

In an attempt to parse out the characteristics that shape the experience of adult learners, Horn and Carroll (1996) suggested that the definition of nontraditional students consider the following characteristics: delaying enrollment after high school, enrolling part time, being financially independent, supporting dependents other than a spouse, being a single parent, working more than 35 hours each week, or not having earned a traditional high school diploma. Horn further acknowledged the cumulative impact of these characteristics and suggested three classifications. A student is "minimally nontraditional" who has one of these characteristics, "moderately nontraditional" when they demonstrate two or three of these characteristics, and "highly nontraditional" when they are managing four or more of these characteristics. Choy's (2002) research identified more than 73% of the undergraduate student population as at least "minimally nontraditional," with most adult learners having at least one or more characteristics. Therefore, while all adults are nontraditional students, the definition of nontraditional student is broader and includes students who may not be (chronologically) classified as "adult students."

The more important issue, however, is that these students exhibit educational goals, learning styles, and background characteristics that differentiate them from traditional-age students. They carry multiple responsibilities (e.g., marriage, children, employment, or social responsibilities) that limit the margin they have for academic pursuits (Kasworm, 2003b; Wlodkowski, Mauldin, & Gahn, 2001). They often return to school to learn specialized skills and meet the demands of the emerging economy and respond to the overall reduction in manufacturing jobs. They may re-engage in higher education out of a desire to increase their earning potential or career prospects. Institutions of higher education need to understand their complex needs and unique characteristics to effectively serve and graduate more adult students.

In addition, career and job progression has changed over time, as well. Careers are less linear than they once were. Educational requirements for entry-level positions have increased (Klein-Collins et al., 2010), and the same is true for mid-career individuals seeking promotions. Credentials that were once sufficient may now fall short. Furthermore, many adults are now finding that mergers, acquisitions, restructuring, downsizing, and outsourcing have created an ever-shifting organizational landscape in which formal credentials are increasingly important (GLI, 2010). Early retirement may be diminishing as well, so older adults find it necessary to retrain and retool.

Adult Degree-Completion Programs

Although enrollment of adult learners has increased (Choy, 2002; Kasworm, 2003a), among individuals 25–29 years old, 53.8% of men and 61%

of women have some college but no degree (U.S. Census Bureau, 2008). In some low-performing states, only 18% of adults have a baccalaureate degree or higher; in the best-performing states, only 41% have at least bachelor's-level credentials (National Center for Public Policy and Higher Education, 2006). This gap creates a significant opportunity for institutions of higher education to serve this population. Meeting this need requires a constellation of services to respond to the realities of adult students returning to school: flexible evening or weekend course schedules, increased online offerings, and targeted student services. The term "adult degree-completion program" encompasses all of these services that are generally housed in an administrative structure that prioritizes retention and persistence-to-degree. The reduced barriers to degree completion are attractive to students who desire to finish their education.

Improving the rate of baccalaureate attainment is critical to competitiveness of the U.S. workforce and economy (Pusser et al., 2007). Increased degree attainment is linked to decreased long-term poverty, a higher base of state taxes, increased per capita personal income, and a stronger economy overall (McMahon, 2000), making this an important policy issue.

Serving adult students in innovative and adult-friendly ways has traditionally been met with reluctance by the academy as a whole. Adult degree-completion programs often operate on the periphery of the institution, but demographic shifts are making it important for colleges and universities to adopt policies that are more adult friendly to maintain their viability (Crouch, 2008; Taylor, 2000). In 2002, Wlodkowski, Mauldin, and Campbell estimated that 25% of adult students would be enrolled in accelerated degree-completion programs within 20 years. The tide may be turning, however, as even many elite and respected institutions—Duke, Harvard, Cornell, and New York University, for example—are now offering online and hybrid programs (Cronin & Bachorz, 2006).

Any successful degree-granting program must be flexible, convenient, and well planned. These programs are designed to be convenient. In addition, the program must deliver robust and rigorous instruction as well as highly effective student services (Wlodkowski et al., 2001). Furthermore, Feldman (2004) suggested that the competitiveness of the workforce could be enhanced when institutions of higher education develop meaningful professional partnerships within the community; these partnerships increase community access to the university and more deeply embed the university within the community it serves, increasing the value of the credential. In addition, most scholars hold that adult learners are very pragmatic in their approach to their education (Thomas & Chickering, 1984), and

they bring real-world experience and well-defined needs that may often result in a utilitarian approach to their academic decision-making (Knowles,
Holton, & Swanson, 2011). At the same time, studies have found a 6-year
graduation rate of 40% (Wlodkowski et al., 2001), meaning that nearly two-
thirds of adults leave (again) before graduation. If this is the case—if the
completion rate of those in these completion-focused programs is the same
or lower than that of traditional students (NCES, 2018)—are adult degree-
completion programs truly helping to remove barriers?

Adult Student Retention

As is evidenced by the research and literature devoted to the topic, student
retention is complex, the result of a combination of environmental, social,
behavioral, and academic factors that are each complex and difficult to
control or "control for" in the statistical sense (Astin, 1975, 1993; Bergman,
Gross, Berry, & Shuck, 2014; McGivney, 2004; Tinto, 1993, 2006). For the
past century, retention rates have remained flat (ACT, 2010; Tinto, 1993),
with about half of all undergraduates not completing their degrees (ACT,
2010; Tinto, 1993; U.S. Department of Education & NCES, 2008).

Most of the retention literature focuses on students between 18 and 21
years old. However, the retention of adult and nontraditional learners may be
even more complex, given the diversity of experience and circumstances of
these learners (Tweedell, 2000). As student demographics shift across higher
education, retention "matters now more than ever" (Tinto, 2006, p. 5). Calls
for more accountability in higher education may also drive a better understanding of adult students and adult student retention (Bonk, 2009).

There have been calls for increased research on persistence in adult-
focused programs, (Kratzer, 2009; Wlodkowski et al., 2001). Even though
research is limited, adult student retention is much lower than traditional-age students (Justice & Dornan, 2001). The National Attitudes Report
(Noel-Levitz, 2015) identified the drop-out[1] rate at 2-year institutions for
nontraditional students at 56.5%; higher than the 43.2% dropout rate for
traditional-age students at 2-year schools. At 4-year institutions, the nontraditional student dropout rate was 56.5%, compared to the traditional-age
student dropout rate of 43.2%. To add to the complexity, the same report
indicated that nontraditional students are likely to study harder—even in
courses they do not like—than traditional students and they enjoy reading
more, all while being considerably more distracted and stressed by finances
and financial problems.

Adult student retention may also be shaped by the type of institution the adult learner is attending. Highly selective institutions have the freedom and privilege to be just that—they can select students with stronger academic credentials than an open-enrollment, 2-year, or for-profit institution, and in general, selective institutions are more likely to retain students. In addition, tuition-driven institutions often struggle to meet budget and enrollment goals and may pursue a strategy of admitting students who may not be adequately prepared, academically, in the hopes of alleviating budget pressures. Furthermore, adult learners generally do not have the luxury of attending highly selective schools, relocating to pursue a college degree, or progressing through the academic experience in a linear fashion. Therefore, they may be more likely to choose a closer-to-home (but perhaps less-adequately-resourced) institution.

The challenge of understanding retention and persistence is further complicated by the fact that much of the student departure literature portrays (and studies) student dropouts in a very stereotypical way, with an incomplete understanding of intersecting and longitudinal factors that lead to dropout decisions (Tinto, 1993). Terms such as transfer-out, stop-out, and dropout can add to precision when discussing the issue, but the fact remains that the research tends to focus on negative outcomes (e.g., stop-out and dropout) rather than on persistence. It is important to understand the decision-making process that adults engage in related to furthering their education (Donaldson & Townsend, 2007). Adult learners have been shown to place a fundamental value on earning a degree (Mishler & Davenport, 1983), and they often have a stronger learning goal orientation rather than a performance orientation often demonstrated by younger learners (Eppler & Harju, 1997).

The Challenge Faced by Higher Education

Changes in the economy—most notably the move away from a strong manufacturing sector toward a technologically focused, knowledge-driven economy—necessitate skilled labor of a different kind (Atkinson & Correa, 2007; Carey, 2004; Childress & Spurgin, 2009). According to Atkinson and Correa (2007), these knowledge-based workers are the engine driving the economic and technological futures of many, if not most, organizations. Higher education can be poised to develop the right workers with the right skills to meet current demands (Kratzer, 2009). Institutions of higher learning need to provide the necessary services that will support these adults as they seek to attain a baccalaureate degree (Bergman et al., 2014; Hoffman & Reindl, 2011).

But what are those necessary supports and services? While there is a significant volume of retention-related research and literature, very little focuses specifically on the persistence of adult students. Research suggests that they are the least understood (Bean & Metzner, 1985; Kasworm, 2005), and there are challenges recruiting (Hadfield, 2003) and retaining adult learners (Donaldson & Graham, 1990; Justice & Dornan, 2001; Noel-Levitz, 2015). When the focus is narrowed even further—to students in degree-completion programs at 4-year colleges—there is even less literature to be found (Tweedell, 2000; Wlodkowski et al., 2002). Retention rates have remained flat or declined (ACT, 2018), and colleges and universities are experiencing little success in addressing this problem.

Student attrition is an expensive problem. Many individuals are currently excelling in the workforce based on their experience alone are being shut out of promotion opportunities because they lack the requisite academic credentials (Kolowich, 2011). There is also a psychological cost for the student who begins an educational journey only to stop-out or dropout as they seek to explain to themselves and others why they were not able to finish. In addition, low graduation rates can have an influence on public perception of the quality of an institution (or, more broadly, the value of higher education in general). That perception may affect recruitment and enrollment, which in turn affects revenue, legislative appropriations, and other external funding and fundraising. There could also be ramifications for accreditation or reaccreditation. Beyond this, there is the cost of recruiting students to "replace" those who were not retained.

One of the underlying motivations for compiling the narratives in this book is to provide a counter-narrative to the stereotypical and monolithic portrayal of adult students in the (sparse) research literature. Students who graduate have faced—and dealt with—multiple threats to their success in the classroom. They have almost certainly overcome a host of factors that could have derailed their educational pursuits. The adult learners in this book were all stop-out students, at least once, but they eventually reached their educational goal. It is incumbent upon colleges and universities to learn everything we can about these persistent learners (Bergman et al., 2014).

Note

1. We understand "dropout" according to Bean and Metzner's (1985) model: "A dropout is considered to be any student who enrolls at an institution one semester but does not enroll the next semester and has not completed his or her formerly declared program of study" (p. 489). This definition does not account for the often nonlinear enrollment patterns of many adult students who "stop in" and "stop out" during the pursuit of their degrees.

8

Building an Updated Model for Adult Student Retention

A s demonstrated in the narratives in this book, it is clear that there can be a variety of factors affecting students' progress to graduation—before and during their enrollment in a degree-completion program. Adult students pursue their college education while managing a unique combination of other roles, responsibilities, and requirements. In addition, they engage (or re-engage) in higher education from wide-ranging academic backgrounds, sometimes returning to college after many years. Some are well prepared for the academic challenges they may face; others may require remediation or developmental-level classes. Many are managing coursework while juggling family schedules and work responsibilities. There really is no such thing as a "typical" adult degree-completion student. This can be challenging for faculty who work to teach these learners, researchers who seek to understand and describe these learners, and administrators who desire to create programs and policies that will serve these learners.

Unfinished Business, pages 145–163
Copyright © 2019 by Information Age Publishing
145

And yet, it is our responsibility to promote retention and persistence for all students—including adult learners. This chapter outlines existing models of retention and persistence, including those that seek to explain adult learner persistence. Drawing from these earlier models, illustrated by the stories presented earlier, and based on a study of those who completed their college education in the context of an adult degree-completion program (Bergman, 2012), we present an updated and streamlined model of adult student retention.

Earlier Retention and Persistence Models

Beginning with McNeely's (1938) study of "College Student Mortality," administrators and policy makers within higher education have been working to understand why students leave college before graduating. McNeely's study, based on data from 60 institutions, examined a variety of factors—attrition rate, institutional size, reasons for departure, time-to-degree—to determine the points of highest attrition during a student's academic career. Research related to retention and attrition was, for the most part, paused during the Great Depression and World War II, but the return of veterans to the classroom following the end of WWII and the introduction of the G.I. Bill reignited broad interest in education, higher education, and retention research.

As researchers sought to better understand student departure, two key theorists built models based on Durkheim's (1951) study of suicide rates and suicide motivations. These early models (Spady, 1971; Tinto, 1975) drew parallels between Durkheim's theory of egotistical suicide and student attrition. As Tinto later suggested (1993), "Egotistical suicide provides the analogue for our thinking about institutional departure from higher education" (p. 100). Also important in this early theory building was the work of Summerskill (1962), who found that persistence and departure decisions were rooted in students' personality attributes, and Spady (1971), who highlighted the connections and interaction between key aspects of the campus environment and student characteristics. Tinto's (1975) model built on the synthesis and conceptual frameworks suggested by Spady (1971).

Astin's (1984) later "Theory of Involvement" drew from national databases to conclude that social and academic pursuits have a direct impact on persistence, suggesting that a student who is more involved will be more likely to persist to graduation. These three theoretical explorations of student retention and persistence (Astin, 1971, 1984; Spady, 1970, 1971; Tinto, 1975, 1993) became the foundation for many empirical studies and a more systematic understanding of student retention (Seidman, 2005). Pascarella and Terenzini (1979, 1983, 2005) conducted numerous studies that operationalized and expanded the earlier theories. In particular, they found that the interaction between student and faculty was a significant factor, promoting student integration and persistence in higher education (Pascarella & Terenzini, 1983). They also found that social and academic integration between student, peers, and faculty may lead to increased persistence.

According to Seidman (2005), Tinto's interactionalist theory of student departure set Tinto apart as the foremost authority in the field; this theory is one of the most cited and well-known theories of student retention. Tinto's (1975, 1993) model is based on the premise that students entering higher education bring pre-established characteristics—academic preparation, gender, family background, and race/ethnicity—with them to college and that these characteristics shape the student's level of commitment to the institution and to the ultimate goal of degree completion. In Tinto's framework, as students participate in the educational community, the corresponding academic and social experiences may lead to greater integration into the institution, and that integration can serve to increase students' commitment to the institution and their goals and potentially reduce their intention to withdraw (Tinto, 1993).

In developing his theory, Tinto (1993) drew from Van Gennep's understanding of rites of passage in tribal communities. Van Gennep suggested that these rites of passage are comprised of three phases: separation, transition, and integration. Tinto suggested the extent to which students "disassociate themselves, in varying degrees, from membership in the communities of the past, most typically those associated with the family, the local high school, and local areas of residence" (Tinto, 1993, p. 95) will have an impact on their integration to the college environment. He also stated that the transition phase "depends on a number of factors, among them degree of difference between the norms and patterns of behavior associated with membership in past communities and those required for integration in to the life of the college" (Tinto, 1993, p. 97). In other words, to be successfully retained, students may need to be willing to separate from membership in previous communities, and if those previous communities are drastically different from the college environment, the separation could require significant transition on the part of the student.

Tinto's model has served as the theoretical framework for many studies. However, it is not free from critique. As is the case with many early theories in higher education and adult development (e.g., Perry, 1999), Tinto's theory has been critiqued because it was based on research conducted at traditional, residential campuses, which calls into question its applicability to minority and nontraditional students or students at commuter schools or community colleges (Cabrera, Nora, & Castaneda, 1993; Nora, 2001; Tierney, 1999). Tierney (1999) also called into question the framework upon which Tinto built his theory (e.g., Van Gennep's concept of rites of passage), asking (a) whether higher education in the United States should be rightly viewed as a rite of passage and (b) whether Tinto's focus on separation from previous communities was a valid construct and assumption when considering the experience and cultural background of students of color (Renn & Reason, 2013).

In seeking to understand the retention and persistence of nontraditional students, Bean and Metzner (1985) hypothesized that Tinto's model overstated the impact of socialization. They suggested that three key factors of nontraditional students—living off campus, often with dependent family members; being 24 years old or older; and enrolling part time—reduce the importance of student–student and student–faculty social interactions (see Figure 8.1). Their model focuses, rather, on finances, occupational goals, external encouragement, and other environmental factors, as well as academic variables like study habits, course availability, and academic advising. Bean and Metzner viewed socialization as having only a marginal influence on nontraditional student departure decisions. They also found that some aspects of employment (e.g., time or money) had an impact on persistence for students from all socioeconomic classes. Working is a necessity for many nontraditional students, even though it has often been shown to be negatively correlated with work and academic persistence, leading to dropout and stop-out behaviors (Berker, Horn, & Carroll, 2003).

Bean and Metzner's (1985) model predicted that four direct variables would have the most impact on a dropout decision: prior academic performance, intent to leave, background and defining goals, and environmental factors (includes number of hours worked, finances, outside encouragement, opportunities to transfer the credit hours earned, and family responsibilities). They also highlighted the indirect impact of several other factors. For example, age, on its own, does not seem to predict retention. At the same time, older students often carry more nonschool responsibilities, which may lead a student to leave. Therefore, it is not precisely age that influences the dropout decision; it is the responsibilities that often correspond with age. They also noted the indirect effect of social integration, stating:

> The model posits that social integration variables should have only minimal effects on retention, partly due to the way nontraditional students were defined and partly because social variables from the outside environment are expected to be of greater importance than college social integration vari-

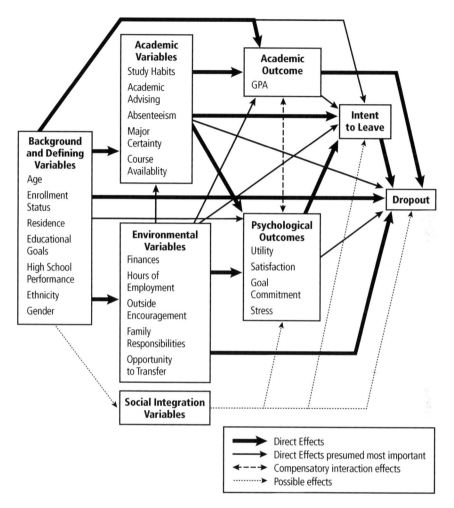

Figure 8.1 Bean and Metzner's (1985) model of nontraditional student attrition (p. 491).

ables. In addition, other environmental variables, such as family responsibilities, can play a significant role in the attrition process for nontraditional students. (p. 530)

Metzner and Bean (1987) further developed this model, finding confirmation for much of the original model, but noting that external/environmental variables did not have a direct effect on dropout. They also found no direct effect between intent to leave (or drop out) and the psychological outcome variables of goal commitment or stress. Therefore, these findings suggest that it may be time to explore the effect of direct and indirect variables at a deeper level—especially for older students.

Braxton and various colleagues (e.g., Braxton & Hirshy, 2005; Braxton, Milem, & Sullivan, 2000; Braxton, Shaw Sullivan, & Johnson, 1997) have researched aspects of Tinto's theory extensively. Most notably, Braxton, Hirschy, and McClendon (2004) studied Tinto's propositions among students at commuter institutions and found very little support for the model. Therefore, they constructed an updated path model to better describe persistence of students at commuter institutions. Commuter students are more likely to enroll part time and live off campus, which changes their drive for and opportunities to participate in social and cocurricular activities highlighted by Tinto's model. In many cases, adult students comprise a larger percentage of commuter students (and students at commuter institutions), which suggests that a model that more effectively describes the stop-out/dropout behavior of commuter students is also likely to address the needs of adult students more effectively.

A New Model of Adult Learner Persistence in Degree Completion Programs

For more than 80 years, scholars and practitioners have been attempting to better understand student retention and persistence (see Table 8.1), with the greatest strides in this research stream occurring within the past 35 years. Spady's (1970) work was expanded by Tinto, and both drew heavily from Durkheim's (1951) theory related to suicide. Tinto (1975) developed a comprehensive framework for understanding college student departure from an interactionalist lens. Tinto's model has been heavily cited and repeatedly tested (Braxton, 2000; Braxton & Hirschy, 2005; Braxton et al., 2004), demonstrating that academic, institutional, and social integration are key elements of student assimilation; they influence student commitment to the institution and student persistence. Bean and Metzner's (1985) model and the theory of student departure in commuter college and universities (Braxton et al., 2004) provide the framework to understand adult learners in degree-completion programs, highlighting the fact that adults pursue degrees concurrent with managing multiple other responsibilities, which is critical for understanding the nuances that both promote and discourage persistence to graduation.

The complexity of these issues, coupled with a desire to simplify and streamline broader understanding of adult learner persistence (specifically in degree-completion programs), provided the rationale for adapting

TABLE 8.1 Summary of Key Retention and Persistence Literature

Article Citation	Major Contribution	Research Type/Sample
McNeely (1938) College Student Mortality	Examined factors in college student retention including time-to-degree, when attrition was most prevalent in student's education, institutional size impact, reasons for withdrawal, and time to degree	Quantitative study involving 60 U.S. institutions
Durkheim (1951) Suicide	Differences in rates of suicide between societies that served as a theoretical basis for future comparison with student departure	Descriptive study well known in the field of sociology
Summerskill (1962) Dropouts from College	Personality attributes of students and their positive and negative influence on student departure	Psychological study focused on personal traits of students
Spady (1970, 1971) Dropouts from Higher Education	Examined interaction between student characteristics and campus environment	Synthesis of census, philosophical, autopsy, case, descriptive, and predictive studies
Astin (1971, 1984) Theory of Involvement	Posited that the more involved a student is at his or her college, the higher the likelihood of persistence to graduation	Theoretical modeling to understand direct influences on student departure
Tinto (1975, 1993) Interactionalist Model and Longitudinal Theory of Departure	Most cited theoretical framework that focuses on academic and social integration with formal and informal academic and social systems of a college	Path models outlining variables that contribute to student departure decisions.
Pascarella & Terenzini (1979, 1983) How College Impacts Students	Found that interaction between the student, peers, and faculty substantially increases the social and academic integration	Numerous empirical studies throughout the 1970s and 1980s
Bean (1980) Model of Work Turnover to Student Attrition	Used concepts from organizational studies of work turnover to equate to student satisfaction and persistence	Theoretical model adapted from Price and Mueller's (1981) Employee Turnover Model
Bean & Metzner (1985) Nontraditional Student Attrition	Found that environmental factors have an impact on departure decisions in nontraditional students more than academic variables	Path model showing interaction of direct and indirect variables on student departure decisions
Braxton, Hirschy, & McClendon (2004) Adapted Interactionalist Model for Commuter Schools	Theory of student departure in commuter colleges and universities	Path model displaying factors that have an impact on student commitment and persistence behavior

these two conceptual models (Bean & Metzner, 1985; Braxton et al., 2004). In addition, shifts in the landscape of higher education, such as the rise and fall of for-profit institutions (e.g., Cronin & Bachorz, 2006; Vasquez & Bauman, 2019) and the increasing ubiquity of online education since these models were initially developed, suggests that it is time to develop a new model of adult learner persistence that accounts for the confluence of events that promote and deter adult learner persistence for those enrolled in adult degree-completion programs at 4-year colleges. The model is the result of an earlier study (Bergman, 2012), in which survey responses from 437 participants were analyzed to isolate and examine the variance explained by each variable. In that study, statistically significant univariate variables were tested in a logistic regression to examine relationships between student entry variables, internal campus environment variables, and external influence variables and the outcome variable student persistence (see Figure 8.2).

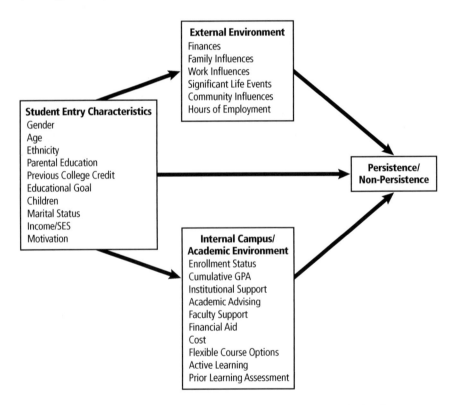

Figure 8.2 Model of Adult Learner Persistence in Degree-Completion Programs (Bergman, 2012)

Components of the Model: Entry Characteristics

No student starts (or restarts) his or her educational journey as a blank slate. Therefore, this model considers the impact of a variety of background variables: gender, age, ethnicity, parental education, previous college credit earned, educational goal, number of children, marital status, income and socioeconomic status, and motivation (goal commitment). Many other models include background characteristics like high school class rank, college prep curriculum, high school friends attending college, or standardized test scores. However, given that these variables are more pertinent to the experiences of traditional-age students, rather than adult learners, they are not included in the model here. The following sections present a brief overview of each of these characteristics. A more complete description of each component—including relevant research and literature—can be found in Bergman's (2012) dissertation.

Gender

Many statistically sound and empirically robust studies have found an association between gender and degree completion (Choy, 2002; Farabaugh-Dorkins, 1991; Horn, 1998; McCormick, Geis, Vergun, & Carroll, 1995). At both 2-year and 4-year institutions, women graduate at higher rates than men (Knapp, Kelly-Reid, & Ginder, 2012). In fact, Knapp et al. analyzed Integrated Postsecondary Education Data System (IPEDS) data and reported that at 2-year institutions, 62% of adult student women graduated, compared to 38% of men adult students; at 4-year institutions, 57.2% of women adult students graduated, compared to 42.8% of men (Knapp et al., 2012). However, several studies (Horn & Berger, 2005; Metzner & Bean, 1987; Shields, 1994; Woosley, 2004) found no significant differences related to gender. As displayed throughout the compelling stories, gender role does have an impact on the adult learner's decision to return to academics after serving their families during their younger years.

Age

Although Bean and Metzner (1985) identified age as having an indirect effect on persistence for nontraditional students, it was not a predictor of retention. In fact, there does not seem to be consensus among scholars and researchers regarding the impact of age on persistence. Students who are older may have more responsibilities that potentially interfere with school and schoolwork, and older students are, perhaps, less likely to have college-educated parents. At the same time, Kasworm (1990) found younger students more likely to complete their degrees and older students more likely to earn higher grades, and Horn (1998) found that those who dropped out tended to be older than those who persisted. These findings are reflected in the narratives as well. Several of the adult completers included here were in their 60s, and their age was a distinguishing factor in stories from Ron Tiller, Amada Skaggs, and Joe Jacoby.

Ethnicity

Ethnicity is included in many studies of educational persistence. However, when this factor has been included within various studies, the results are mixed. Neither Choy (2002) nor St. John and Starkey (1995) found ethnicity to be statistically significant. At the same time, Byrd (1990), Horn (1998), and Webb (1989) found a statistically significant connection between ethnicity and persistence.

Parent's Educational Attainment

The impact of parental education on student persistence—especially for first-generation college students—has been an increasing focus of researchers and scholars. Both Choy (2002) and Horn (1998) found that first-generation students, both adult and traditional-age, are more likely to leave before their studies are completed than students whose parents completed a higher education degree. Adult students are more likely than traditional-age students to also be first-generation college students.

Previous College Credit

It is logical that students with more prior college credits are more likely to persist to graduation (Christensen, 1991; Hanniford & Sagaria, 1994; Harrington, 1993; Martin 1990; Simmons, 1995), because the road to graduation is shorter for those with more credits. Wlodkowski et al. (2001) suggested that adult students with significant prior college experience (before enrolling in 4-year colleges) do better than those who do not have this educational background, regardless of whether the student enrolled in an accelerated or conventional program. More student-friendly transfer credit and admissions policies have also been connected to adult learner persistence (Calcagno, Jenkins, Bailey, & Crosta, 2006; Simmons, 1995).

Educational Goals

Adult students who approach their studies with wavering self-image or limited self-confidence (Kasworm, 2005) may find the college or university experience to be particularly challenging. With weak goals and motives, the adult learner may find the competitive college environment overwhelming, leading to a drop-out decision. Adults with a higher level of commitment to their educational goals tend to persist at much higher rates than those with lower educational attainment goals. Bergman (2012) found educational goal to be strongly correlated ($p < .01$) with adult student persistence.

Marital Status and Children

In many cases, the presence of children has been found to have a negative effect on persistence (Horn, 1998; McCaffrey, 1989; McGivney, 1996; Mercer, 1993; Shields, 1994). And yet, with many jobs now requiring bachelor's-level credentials, working adults with children are returning to American colleges and universities (Cabrera et al., 2005). In some studies, marital status is positively correlated with persistence (Mercer, 1993). At the same time, Mercer's results indicate no difference in persistence—when controlling for other factors—based on the presence of children or marital status. At the same time, another study (Hanniford & Sagaria, 1994) found that while women with children were more likely to complete their degrees, school-age children seemed to be more of a barrier than children who were older. This was evidenced in the narratives in many stories throughout the chapters. As mentioned in the story James Sauders shared, the impact of his daughter's viewpoint was a positive driver toward completing the degree. While time is an incredibly valuable resource with one's children, the ability to model positive behavior toward educational achievement outweighs the time away from family when pursuing a degree. The narratives shared in this book reflect the importance of flexible and convenient options to lessen the overall time away from family. Yet, the stories also highlight the importance of the process of allowing the returning adults to "walk the walk" as they convey the need for their children to focus on their studies in primary school.

Income/Socioeconomic Status (SES)

As with many other factors described here, the impact of income and socioeconomic status (SES) on adult student persistence is complex. SES was found to have a significant impact on the persistence of female adult students (Scott, Burns, & Cooney, 1996), and when adults report increased financial commitments and SES/income, this also has a direct effect on persistence (Ashar & Skenes, 1993). In addition, Hunt and Tierney (2006) found that when adult learners have access to increased financial assistance, they achieve higher rates of degree completion. As displayed throughout the narratives in this book, students with fewer concerns for meeting basic living expenses have more margin to respond to unexpected expenses that would likely lead to departure decisions for those with lower incomes and less financial margin. While many students indicated they faced financial challenges during their trajectory to a degree, their sheer fortitude helped them overcome barriers experienced throughout their time before, during, and after pursuing a degree.

Motivation

In Tinto's (1993) research, he suggested that goal commitment "becomes a motivating force" (p. 38) toward degree completion, even when students were marginally academically prepared. Motivation and commitment have been shown as a strong predictor of college students' ability to persist (Braxton et al., 2000; Cabrera, Nora, & Castaneda, 1993; Sadler, Cohen, & Kockesen, 2000). Bean (1980) highlighted intent and/or motivation to leave or stay as the best predictor of actual student departure. It is also important to help returning students set realistic expectations and goals. While returning students may be motivated enough to enroll in degree-seeking programs and value education, at times, past negative school experiences may overpower that motivation, leading to non-persistence (Quigley & Uhland, 2000).

Components of the Model: Internal Campus/Academic Environment

Given the focus on the needs and experiences of the *adult* learner, this model does not include internal campus factors like housing or dining policies and services, student government involvement, or membership in student organizations, as these are generally more pertinent to traditional-age learners. At the same time, there is evidence that many university policies, procedures, and services do not adequately support adult student success, leading to a problematic relationship between the institution and the student (Kasworm, Sandmann, & Sissel, 2000; Osam, Bergman, & Cumberland, 2017). Therefore, this model includes internal variables such as grade point average, part/full-time enrollment status, counseling, course scheduling (e.g., evening and weekend class times), and financial aid. Bergman (2012) found each of the variables listed here to be significantly correlated with adult student persistence.

Enrollment Status

For many students, attending school full-time is neither practical nor feasible. In these cases, part-time attendance can provide opportunities for a wider array of students (McCormick et al., 1995). However, there is no such thing as a "typical" part-time student. These students may be taking courses casually, one or two at a time for personal enrichment rather than degree attainment; returning students who want to upgrade their skills without leaving their current employment; high-school graduates who need to work full-time while pursuing a degree or credential in pursuit of increased employment prospects; or students who are "trying out" postsecondary education but unsure of their educational goals. Furthermore, students sometimes move back and forth between full-time and part-time status, depending on course offerings or life, work, and family situations. However, students who can enroll full-time, rather than part time, are more likely to persist, and students who take more hours per term are more likely to persist (Bean & Metzner, 1987; Choy & Premo, 1995; Cuccaro-Alamin, Choy, & Carroll, 1998; Horn & Carroll, 1996; McCormick et al., 1995; McGivney, 1996; Mercer, 1993; St. John & Starkey, 1995). This also translates to extended time-to-degree (Taniguchi & Kaufman, 2005), and there is a negative correlation between the number of hours worked and credit hours taken (Ahson, Gentemann, & Phelps, 1998).

Cumulative GPA

Bean and Metzner (1987) confirmed that GPA is a factor in persistence. Since that time, other studies have supported this conclusion (Farabaugh-Dorkins, 1991; Horn, 1998; Kasworm, 1990; McCaffrey, 1989; Mercer, 1993; St. John & Starkey, 1995), and this association has been shown regardless of the age of students (Cuccaro-Alamin, Choy, & Carroll, 1998). At the same time, there is some evidence that GPA may not affect adult student persistence (Shields, 1994), perhaps because adults have a stronger commitment to learning that may be less dependent on the external validation of a grade.

Institutional Support, Academic Advising, and Faculty Support

Traditionally, American colleges and universities do not have a reputation for being exceptionally "adult learner friendly." However, academic advising and interaction with faculty have been shown as critical to retention, persistence, and student success (Kuh, 2008), because these interactions help students learn about and utilize available campus and classroom resources. In previous studies, adult learners have called for better academic advising (Wlodkowski et al., 2002), and they see both advising and faculty support as services that need to be prompt, efficient, and accurate.

These items also promote a student's sense of community, which can promote persistence, as well. As displayed in many stories in this book, a sense of community includes two distinct aspects including classroom and community. A sense of community in the online classroom has been the focus of much research in distance learning (Childress & Spurgin, 2009; Rovai, Wighting, & Lucking, 2004). However, less attention and research has been given to the culture and climate that makes up a school community in the online environment (Childress & Spurgin, 2009; Rovai, Wighting, & Liu, 2005).

Financial Aid and Cost

Virtually every conversation about contemporary issues facing higher education includes the topics of financial aid and cost of attendance. For adult students, these costs are added to the other financial responsibilities they shoulder, and financial challenges are often highlighted as a factor in attrition (Aslanian, 2001; Kasworm, 1990; McCormick et al., 1995). Grants are limited for adult, part-time, and independent students (Lumina Foundation, 2011). Other funding is also limited: Only 20% use loans, only 19% are awarded scholarships, and only 18% have access to tuition reimbursement (NCES, 2018). Therefore, most undergraduates pay for their studies from personal funds (Aslanian, 2001).

As one would assume, being awarded financial aid is correlated with higher persistence rates (Cuccaro-Alamin, 1997; Kasworm, 1990; McCormick et al., 1995). For part-time students, especially, the type of aid can be a contributing factor—grants are positive while loans tend to be more negative (McCormick et al., 1995; St. John & Starkey, 1995). Merisotis (2018) has called for increased student aid for adult students—especially students of low SES—to increase opportunity for adult students and reduce the effects of rising tuition.

Flexible Course Options

Nearly every major American university and many colleges and community colleges offer distance education. The flexibility offered by online learning, in particular, allows colleges and universities to better address student needs, reach a broader audience, and employ updated learning pedagogy. It also allows students to arrange their studies around other life commitments (Sikora, 2002). Online education is not a panacea, however (Ashburn, 2010). Many adult learners indicate a preference for face-to-face classes, and institutions of higher education that can find a way to effectively schedule weekend and evening courses will also be effectively meeting the needs of their adult students.

Active Learning

It is important for students to be both intellectually and socially connected to their learning. Tinto (1993) suggested that a student who was connected intellectually but not socially was just as likely to not persist as students who were connected socially but not intellectually. Likewise, Horn and Carroll (1996) found that persistence was positively associated with active learning and academic integration, and other studies have demonstrated the positive impact of positive involvement with peers and faculty upon persistence (New England Adult Research Network, 1999; Tinto, 1998). In fact, it may be helpful to define active learning in terms of how a student integrates the pursuit of education into his or her overall life (Kerka, 1997).

Knowles et al. (2011) described adult learners as self-directed, problem-centered, internally motivated, and experientially oriented. Therefore, adult students often exhibit a problem-centered or skills-development focus while in academic, formal environments. These active learning tasks and the social connections that may result can positively shape persistence (Vann & Hinton, 1994). Universities committed to student success—holding high expectations as well as providing needed financial, social, and academic policies and supports on campus—are places where students tend to succeed (Tinto, 2006). Feedback and engagement with both staff and faculty leads to increased levels of institution commitment; it is important that this active involvement is valued both in and outside of the classroom.

Prior Learning Assessment

The Council for Adult and Experiential Learning (CAEL, 2010) describes Prior Learning Assessment (PLA) as a systematic process that colleges can use to evaluate college-level learning (i.e., knowledge, skills, and abilities) gained in outside-of-classroom settings for the purpose of granting credit for that learning. It is important to recognize (and validate, wherever possible) what the adult student has already learned and brings with them to their pursuit of a college degree. Smith and McCormick (1992) went so far as to suggest that this learning from experience is often equivalent and may surpass college-level learning gained through more traditional, formal settings. Students who earn credits through PLA processes are more likely to graduate, and graduate sooner, than non-PLA students (CAEL, 2010; Snyder, 1990). The College Board (College Board Advocacy, 2009) indicated that survey participants rated PLA strategies as more important to their educational pursuits than small classes or available financial aid. In considering factors that have an impact on the success and retention of adult students, PLA is a critical component.

Components of the Model: External Environment Variables

No student pursues an education from within a vacuum. For adult students, the external environmental variables are more salient, and often more pressing, than for traditional-age learners. These environmental factors may include family or employer support, finances, child care, job demands, or significant life events. Kasworm (2001) highlighted the challenges of being an adult student as "fraught with time and resource issues related to actively pursuing homework assignments and final projects, getting to and from courses and the library, typing papers, collaborating with study groups, and engaging in other activities to support academic success" (p. 33). There is often not enough time in any given day to devote to academic pursuits. When academic responsibilities slide to the bottom of the priority list, the result is often guilt and frustration. Navigating these factors requires a careful balancing act to meet family, community, work, and academic responsibilities; these factors are (and should be) weighed carefully as adult learners consider and pursue degree programs (Kasworm, 2003b; Kazis et al., 2007; Woosley, 2004).

Finances

Bean and Metzner (1985) included finances as a significant factor in adult student persistence, but they did not find it statistically significant in their later study (Metzner & Bean, 1987). At the same time, many other studies have observed finances or low income as a significant factor related to persistence (Christensen, 1991; Hall, 1997; Horn & Caroll, 1996; Losty & Kreilick, 1982; McCaffrey, 1989; Mercer, 1993; Zajkowski, 1997). Ryder, Bowman, and Newman (1994) found that men do not persist as often as women, even though they generally express fewer financial problems than women do. Bergman (2012) found finances to be significantly correlated with persistence in adult degree-completion programs.

Although money concerns are real and do need to be considered—and alleviated whenever possible—it is important to remember that saying "I can't afford it" may also be a face-saving measure. It is much easier to say "I didn't get enough financial aid to be able to continue" than to admit to very real fears of not being competent to finish or to recognize a diminishing commitment to pursue one's degree. It is also important to remember that the cost of pursuing a degree extends beyond tuition and fees. For all students this cost includes books, materials, and technology; for adult students the cost of education also likely includes child care (Malhotra, Shapero, Sizoo, & Munro, 2007), convenience foods, and opportunity costs (i.e., time taken for education that might have otherwise been committed to immediate job advancement). For some, tuition assistance can ease the financial burden, but reimbursement that is contingent on academic performance, such as needing to earn a B to be reimbursed for a class, can mean that the student trades financial pressure for academic pressure.

Family and Community Influences

Adult students are often motivated to complete a degree to create better opportunities for their families and to highlight the importance of education for their family members. At the same time, the responsibilities and pressures of family life often place pressure on the pursuit of education (Sorey & Duggan, 2008). Wlodkowski et al. (2001) reported that adult students in an accelerated program listed managing home and community responsibilities as one of the top two reasons for leaving college; his participants repeatedly cited the challenge of not having time to meet competing demands and priorities from work, family, community, and school. Kimmel and McNeese (2006), likewise, highlighted family care and financing as significant deterrents to academic pursuits. Therefore, it is perhaps not surprising that Bergman (2012) found that survey respondents identified various types of "encouragement" (from spouse, friends, employer, etc.) as statistically significantly correlated with persistence.

Work Influences and Hours of Employment

Like so many of the factors in the model, employment can have both motivational and detrimental influences on adult student participation and persistence (Kasworm, 2003b). Although an adult learner may cite career advancement and higher wages as motivating factors for returning to school, they also likely have a stronger tie to their career/employment culture than to academic culture (Riggert, Boyle, Petrosko, Ash, & Rude-Parkins, 2006). Therefore, when the two arenas (work and school) are in conflict, the adult student may feel pressure to prioritize work demands over school demands (Berker et al., 2003). Likewise, students in Wlodkowski et al.'s (2002) study indicated that job responsibilities and other competing priorities often lead to general feelings of being overwhelmed and being ineffective as a student. When students feel support from work, they report significantly lower levels of stress (Kirby, Biever, Martinez, & Gomez, 2004). Support systems—at work and at home—are important factors for adult learner persistence and success (Aslanian, 2001; Elkins, Braxton, & James, 1998). Bergman (2012) found work influences (but not hours employed) to be a statistically significant correlate of persistence for those enrolled in adult degree-completion programs.

Significant Life Events

Situations such as health issues (for the student or within the family), marriage or divorce, employment changes (e.g., job loss, promotion, or relocation), military deployment, or death in the family can have an impact on a student's educational journey. A significant life change may propel a return to college (Aslanian, 2001) and a non-event, such as not receiving a hoped-for promotion, may also trigger the pursuit of a long-delayed educational goal (Anderson, Goodman, & Schlossberg, 2012). Although the impact of significant life events is a complex topic and challenging to pursue empirically, these events do shape the educational journeys of many students and need to be acknowledged. As illustrated in this book—ranging from Phillip Allier's a journey of 1,000 miles to multiple overseas deployments faced by several military personnel in this book—adults are bound to experience significant life events based solely on their reality in the world. With adulthood, comes challenge. Consequently, the vast majority of adult learners that the authors have taught, advised, and mentored have described crazy things occurring in their lives. The real challenge, for the educator, is to respond well to these significant events in the lives of students, promoting the educational aspirations of students while simultaneously preserving the integrity of the academic process. Adult educators can continue to promote and establish a culture of "solidarity" among formal or informal cohorts. Then, if someone experiences challenges, the group lifts those individuals up and supports them through the inevitable twists and turns that life throws. When this culture exists, persistence to graduation follows.

Summary of the Model

Student persistence and retention has been studied extensively (Bean, 1990; Braxton et al., 2004; Cope & Hannah, 1974; Iffert, 1957; Lang & Ford, 1988; McNeely, 1938; Pantages & Creedon, 1978; Ramist, 1981; Spady, 1970, 1971; Summerskill, 1962; Tinto, 1975, 1993), but many students—especially adult students—still struggle to meet their educational goals. When it comes to adult students, the heterogeneity of the population makes empirical modeling of attrition behavior difficult (Metzner & Bean, 1987), and retention strategies specifically related to students in degree-completion programs have not been extensively studied.

More students in the United States attain degrees of higher education than anywhere else in the world, but while degree attainment levels are increasing in other industrialized or post-industrial countries, levels in the United States have yet to improve (Merisotis, 2018). With policy makers and higher education administrators and researchers alike making louder and more frequent calls for an increase in baccalaureate degree attainment, it is increasingly important to understand—and ameliorate—the obstacles that returning adult learners encounter. Work, family, finances, responsibilities, and educational history all have an impact on adult learner attrition and persistence as displayed throughout the compelling narratives. Adults who seek degree-completion programs and re-engage in their education do so for a variety of reasons, and they bring a wide range of experiences, support systems, and educational baggage. The model presented in this chapter is our contribution to helping institutions of higher education more effectively respond to the factors that shape the experience of adults in degree-completion programs. Furthermore, we hope that future research considers and tests this model to enhance the experience of all adult learners that return to the academic setting.

9

What Might This Mean for Higher Education?

Enrollment trends in U.S. higher education are not signaling a great deal of optimism across American college campuses. Between 2016 and 2018, there was an overall decrease of 2.6% in nationwide enrollment, with for-profit institutions experiencing the greatest decline (15.1%). There has been a string of closures of small private liberal arts colleges across the country (Hunter, 2012). In addition, while 4-year public institutional enrollment is flat, the coming decline in high school to college transition is signaling alarm about current budget and funding models. If higher education administrators do nothing, they are likely to see a 15% decline in overall enrollment because of the lower birth rate during the Great Recession. On the flip side of this looming decline is the advent of national, state, and regional degree-completion initiatives. Organizations like Complete College America, the Graduate! Network, Complete Florida, Prior Learning Assessment Network, KC Graduates, IHEP Degree Reclamation, TN Reconnect, and many more are promoting avenues that are both efficient and flexible for adults to return to finish degrees. The traditional way of doing business in higher education

Unfinished Business, pages 165–171
Copyright © 2019 by Information Age Publishing
165

is adapting to meet the needs of the modern learner and the realities of con-temporary demographics. These new approaches untether learners from the need to go to class in person at a specific time, create a collaborative environ-ment for on-demand learning, and open up an inclusive and collaborative virtual environment that can occur anytime day or night.

These advancements have resulted in slight growth in retention to graduation at innovative colleges and universities focused specifically on this population. However, understanding retention is complex. A student who persists to graduation encounters academic, behavioral, social, and environmental factors—both positive and negative—that are not easily defined and difficult to "control for" statistically (Astin, 1975, 1993; Mc-Givney, 2004; Tinto, 1993, 2006). The purpose of this book is to examine the experiences of adult students who successfully completed a baccalau-reate degree. The numerous variables that had an impact on that even-tual completion—including background and entry characteristics, internal campus and academic environment, and external environment variables—influenced the pursuit of the long-held dream of a college degree. Con-sequently, the Bergman model (theory of adult student persistence in de-gree completion programs; see Chapter 8, this volume) serves as a positive theoretical framework to identify variables that may combine to increase or decrease the likelihood of adult student persistence. Administrators of adult degree-completion programs can use this model to consider the im-pact of these empirically tested variables as they implement policies and procedures and seek to raise retention and graduation rates. The stories in this book, alongside the empirical literature, suggest that the most signifi-cant variables for predicting degree completion for working adults include educational goal, finances, and active learning.

What Does This Mean for Theory?

The stories in the earlier chapters of the book support the idea that adults often exhibit a problem-centered or performance-centered mind-set as they pursue their education. Knowles et al. (2011) suggested that many adult learners pursue learning environments to deal with a current (prob-lem-centered) or desired (performance-centered) situation. Adult learners have been described as experiential, internally motivated, self-directed, and problem-centered (Knowles, 1980; Merriam, Caffarella, & Baumgartner, 2007), and the adult learners who tell their stories in this book illustrate these characteristics in the context of adult degree-completion programs. As indicated in many stories, these working adults placed a strong emphasis on maintaining a high GPA throughout their programs when they returned after previous failings in the classroom. Given that adult learners often identify personal fulfillment as a primary reason for returning to complete a bachelor's degree, a high GPA is also likely an outcome of their self-direction and internal motivation as well.

Students believe in the value of experiential learning. Therefore, prior learning assessment (PLA) is a mechanism that many adult completers describe as an important time-saving avenue in the pursuit of their degree. Many of these completers noted that the credits awarded from PLA processes facilitated faster degree completion. While they generally understand the intrinsic value of what they have gained from their life and professional experience, they also highly value any credit awarded to validate that learning and expedite their degree completion. Finally, andragogy (Knowles, 1980) is evidenced in the active learning nature of many programs featured in this book. These stories displayed a strong value placed on developing critical thinking, interpersonal skills, and problem-solving skills within adult degree-completion programs. Many of the stories highlighted the benefit of applying relevant content to real-world practice; individuals whose stories are highlighted here also described an appreciation for working in teams to solve problems.

These stories and the earlier study (Bergman, 2012) also support the tenets of Bean and Metzner's (1985) theory of adult student persistence and Braxton, Hirschy, and McClendon's (2004) model. The model proposed by Braxton et al. (2004), who sought to respond to the unique characteristics of commuter schools rather than more traditional residential institutions, more closely connected to the students and programs represented by the stories presented here. In addition, these path models of student persistence all highlight the importance of finances, academic support, and institutional support systems. The stories presented here work to illustrate many of the elements suggested by Bean and Metzner (1985) and Braxton et al. (2004) for improving the effectiveness of any adult-friendly program or practice. Furthermore, the Bergman model—theory of adult learner persistence in degree completion programs is also supported as a valuable path model worthy of consideration in developing and executing adult-friendly practices at colleges and universities across the country.

Innovative practices related to evening and online course work, compressed scheduling, PLA, and strong financial aid structures for adults are important, especially in the context of rigorous and relevant adult degree programs. Researchers and practitioners alike must increasingly recognize the value of strong curriculum, quality instructors, robust support systems, and acknowledgement of prior experience (i.e., PLA) to promote the success of returning adult learners. In addition, to gain visibility and validation among more traditional college and university programs, these degree-completion programs must continue to provide proper oversight, consistent and relevant course and program offerings, academic rigor and integrity, and support services.

What Does This Mean for Research?

When studying student retention, it is easy to get lost in the dismal statistics surrounding student attrition and non-completion. Above all, the stories here challenge researchers and administrators alike to remember that each data point represents a real-world individual, pursuing additional education and credentials and seeking to change at least one trajectory of his or her life. The challenges are real and the battles are hard-fought, but the successes should be celebrated.

In addition, it is important to remember that "adult students" do not comprise a homogeneous population. What do we lose if we simply categorize all students over the age of 25 as "adults" and fail to consider the broad spectrum of adult development patterns? Therefore, future research should seek to disaggregate age groups, to understand recruitment and retention strategies in a more nuanced way. Alternately, previous studies have confirmed correlation between adult student persistence and many internal campus and academic influences (e.g., status of enrollment, GPA, institutional support, academic advising, faculty support, financial aid, flexible scheduling, active learning, and PLA). However, these variables have not been considered collectively, so further path analysis of the Bergman model may deepen understanding of the cumulative effect of these variables.

Tinto (1993) highlighted the importance of social integration in relation to student assimilation and persistence to graduation, and research related to traditional-age student retention highlights the importance of student engagement (i.e., integration; Horn & Carroll, 1996; New England Adult Research Network, 1999; Tinto, 1998). At the same time, other studies have challenged a simplistic understanding of "social integration" (Braxton et al., 1997), and the stories here demonstrate the myriad types of "integration" that these successful students experienced. Therefore, in considering adult student retention, it may be helpful to define social integration in terms of integrating the pursuit of education into one's overall life (Kerka, 1997). Future research should explore the concept of integration more fully, perhaps through the lens of active learning, given that these adult learners highly valued the development of critical thinking, interpersonal skills, teamwork, and problem-solving.

Regardless of the age or life-stage of the student, no student's pursuit of a college degree happens in isolation, and significant research has highlighted the impact of the external environment on student persistence (Bean & Metzner, 1985; Bergman, Strickler, Osam, & Ash, 2018; Christensen, 1991; Hall, 1997; Hammer, Grigsby, & Woods, 1998; Horn & Carroll, 1996; Mercer, 1993; Wldokowski et al., 2001; Zajkowski, 1997). Therefore, it is important to consider the influence of those external factors such as work conflicts or finances—especially as they affect adult learners—as they may be important predictors of adult student persistence. In addition, future research should explore variations in persistence related to institution and degree-completion program types to determine the impact of these variables on adult learners as a whole.

At the same time, these stories demonstrate that "history is not destiny"; these adult learners persisted in spite of challenging family influences (conflict), life-changing events, community influences, and challenging work settings and hours. It is incredibly important to acknowledge that "life happens" to just about every returning adult student. However, while these events certainly present a challenge for any student, they are not necessarily (or fatalistically) catastrophic to one's path to completion. Why did *these* adult students persist when so many are not able to overcome these external factors? Further study of successful students who persisted to graduation to better understand how individuals respond to the variable and wide-ranging life events they may encounter may provide greater understanding of the nuances within the significant life event variable and suggest strategies or programming options that may foster increased retention and persistence. Barriers will always arise while the adult learner is working to create a better quality of life through additional educational attainment. Those who are willing to work through those barriers and find advocates and advisors to help navigate those barriers can make it to the finish line!

What Does This Mean for Practice?

Adult degree-completion programs looking to increase persistence should dig into the repository of students who successfully completed their programs. The insights from these students who successfully navigated the challenges of higher education as returning as adults will continue to provide insight into what institutions are doing wrong and doing right to serve their respective population of students. This book provides support for action-oriented interventions that will promote the persistence of adult students. One such intervention for innovative student tracking could be an early-alert system related to barriers presented by these narratives. Promoting proactive communication between students, faculty, advisors, and other staff may alert those involved to "minor issues" (with attendance or writing skills, for example) before they become insurmountable. It may be helpful to consider how technology and social media can be utilized for ongoing student support. Text alerts, web-based calendars, mobile apps for the campus learning management system, and social media provide multiple ways to meet students where they are at, to maintain contact with adult students, and to help them stay engaged in their academic progress. This sort of intrusive intervention may also serve traditional-age students, as well, leading to improved retention and graduation rates for the institution as a whole.

At the very least, adult degree-completion programs should be compiling the graduation tracking and employment statistics that will help incoming students evaluate the learning outcomes and value of each particular degree or credential. In addition, exit interviews with students who are successfully completing their programs—much like the narratives presented in this book—may be a low-cost way to better understand the support and encouragement students need.

We are certainly not the first to say it, and we won't be the last, but this book once again highlights the importance of adding course and schedule options that increase flexibility for students while also maintaining academic rigor. Those who are returning to complete a degree that was previously started may be battling insecurity, educational baggage, and fears of failure. Accelerated course formats (e.g., 8-week sessions) and online offerings are key components of serving students in a flexible way, while preserving the integrity of the degrees they are seeking. Robust orientation sessions tailored to the needs of adult learners will help returning students better understand and navigate the bureaucracy inherent to any institution of higher education. Prior learning assessment validates the adult student's work and learning experience, expedites credit accumulation, and may serve to dissipate the students' fears about being capable of college-level learning.

Within the stories presented here, those who believed they had sufficient financial resources to complete their degree did make it to the finish line. To be successful, students in adult degree-completion programs need to be convinced that (a) they can afford the education and (b) there will be sufficient return on that investment in terms of increased career opportunities and salary possibilities. This means at least two things for adult degree-completion program administrators. First, with adult learners returning to higher education at increasing rates and many institutions increasingly reliant on these students to meet enrollment goals, institutions and legislatures need to be vigilant about designating more financial aid for this growing population of students. Recent revisions to the G.I. Bill have expanded options for veterans and military families, but many other students find it difficult to secure sufficient scholarships, grant, or loans (Bergman et al., 2018). Second, it is imperative that colleges and universities pay attention to the career development needs of these returning adults. These students will need concrete and targeted assistance to write or rework resumes, so as to best capitalize on previous work experience while also potentially preparing for career changes. A generic "how to write your resume" session, created with 22-year-old, first-time entrants into the workforce as the target audience, will not serve the needs of adult students. In addition, while returning adult students often have a clear idea of their educational and career goals, this is not always the case (e.g., Schultz, 1997), so it is important that career services professionals are available and accessible for *all* students, including those in degree-completion programs.

Woven through each page of this book is the theme that relationships matter. The support of a family member, the prompting of an employer, or the encouragement of a mentor can make all the difference for the student navigating a degree-completion program. When it comes to relationships on campus, most adult students have very little time or relational margin to get involved in cocurricular activities or relationships. The initial enrollment counselor or first professor might not continue to be the student's key contact after the student has enrolled in classes, but for many, having a single point of contact or a connection with one specific office fosters those relationships that may anchor the student to the institution when things get challenging. Therefore, it is essential that any degree-completion program employ dedicated staff and advisors who are available and accessible to give support and feedback that is timely and accurate.

In conclusion, the complexities of the contemporary workforce are driving the need for more highly skilled and credentialed workers. As adult students return to finish what was once started, they will be expecting programs that are relevant in the real world. They will be expecting superior service, just as they would expect from any other institution where they do business. They will be expecting colleges and universities to be flexible and to provide programs, schedules, and strategies (e.g., PLA) that help them meet their career and educational goals quickly and simply. What they once started, we can help them finish.

10

Call to Action

To strengthen the nation, we must help people find a pathway to educational credentials that fit their life. The variety and accessibility of programs at local education institutions is expanding and whether a student wants a certificate in IT or a bachelor's degree in management, there are likely local (or online) options that provide convenient and flexible pathways to achieving these goals. There is a fundamental shift in the historic way of doing business in the academy. The entrepreneurial spirit is finally making inroads into the fabric of many of the nation's traditional institutions. From accelerated formats, to evening and online programs, to innovative partnerships with corporate collaborators, to prior learning assessment, many institutions are getting ahead of the statistically unavoidable, upcoming demographic shift. As these innovations become more readily apparent to the general public, it is likely that adults with some college and no degree will realize that the old university model that they experienced is no longer prevalent. Higher education has changed, and most colleges or universities should no longer be seen as a big scary entity holding them back from realizing their potential. Entrepreneurial strategies employed by

Unfinished Business, pages 173–181
Copyright © 2019 by Information Age Publishing

these traditional institutions can present pathways that can be integrated into life despite the many competing responsibilities that working adults face. So, what can you do to get started, if you or your loved one needs (or wants) more education? Below are five tips on how to get started on the journey to finish your degree.

Identifying the Best Adult-Friendly Degree Program

1. *Reflect and research:* What do you plan to do in your career, and what skills and credentials are required? Once you know the answers to these questions, you can narrow the search and examine schools that offer the program that is right for you.
2. *Find the appropriate delivery method for your needs:* Decide what type of classes (online, face-to-face, blended, accelerated) you want to take. Explore the times and days that courses are offered and choose a program that works with your schedule.
3. *Regional accreditation:* It is very important to make sure your degree or certification will be valued and credits will transfer in the event that you want to switch schools or advance from a 2-year to a 4-year college. Be sure to ask if the institution you are interested in is "regionally accredited." This is a perfectly acceptable question to ask of any recruiter or program director you speak with, and they should be able to give a concise and straightforward answer to this question and tell you which organization has given the accreditation. If they hedge *at all* in their response, be very cautious. Also note that "national accreditation" is actually *less* rigorous and likely to create *more* restrictions for you. If the recruiter implies (or tells you) that "national accreditation is better" or "accreditation doesn't mean that much anyway," do not be fooled. Start looking for a different institution right away.
4. *Create a "top picks" list:* Once you have some regionally accredited options that match your interests, contact those institutions to make a virtual or in-person appointment. See if the institution has people who seem welcoming and committed to your goal fulfillment. Talk with some staff, faculty, and students to get a sense of the campus culture. Is the atmosphere inclusive and considerate of your schedule? If not, consider expanding your search.
5. *Financial aid and cost:* Cost has to be a consideration, but do not unnecessarily limit your search by looking only at cost. Nationally, degrees have been shown to produce a 15% return on investment during your career. Are there options for financial assistance through loans, grants, or scholarships? Consider the price of the

institution and make sure the investment matches the investment you are making. If you feel comfortable with the investment you are about to make, you are more likely to complete your degree or certificate.

While these recommendations are not all-encompassing, they will reframe working adults' minds into an understanding that this process can be methodical and manageable despite their reservations about past failure in higher education.

Research has highlighted a few things that tend to be predictors of success in college. Making the right connections, being adaptable and resilient, developing high emotional intelligence, and having clearly defined goals all predispose a company for marketing success. So how do you stack up in those critical areas? Are you connecting with the right referral sources to find a program that is a great fit for you? Are you able to challenge yourself to adapt to the new learning economy? Are you ready to bounce back quickly when something does not go as planned? Do you manage yourself well, and can you apply that to an academic program? Are you socially aware, and will you read the cues that help you assimilate into your program of choice? Do you have specific career objectives that can be met as a result of finishing your degree? If the answer is no to any or all of these questions, where do you need to improve? And how can you get started? If you or a loved one are considering a return to finish what was started last year or long ago, take the time to explore these important questions. The individuals featured in this book found a way to convince themselves that the sacrifice of returning to college was worth it, and they had a solid belief that they could do it.

Creating Opportunities for Adult Learners

Unfortunately, we often hear a negative portrayal of adult learners who return to college. Research highlights that they are more likely to be first-generation college students, to come from lower socioeconomic backgrounds, to have low grades from the past, to need developmental education, and more likely to fail or drop out. We view this as the "same old story" that is a very limited view of potential returning students who could thrive given a convenient and flexible pathway. In our view, the "real story" about adult learners is more focused on an appreciative inquiry of their prior experiences and how those experiences will propel adults forward into a successful return to the academic setting. The stories in this book were written by high-performing working professionals who have been employed for years in various industries. They have strong family backgrounds and support that make the return not only possible but favorable to that of traditional students who don't bring much context to the learning exchange. These learners find necessary finances to pursue priorities in their lives. They have large networks and are highly connected to people and organizations that can assist them along the way. Furthermore, they can draw on a laundry list of previous nonacademic success to keep them motivated and resilient through the process. These appreciative aspects of working adults are often not the focus as higher education recruits, retains, and graduates adult learners along the way. We view the shortcomings first and neglect the immense amount of benefit that these individuals bring to our colleges and universities. Instead of colleges and universities saying, "We will give you another chance," we need to say, "Will you give us another chance?"

Higher education institutions that can create flexible course options with convenient availability and tap into the prior knowledge that adults bring to the classroom are more likely to retain these highly motivated individuals in relevant, rigorous, and research-based programs that will address the needs of the American workforce. Adults are often going to work every day to produce a good or service for their employers. If we can leverage that motivation to help adults advance in their current or future roles, develop new skills to remain competitive, help them develop greater self-efficacy, and aid in the inspiration or modeling that education is important to their family, we are far more likely to have engaged, motivated, and potentially happier workers in our economy.

Promoting Prior Learning Assessment

Consequently, we now have a recipe for innovative approaches to fuel the enrollment goals of America's colleges and universities of the future. Adult learners are becoming increasingly central to the viability of many institutions. This fierce competition for student tuition dollars is poised to breed new economic realities that also influence academic programs. Therefore, prior learning assessment (PLA) has the potential to re-engage a dormant student population waiting for an opportunity to finish a long-held goal started last year or long ago (Bergman & Herd, 2017).

The Council for Adult and Experiential Learning (CAEL) has been a leading voice in promoting the evaluation of college-level learning as a means of accelerating adult degree completion. Their standards highlight that this is not "credit for life experience," which is at the root of many administrators' resistance to PLA processes. Given this, CAEL promotes the following standards for PLA programs:

1. Credit should be awarded only for learning and not for experience.
2. College credit should be awarded only for college-level learning.
3. Credit should be awarded only for learning that has a balance, appropriate to the subject, between theory and practical application.
4. Competence levels and credit awards must be made by subject matter/academic experts.
5. Credit should be appropriate to the academic context in which it is accepted.
6. Credit awards and transcript entries should be monitored to avoid duplicate credit.
7. Policies and procedures (including appeals) should be fully disclosed and prominently available.
8. Fees charged for assessment should be based on services, not on the amount of credit.
9. Personnel involved in assessment should receive adequate training.
10. Assessment programs should be regularly monitored, reviewed, evaluated, and revised (Colvin, 2012).

When an institution adopts and follows these standards, it can use PLA rigorously to evaluate and validate college-level learning—the knowledge, skills, and abilities gained outside the confines of the classroom—to award academic credit (CAEL, 2010) for the benefit of adult learners. Most PLA efforts provide constructivist and narrative storytelling approaches, which help increase self-awareness, self-efficacy, career identity, and goal orientation.

The two primary forms of PLA include course-specific assessment (test-out) and a broader form of portfolio submission. Course-specific PLA allows adult learners to take "challenge exams" to test out of courses or take College Level Examination Program (CLEP) or DANTES Subject Standardized Test (DSST) exams that are broadly accepted by most institutions. Students who achieve a certain score in the requisite exam are awarded college credit toward their program of study and are exempted from those courses. In the second form of PLA—portfolio compilation—students who are eligible for elective or major-specific course credit assemble documents to demonstrate competency in a specific area of knowledge that is deemed college-level equivalent (Bergman & Herd, 2017). A portfolio typically includes a statement of goals, learning chronology (e.g., resume, learning chart, autobiography), learning narrative, and competency statements that match learning outcomes. Students also include supporting documentation to validate that the learning has actually occurred (Colvin, 2012). Quite often, the degree-completion program offers a structured PLA class or some other guided process that assists the learners as they work through the process of documenting college-level learning outcomes from noncollege settings. The PLA process recognizes and legitimizes learning in which adults have engaged in many parts of their lives, such as nonformal instructional programs, civic or volunteer engagement, military training, and employment (CAEL, 2010).

The portfolio process is sometimes met with ambivalence by faculty and administrators, due to a lack of publicity and awareness, a sense that students are not adequately supported while assembling the portfolio, or concerns that the process lacks rigor or academic integrity (Fisher, 1991; Topping, 1996). At times, students choose to not utilize the process; some feel it requires too much work and others assume their experience or prior learning is not sufficient to be awarded credit. Those who choose to complete the process express accomplishment, satisfaction, and appreciation for the time and money they saved once credits were awarded (Dagavarian & Walters, 1993; Fisher, 1991). The portfolio process strengthens core values: freedom and independence, learning, tenacity and hard work, pride, aspiration, and commitment to goals (Burris, 1997). McGinley (1995) suggested that when a PLA process is structured well, students' thinking—about their present and their futures, as well as about their pasts—can be changed. Many times, students are eager to share the portfolio with children and other family members; it becomes a source of pride.

PLA Can Lead to Increased Graduation Rate and Pace to Graduation

Portfolio development for PLA is becoming a more readily used form of demonstrated mastery of college level subject matter expertise, but it is also still met with wide skepticism from faculty and administrators. However, PLA has been empirically shown to increase graduation rate and pace to graduation. A 48-institution study conducted by CAEL in 2010 demonstrated that graduation and persistence/retention rates are 2.5 times higher for students with PLA credit than for those without. Also, among 62,475 in the study, students saved an average of between 2.5 and 10.1 months in earning their degrees (CAEL, 2010).

Adult Learners who Complete PLA Portfolios are More Engaged and Assimilated

Students are more engaged and ready for academics after the portfolio writing process. Much of the baggage a returning adult brings to the academic setting is unpacked in this reflective writing process. Students who complete a portfolio begin to make substantive connections to the academic community and gain confidence in their ability to become a high-performing adult student as well as a competent working professional. For approximately 36 million nontraditional students, a few more credits can be a powerful motivator to persist when competing responsibilities from life intervene.

Students with Access to PLA Take More Credits

According to recent findings from the Council for Adult and Experiential Learning, students earning PLA credit take an average of 9.9 more course credits than their peers without access to PLA. While that may seem counterintuitive, if adults are recognized for their prior knowledge, skills, and abilities, they are more likely to persist, which generates more credits toward the degree.

PLA is Generally Awarded for Non-Major Credit

PLA is designed to acknowledge subject areas where adults can demonstrate mastery. While adult learners may have extensive experience in certain fields, they must engross themselves in a discipline to earn the requisite degree. Consequently, returning adults are focused on immersing themselves into the major of their choice so they can apply the research to practice in their area of study. There may be an instance of gaining credit for certain areas of subject matter expertise, but this process does not circumvent the exposure and immersion into the discipline.

The added credit also provides momentum to move efficiently and effectively toward graduation in their selected major. The most effective degree-granting programs offer excellent instruction and high-level student services, and they are planned well, flexible, and convenient. Using PLA to examine an adult student's previous learning experiences from workplace experiences or military training, as well as certifications and licenses the individual may have earned, can lay the groundwork for a very engaged and satisfied adult learner population. While PLA takes a different approach than a traditional college class, it arrives at the same result of demonstrated mastery in a particular college-level subject area. The learning objectives are assessed, met, and validated just like a standard college course taught on campus.

This process still makes people nervous. Therefore, standardization of policy and process are a key driver in greater acceptance and understanding of PLA. Just as young people are "our future," the adult population is "our present." Completing a baccalaureate education challenges adults who have some college but no degree to pursue deeper engagement in critical thought. The corresponding increase in knowledge and skills will likely trickle down; "our present" (i.e., adult learners) may well, in turn, serve to inspire "our future" (i.e., younger students) and validate the importance, value, and necessity of higher education for meeting the needs of contemporary society and attain local, state, and national goals for increased educational attainment and completion (Bowers & Bergman, 2016).

Conclusion

Research and literature relating to retention and persistence tends to highlight the experiences of traditional-age students. Likewise, the performance and retention of first-year, full-time freshmen have been the focus of reporting requirements and state-level funding formulas, which discounts—if not ignores completely—the experience and retention of part-time and/ or nontraditional students. Understanding the factors that influence the retention and persistence of nontraditional adult learners is a complex endeavor, due in large part to the variety of responsibilities that adult students manage while also pursuing their education. The narratives included in this book display many of the variables that have an impact on the adults who return to the formal academic setting to complete a bachelor's degree, as outlined in the model presented in Chapter 8.

Each student who leaves college prior to graduation does so for a constellation of reasons unique to that student. However, research and the resulting body of literature suggests that, broadly speaking, background, academic, and environmental variables have an impact on the likelihood of retention (Pascarella & Terenzini, 2005; Pascarella, Terenzini, & Wolfle, 1991). The first six to eight weeks of a student's program may be the most critical attrition point for students. Tinto (1993) highlighted the importance of academic or social integration for student persistence. However, many adult students have limited opportunities for academic and social integration (Taylor, 2000); therefore, strategies that work for retaining traditional students may have limited utility for adult students.

There will always be some attrition, due to unplanned life events, inadequate commitment, lack of time, or an incomplete understanding of the time and intellectual demands inherent in pursuing higher education. However, many who stop out, withdraw, or drop out completely might have been retained if they had encountered the right services, programs, or staff person before they made the decision to step away from their educational pursuits. At the same time, many colleges and universities face growing pressure to retain students to degree completion. Researchers and practitioners need theories that more clearly describe the longitudinal process of student departure and account for the complex behaviors leading to that departure (Tinto, 1993).

The secret to successful retention may well be the willingness of colleges and universities to get involved in both the intellectual and social development of students (Tinto, 1993). Knowles (1980) suggested that a departure from a human community may reflect the attributes and actions of both the individual who leaves and the other participants in the community. In other words, a decision to withdraw may be less a function of what occurred before the student enrolls and more a function of what happens after entry. If this is the case, then institutions that enroll students in adult degree-completion programs must be intentional to attend to the needs of the entering (or re-entering) students. This is a dynamic relationship. As institutions commit to student success and completion, students become more involved and committed to their own educational pursuits. It can be a win–win.

The need is critical. The U.S. workforce will need one million more college graduates than produced, by the year 2025. At the same time, birth rates are declining; therefore, the population of traditional-age students will shrink. Adult students—both those enrolling for the first time and those who return to complete their degrees—will become a growing and increasingly important component of college students. If, as Kasworm (2003a) suggested, the college experience is different for adult students, especially when compared to traditional-age students, we need an increasingly nuanced understanding of the institutional, personal, and environmental factors that shape their persistence. We need to help them finish their "unfinished business."

References

Aaker, J. (2013). *Harnessing the power of stories* [Video file]. Stanford Graduate School of Business Clayman Institute for Gender Research Online Institute. Retrieved from: https://womensleadership.stanford.edu/stories

Abel, J. R., & Deitz, R. (2014). Do the benefits of college still outweigh the costs? *Reserve Bank of New York Current Issues in Economics and Finance, 20*(3), 1–9.

Adult Higher Education Alliance. (1998, October). *The principles of good practice for alternative and external degree programs for adults* [The Alliance Monograph]. Washington, DC: American Council on Education.

Ahson, N. L., Gentemann, K. M., & Phelps, L. (1998, May). *Do stop outs return? A longitudinal study of re-enrollment, attrition and graduation.* Paper presented at the 38th Annual Forum of the Association for Institutional Research. Retrieved from the ERIC database. (ED424800)

American Association of Colleges of Nursing). (n.d.). *Nursing education pathways.* Retrieved from https://www.aacnnursing.org/Students/Nursing -Education-Pathways

American College Testing. (2010). *What works in student retention? Fourth national survey: Report for all colleges and universities.* Iowa City, IA: Author.

Anderson, M. L., Goodman, J., & Schlossberg, N. K. (2012). *Counseling adults in transition: Linking Schlossberg's theory with practice in a diverse world* (4th ed.). New York, NY: Springer.

Ashar, H., & Skenes, R. (1993). Can Tinto's student departure model be applied to nontraditional students? *Adult Education Quarterly, 43*(2), 90–100.

Unfinished Business, pages 183–196
Copyright © 2019 by Information Age Publishing
All rights of reproduction in any form reserved.

Ashburn, E. (2010, April 18). City U. of New York plans "a grand experiment": A new college. *The Chronicle of Higher Education.* Retrieved from https://www.chronicle.com/article/City-U-of-New-York-Plans-a/65054

Aslanian, C. B. (2001). *Adult students today.* New York, NY: The College Board.

Astin, A. (1971). *Predicting academic performance in college: Selectivity data for 2300 American colleges.* New York, NY: The Free Press.

Astin, A. (1975). *Preventing students from dropping out.* San Francisco, CA: Jossey-Bass.

Astin, A. (1984). Student involvement: A developmental theory for higher education. *Journal of College Student Personnel, 25*(4), 297–308.

Astin, A. (1993). *What matters in college? Four critical years revisited.* San Francisco, CA: Jossey-Bass.

Atkinson. D., & Correa, D. K. (2007). *The 2007 state new economy index: Benchmarking economic transformation in the states.* Washington, DC: Ewing Marion Kauffman Foundation and Information Technology and Innovation Foundation.

Baum, S., & Ma, J. (2007). *Education pays: The benefits of higher education for individuals and society.* New York, NY: The College Board.

Bean, J. P. (1980). Dropouts and turnover: The synthesis and test of a causal model of student attrition. *Research in Higher Education, 12*(2), 155–187.

Bean, J. P., & Metzner, B. S. (1985). A conceptual model of nontraditional student attrition. *Review of Educational Research, 55*(4), 485–540.

Bergman, M. (2012). *An examination of factors that impact persistence among adult students in a degree completion program at a four-year university* (Doctoral dissertation). University of Louisville, Louisville, KY. Retrieved from https://ir.library.louisville.edu/etd/102/

Bergman, M. (2016). From stopout to scholar: Pathways to graduation through adult degree completion programs. *International Journal of Information Communication Technologies and Human Development, 8*(4), 1–12.

Bergman, M., Gross, J. P. K., Berry, M., & Shuck, M. B. (2014). If life happened but a degree didn't: Examining factors that impact adult student persistence. *Journal of Continuing Higher Education, 62*(2), 90–101.

Bergman, M., & Herd, A. (2017). Proven leadership = college credit: Enhancing employability of transitioning military members through prior learning assessment. *Advances in Developing Human Resources, 19*(1), 78–87.

Bergman, M., Strickler, B., Osam, K., & Ash, D. (2018). Engineering the benefits of learning in the new learning economy. *The Journal of Continuing Higher Education, 66*(2), 67–76.

Berker, A., Horn, L., & Carroll, C. (2003). *Work first, study second: Adult undergraduates who combine employment and postsecondary enrollment* (NCES

2003–167). Washington, DC: U.S. Department of Education. Retrieved from https://nces.ed.gov/pubs2003/2003167.pdf

Bonk, C. J. (2009). *The world is open: How web technology is revolutionizing education.* San Francisco, CA: Jossey-Bass.

Bowers, A., & Bergman, M. (2016). Affordability and the return on investment of college completion: Unique challenges and opportunities for adult learners. *Journal of Continuing Higher Education, 64*(3), 144–151.

Bragg, D. D., Townsend, B. K., & Ruud, C. M. (2009, January). *The adult learner and the applied baccalaureate: Emerging lessons for state and local implementation.* Champaign, IL: Office of Community College Research and Leadership University of Illinois. Retrieved from ERIC database. (ED504447)

Braxton, J. M. (Ed). (2000). *Reworking the student departure puzzle.* Nashville, TN: Vanderbilt University Press.

Braxton, J. M., & Hirschy, A. S. (2005). Theoretical developments in the study of college student departure. In A. Seidman (Ed.), *College student retention* (pp. 61–88). Westport, CT: Praeger.

Braxton, J. M., Hirschy, A. S., & McClendon, S. A. (2004). Understanding and reducing college student departure: ASHE-ERIC Higher Education Report. San Francisco, CA: Wiley Periodicals.

Braxton, J. M., Milem, J. F., & Sullivan A. S. (2000). The influence of active learning on the college student departure process. *The Journal of Higher Education, 71*(5), 569–590.

Braxton, J. M., Shaw Sullivan, A. V., & Johnson, R. M. (1997). Appraising Tinto's theory of college student departure. In J. C. Smart (Ed.), *Higher education: Handbook of theory and research* (Vol. 1; pp. 107–164). New York, NY: Agathon Press.

Bureau of Labor Statistics. (2018). United States Department of Labor census data. Retrieved from https://www.bls.gov/opub/mlr/2012/01/art3full.pdf

Burleson, D., Hallett, R., & Park, D. (2008). College knowledge: An assessment of urban students' awareness of college processes. *College and University, 84*(2), 10–17.

Burris, J. (1997). The adult undergraduate's experience of portfolio development: A multiple case study. *Dissertation Abstracts International, 58,* 2742.

Byrd, S. (1990). *Perceptions of barriers to undergraduate education by nontraditional students at selected non-public, liberal arts institutions in the mid-south* (Doctoral dissertation). Louisiana State University, Baton Rouge, LA.

Cabrera, A. F., Burkum, K. R., & LaNasa, S. M. (2005). Pathways to a four-year degree: Determinants of transfer and degree completion. In A. Seidman (Ed.), *Student retention: Formula for student success* (pp. 155–214). New York, NY: Rowman & Littlefield.

Cabrera, A. F., Nora, A., & Castaneda, M. B. (1993). College persistence: Structural equations modeling test of an integrated model of student retention. *Journal of Higher Education, 64*(2), 123–139.

Calcagno, J., Jenkins, D., Bailey, T., & Crosta, P. (2006). *Stepping stones to a degree: The impact of enrollment pathways and milestones on community college student outcomes.* New York, NY: Community College Research Center. Retrieved from https://ccrc.tc.columbia.edu/publications/impact-enrollment-pathways -milestones.html

Canja, E. T. (2002). Lifelong learning: Challenges & opportunities. *CAEL Forum and News,* 26–29.

Carey, K. (2004). *A matter of degrees: A report by the Education Trust.* Washington, DC: Education Trust.

Carnevale, A., Jayasundera, T., & Gulish, A. (2016). *America's divided recovery: College haves and have-nots.* Washington, DC: Georgetown University Center on Education and the Workforce. Retrieved from https:// 1gyhoq479ufd3yna29x7ubjn-wpengine.netdna-ssl.com/wp-content/ uploads/Americas-Divided-Recovery-web.pdf

Carnevale, A., Smith, N., & Strohl, J. (2010). *Help wanted: Projections of jobs and education requirements through 2018.* Washington, DC: Georgetown University Center on Education and the Workforce. Retrieved from https://cew .georgetown.edu/cew-reports/help-wanted/#report

Childress, M. D., & Spurgin, D. G. (2009). Effects of university and departmental community on online learners. *Educause Quarterly, 32*(4). Retrieved from http://www.learntechlib.org/p/106946/

Choy, S. (2002). *Nontraditional undergraduates: Findings from the condition of education 2002 (NCES 2002–012).* Washington, DC: U.S. Department of Education. Retrieved from https://nces.ed.gov/pubs2002/2002012.pdf

Choy, S., & Premo, M. (1995). *Profile of older undergraduates: 1989–90.* (NCES 95-167). Washington, DC: U.S. Department of Education. Retrieved from http://nces.ed.gov/pubs95/web/95167.asp

Christensen, P. (1991, October). *Comparison of adult baccalaureate graduates and nonpersisters.* Paper presented at the Midwest Research-to-Practice Conference, St. Paul, MN. Retrieved from ERIC database. (ED378307)

College Board Advocacy. (2009). *How colleges organize themselves to increase student persistence: Four-year institutions.* Bloomington: Indiana University Project on Academic Success. Retrieved from http://pas.indiana.edu/ pdf/How%20Colleges%20Organize.pdf

Colvin, J. (2012). *Earn college credit for what you know* (5th ed.) Chicago, IL: Kendall/Hunt.

Cope, R. G., & Hannah, W. (1974). *Revolving college doors.* New York, NY: Wiley.

Council for Adult and Experiential Learning. (2010). *Fueling the race to postsecondary success: A 48-institution survey of prior learning assessment and adult student outcomes*. Retrieved from https://www.cacl.org/pla/publication/fueling-the-race-to-postsecondary-success

Cronin, J. M., & Bachorz, P. M. (2006). The rising of Phoenix, and what it means for higher education. *Journal of Education, 186*(1), 11–21.

Crouch, R. (2008). Debunking the myths: Immigration. *Diversity Forum Series*. University of Louisville, Louisville, KY.

Cruse, L., Holtzman, T., Gault, B., Croom, D., & Polk, P. (2019). *Parents in college by the numbers*. Institute for Women's Policy Research. Retrieved from https://iwpr.org/publications/parents-college-numbers/

Cuccaro-Alamin, S. (1997). *Postsecondary persistence and attainment (NCES 97–984)*. Washington, DC: U.S. Department of Education. Retrieved from https://nces.ed.gov/pubs97/97984.pdf

Cuccaro-Alamin, S., Choy, S. P., & Carroll, C. D. (1998). *Postsecondary financing strategies: How undergraduates combine work, borrowing, and attendance* (NCES 98-088). Washington, DC: U.S. Department of Education. Retrieved from https://nces.ed.gov/pubs98/98088.pdf

Dagavarian, D., & Walters, W. (1993). Outcomes assessment of prior learning assessment programs. In D. Dagavarian (Ed.), *In support of prior learning assessment and outcomes assessment of prior learning assessment programs* (pp. 3–8). Proceedings of the National Institute on the Assessment of Experiential Learning. Princeton, NJ. Retrieved from the ERIC database. (ED387613)

Dinmore, I. (1997). Interdisciplinarity and integrative learning: An imperative for adult education. *Education, 117*(3), 452–467.

Donaldson, J. E., & Graham, S. (1990). A model of college outcomes for adults. *Adult Education Quarterly, 50*, 24–40.

Donaldson, J. F., & Townsend, B. K. (2007). Higher education journals' discourse about adult undergraduate students. *The Journal of Higher Education, 78*(1), 27–50.

Durkheim, E. (1951). *Suicide*. New York, NY: Free Press.

Elkins, S. A., Braxton, J. M., & James, G. W. (1998, May). *Tinto's separation stage and its influence on first-semester college student persistence*. AIR 1998 Annual Forum Paper. Paper presented at the Annual Forum of the Association for Institutional Research Minneapolis, MN. Retrieved from ERIC database. (ED424799)

Eppler, M., & Harju, B. (1997). Achievement motivation goals in relation to academic performance in traditional and nontraditional college students. *Research in Higher Education, 38*(5), 557–573.

Ewell, P., Kelly, P., & Klein-Collins, R. (2008). *Adults learning in focus: National and state-by-state data CAEL and NCHEMS published report*. Retrieved from https://lincs.ed.gov/professional-development/resource-collections/profile-218

Farabaugh-Dorkins, C. (1991). Beginning to understand why older students drop out of college: A path analytic test of the Bean/Metzner model of nontraditional student attrition. *AIR Professional File, 39*, 1–12.

Feldman, P. A. (2004). *Bachelor's degree completion programs: Factors influencing success for adult students* (Unpublished doctoral dissertation). Arizona State University, Tempe, AZ.

Fisher, V. (1991). An institutional evaluation of perceptions and expectations of a portfolio assessment program (life experience). *Dissertation Abstracts International, 57*, 2908.

Gallup, Inc. (2013). *21st century skills and the workplace: A 2013 Microsoft Partners in Learning and Pearson Foundation study.* Washington, DC: Author. Retrieved from https://www.gallup.com/services/176699/21st-century-skills-workplace.aspx

Graduate! Network. (2019). *Why it Matters! Philadelphia, PA.* Retrieved from https://graduate-network.org/why-it-matters/

Greater Louisville Inc. (2010). *Fifty-five thousand degrees initiative: Greater Louisville's education commitment.* Retrieved from http://www.55000degrees.org/about-55k/our-objectives/

Gurin, P., Dey, E. L., Hurtado, S., & Gurin, G. (2002). Diversity and higher education: Theory and impact on educational outcomes. *Harvard Education Review, 72*, 330–366.

Hadfield, J. (2003). Recruiting and retaining adult students. In D. Kilgore & P. J. Rice (Eds.), *New directions for student services: No. 102: Meeting the special needs of adult learners* (pp. 17–25). San Francisco, CA: Jossey-Bass. https://doi.org/10.1002/ss.85

Hall, N. (1997). Variables that enhance the persistence of older female graduate students. *Dissertation Abstracts International, 53*, 1610.

Hammer, L. B., Grigsby, T. D., & Woods, S. (1998). The conflicting demands of work, family, and school among students at an urban university. *The Journal of Psychology, 132*(2), 220–226.

Hanniford, B., & Sagaria, M. (1994, April). *The impact of work and family roles on associate and baccalaureate degree completion among students in early adulthood.* Paper presented at the annual meeting of the American Educational Research Association, New Orleans, LA. Retrieved from ERIC database. (ED370520)

Harrington, J. (1993). Why they stay: A study on the persistence of re-entry women. *Initiatives, 55*(4), 17–24.

Hoffman, L., & Reindl, T. (2011). *Compete to complete: Improving postsecondary attainment among adults.* Washington, DC: National Governor's Association Center for Best Practices.

Horn, L. (1998). *Stopouts or stayouts? Undergraduates who leave college in their first year* (NCES 1999-087). Washington, DC: U.S. Department of Education.

Horn, L., & Berger, R. (2005). *College persistence on the rise? Changes in 5-year degree completion and postsecondary persistence rates between 1994 and 2000* (NCES 2005-156). Washington, DC: U.S. Department of Education.

Horn, L., & Carroll, C. D. (1996). *Nontraditional students: Trends in enrollment from 1986 to 1992 and persistence and attainment among 1989–90 beginning postsecondary students* (NCES 97-578). Washington, DC: U.S. Department of Education. Retrieved from https://nces.ed.gov/pubs/97578.pdf

Hoyt, J. E., & Allred, E. (2008). Educational and employment outcomes of a degree completion program. *Journal of Continuing Higher Education, 56*(2), 26–33. https://doi.org/10.1080/07377366.2008.10400150

Hunt, J. B., & Tierney, T. J. (2006). *American higher education: How does it measure up for the 21st century?* San Jose, CA: The National Center for Public Policy and Higher Education.

Hunter, J. M. (2012). *An integrated framework for understanding the financial health of small, private colleges* (Doctoral dissertation). University of Minnesota, Minneapolis, MN. Retrieved from https://conservancy.umn.edu/bitstream/handle/11299/137149/Hunter_umn_0130E_13034.pdf?sequence=1

Iffert, R. E. (1957). *Retention and withdrawal of college students: U.S. Office of Education, Bulletin 1957, no. 1.* Washington, DC: U.S. Government Printing Office.

Institute of Medicine of the National Academies. (2010). *The future of nursing: Leading change, advancing health.* Washington, DC: The National Academies Press. Retrieved from https://www.nap.edu/read/12956/chapter/1

Justice, E. M., & Dornan, T. M. (2001). Metacognitive differences between traditional age and non-traditional age college students. *Adult Education Quarterly, 51*(3), 236–249.

Kasworm, C. (1990). Adult undergraduates in higher education: A review of past research perspectives. *Review of Educational Research, 60*, 345–372.

Kasworm, C. (2001, April). *A case study of adult learner experiences of an accelerated degree program.* Paper presented at the American Educational Research Association Conference, Seattle, WA.

Kasworm, C. (2003a). Adult meaning making in the undergraduate classroom. *Adult Education Quarterly, 53*, 81–98.

Kasworm, C. (2003b). Setting the stage: Adults in higher education. In D. Kilgore & P. J. Rice (Eds.), *New directions for student services: No. 102: Meeting the special needs of adult learners* (pp. 3–10). San Francisco, CA: Jossey-Bass. https://doi.org/10.1002/ss.83

Kasworm, C. (2005). Adult student identity in an intergenerational community college classroom. *Adult Education Quarterly, 56*, 3–20.

Kasworm, C., Sandmann, L. R., & Sissel, P. A. (2000). Adult learners in higher education. In A. L. Wilson & E. R. Hayes (Eds.), *Handbook of adult and continuing education* (pp. 449–463). San Francisco, CA: Jossey-Bass.

Kazis, R., Vargas, J., & Hoffman, N. (2007). *Double the numbers: Increasing postsecondary credentials for underrepresented youth.* Boston, MA: Harvard Education Press.

Kelly, M. (2017). *Perfectly yourself: Discovering God's dream for you.* North Palm Beach, FL: Beacon.

Kerka, S. (1997). *Adult career counseling in a new age: Social integration for adults.* Columbus, OH: ERIC Clearinghouse on Adult Career and Vocational Education. (ERIC Digest No. 167).

Kimmel, S. B., & McNeese, M. N. (2006). Barriers to business education: Motivating adult learners. *Journal of Behavioral and Applied Management, 7*(3), 292–303.

Kirby, P. G., Biever, J. L., Martinez, I. G., & Gomez, J. P. (2004). Adults returning to school: The impact on family and work. *The Journal of Psychology, 138*(1), 65–76.

Klein-Collins, R. (2018). *Never too late: The adult student's guide to college* (1st ed.). New York, NY: The New Press, Washington Monthly.

Klein-Collins, R., Sherman, A., & Soares, L. (2010). *Degree completion beyond institutional borders: Responding to the new reality of mobile and nontraditional learners.* Washington, DC: Center for American Progress: The Council for Adult and Experiential Learning. Retrieved from https://www.americanprogress.org/issues/economy/reports/2010/10/28/8567/degree-completion-beyond-institutional-borders/

Knapp, L. G., Kelly-Reid, J. E., & Ginder, S. A. (2012). *2011–12 Integrated Postsecondary Education Data System (IPEDS) methodology report* (NCES 2012-293). Washington, DC: National Center for Education Statistics/U.S. Department of Education. Retrieved from https://nces.ed.gov/pubs2012/2012293.pdf

Knowles, M. (1980). *The modern practice of adult education: From pedagogy to andragogy.* New York, NY: Association Press.

Knowles, M. S., Holton, E. F., & Swanson, R. A. (2011). *The adult learner: The definitive classic in adult education and human resource development.* Abingdon, England: Routledge.

Kolowich, S. (2011, May 9). Model of the moment. *Inside Higher Education.* Retrieved from https://www.insidehighered.com/news/2011/05/09/model-moment

Kratzer, D. F. (2009). *Factors influencing adult learner intentions to complete a bachelor's degree* (Doctoral dissertation). University of Louisville, Louisville, KY.

Kuh, G. (2008). Diagnosing why some students don't succeed. *Chronicle of Higher Education, 55*(16), A72.

Lang, M., & Ford, C. A. (1988). *Black student retention in higher education.* Springfield, IL: Charles C. Thomas.

Losty, B., & Kreilick, D. (1982). Who succeeds? Perceptions of graduates and inactive students of a nontraditional Bachelor of Arts degree program. *Alternative Higher Education: The Journal of Nontraditional Studies, 6,* 258–267.

Lumina Foundation. (2011). *Goal 2025: Increasing postsecondary attainment.* Retrieved from https://www.luminafoundation.org/lumina-goal

Malhotra, N. K., Shapero, M., Sizoo, S., & Munro, T. (2007). Factor structure of deterrents to adult participation in higher education. *Journal of College Teaching and Learning, 4*(12), 81–90. Retrieved from https://clutejournals .com/index.php/TLC/article/download/1515/1495/

Marcus, J. (2019, February 25). Americans don't realize state funding for higher ed is falling, new poll finds. *Hechinger Report.* Retrieved from https://hechinger report.org/americans-think-state-funding-for-higher-ed-has-held-steady -or-risen-survey-finds/

Martin, L. (1990). Dropout, persistence, and completion in adult secondary and prevocational programs. *Adult Literacy and Basic Education, 14,* 159–174.

McCaffrey, S. (1989, November). *A key to survival: The retention of adult students in an external degree program.* Paper presented at the annual meeting of the Association for the Study of Higher Education, Atlanta, GA. Retrieved from ERIC database. (ED313974)

McCormick, A., Geis, S., Vergun, R., & Carroll, D. (1995). *Profile of part-time undergraduates in postsecondary education: 1989–90.* (NCES 95-173). Washington, DC: U.S. Department of Education.

McGinley, L. (1995, October). *Transformative learning and prior learning assessment.* Paper presented at the National Conference on Alternative and External Degree Programs for Adults, Columbus, Ohio. Retrieved from ERIC database. (ED402510)

McGivney, V. (1996). *Staying or leaving the course: Non-completion and retention of mature students in further and higher education.* Leicester, England: National Institute of Adult Continuing Education.

McGivney, V. (2004). Understanding persistence in adult learning, *Open Learning, 19*(1), 33–46.

McMahon, W. W. (2000). *Education and development: Measuring the social benefits.* London, England: Oxford University Press.

McNeely, J. H. (1938). *College student mortality.* Washington, DC: U.S. Government Printing Office.

Mercer, D. (1993). Older co-eds: Predicting who will stay this time. *Journal of Research and Development in Education, 26,* 153–163.

Merisotis, J. P. (2018). *President's Message: Fall 2018*. Indianapolis, IN: Lumina Foundation. Retrieved from https://focus.luminafoundation.org/presidents-message-fall-2018/

Merriam, S. B., Caffarella, R. S., & Baumgartner, L. (2007). *Learning in adulthood: A comprehensive guide*. San Francisco, CA: Wiley.

Metzner, B., & Bean, J. (1987). The estimation of a conceptual model of nontraditional undergraduate student attrition. *Research in Higher Education, 27*(1), 15–38.

Mishler, C., & Davenport, M. (1983). *The mixed-age college classroom: Report of a pilot study at UW-Green Bay*. Green Bay: University of Wisconsin-Green Bay Assessment Center. Retrieved from ERIC database. (ED240364)

Murphy, J. L. (2012). *Increasing degree attainment in California: Policy factors affecting the near completion population* (Doctoral dissertation). Sacramento State, Sacramento, CA. Retrieved from http://csus-dspace.calstate.edu/handle/10211.9/1881

National Center for Education Statistics. (2018). *The condition of education 2018* (NCES 2018-144). Washington, DC: U.S. Department of Education.

National Center for Public Policy in Higher Education. (2006). *Measuring up 2006*. San Jose, CA: Author.

New England Adult Research Network. (1999). *Factors influencing adult student persistence in undergraduate degree programs*. Amherst: Victoria Dowling, University of Massachusetts.

Noel-Levitz, Inc. (2015). *National freshmen attitudes report*. Retrieved from http://learn.ruffalonl.com/rs/395-EOG-977/images/2015_National_Freshman_Atttitudes_Report.pdf

Nora, A. (2001). The depiction of significant others in Tinto's "rites of passage": A reconceptualization of the influence of family and community in the persistence process. *Journal of College Student Retention, 3*(1), 41–56.

Osam, K., Bergman, M., & Cumberland, D. (2017). An integrative literature review on the barriers impacting adult learners' return to college. *Adult Learning, 28*(2), 54–60.

Pantages, T. J., & Creedon, C. F. (1978) Studies of college attrition: 1950–1975. *Review of Educational Research, 48*(1), 49–101.

Pascarella, E. T., & Terenzini, P. T. (1979). Interactive influences in Spady and Tinto's conceptual models of college dropout. *Sociology of Education, 52*, 197–210.

Pascarella, E. T., & Terenzini, P. T. (1983). Predicting voluntary freshman year persistence/withdrawal behavior in a residential university: A path analytic validation of Tinto's model. *Journal of Educational Psychology, 75*(2), 215–226.

Pascarella, E. T., & Terenzini, P. T. (2005). *How college affects students: A third decade of research* (Vol. 2). San Francisco, CA: Jossey-Bass.

Pascarella, E. T., Terenzini, P. T., & Wolfle, L. M. (1991). Orientation to college and freshman year persistence/withdrawal decisions. *The Journal of Higher Education, 57,* 155–175.

Perna, L. (2005). The benefits of higher education: Sex, racial/ethnic, and socioeconomic group differences. *The Review of Higher Education, 29,* 23–52. https://doi.org/10.1353/rhe.2005.0073

Perry, W. G. (1999). *Forms of intellectual and ethical development in the college years: A scheme.* San Francisco, CA: Jossey-Bass.

Pew Research Center. (2016). *The state of American jobs: Social and demographic trends.* Washington, DC: Author. Retrieved from https://www.pewsocial trends.org/2016/10/06/1-changes-in-the-american-workplace

Phillips, C. (1833). Speech of Mr. Phillips in the case of O'Mullan v. M'Korkill. From *Irish eloquence: The speeches of the celebrated Irish orators Phillips, Curran, and Grattan* (pp. 83–99). Philadelphia, PA: Key & Biddle.

Pusser, B., Breneman, D. W., Gansneder, B. M., Kohl, K. J., Levin, J. S., & Milam, J. H. (2007, March). *Returning to learning: Adults' success in college is key to America's future.* Indianapolis, IN: Lumina Foundation for Education.

Quigley, B. A., & Uhland, R. L. (2000). Retaining adult learners in the first three critical weeks: A quasi-experimental model for use in ABE programs. *Adult Basic Education, 10*(2), 55.

Ramist, L. (1981). *College student attrition and retention* (College Board Report No. 81-1). New York, NY: College Entrance Examination Board.

Renn, K. A., & Reason, R. D. (2013). *College students in the United States: Characteristics, experiences, and outcomes.* San Francisco, CA: Jossey-Bass.

Riggert, S. C., Boyle, M., Petrosko, J. M., Ash, D., & Rude-Parkins, C. (2006). Student employment and higher education: Empiricism and contradiction. *Review of Educational Research, 76,* 63–92.

Rosling, H. (2018). *Factfulness: Ten reasons we're wrong about the world—and why things are better than you think.* New York, NY: Flatiron Books.

Rovai, A. P., Wighting, M. J., & Liu, J. (2005). School climate: Sense of classroom and school communities in online and in-campus higher education courses. *Quarterly Review of Distance Education, 6*(4), 361–374.

Rovai, A. P., Wighting, M. J., & Lucking, R. (2004). The classroom and school community inventory: Development, refinement, and validation of a self-report measure for educational research. *Internet and Higher Education, 7*(4), 263–280. https://doi.org/10.1016/j.iheduc.2004.09.001

Ryder, R., Bowman, R., & Newman, P. (1994). Nontraditional students: Perceived barriers to degree completion. *College Student Affairs Journal, 13*(2), 5–13.

Sadler, W., Cohen, F., & Kockesen, L. (1997, May). *Factors affecting retention behavior: A model to predict at-risk students.* Paper presented at the Annual Forum of the Association for Institutional Research, Orlando, FL. Retrieved from ERIC database. (ED410885)

Schultz, M. B. (1997). *Major matters: How adult undergraduate students select their academic majors* (Doctoral dissertation). Pennsylvania State University, State College, PA.

Scott, C., Burns, A., & Cooney, G. (1996). Reasons for discontinuing study: The case of mature age female students with children. *Higher Education, 31,* 233–253.

Seidman, A. (2005). *College student retention: Formula for student success.* Westport, CT: Praeger.

Shields, N. (1994). Retention, academic success, and progress among adult, returning students: A comparison of the effects of institutional and external factors. *NACADA Journal, 14,* 13–24.

Sikora, A. C. (2002). *A profile of participation in distance education: 1999–2000* (NCES 2003-154). Washington, DC: U.S. Department of Education.

Simmons, D. (1995). Retraining dislocated workers in the community college: Identifying factors for persistence. *Community College Review, 23*(2), 47–58.

Smith, K., & McCormick, D. (1992). Translating experience into learning. *Adult Learning, 3*(5), 22–25.

Snyder, G. (1990). *Persistence of community college students receiving credit for prior learning* (Doctoral dissertation). University of Pennsylvania, Philadelphia, PA.

Snyder, T. D., & Dillow, S. A. (2007). *Digest of education statistics 2006* (NCES 2007-017). Washington, DC: U.S. Department of Education.

Sorey, K. C., & Duggan, M. H. (2008). Differential predictors of persistence between community college adult and traditional-aged students. *Community College Journal of Research and Practice, 32*(2), 75–100. https://doi.org/10.1080/10668920701380967

Spady, W. (1970). Dropouts from higher education: An interdisciplinary review and synthesis. *Interchange, 1,* 64–85.

Spady, W. (1971). Dropouts from higher education: Toward an empirical model. *Interchange, 2,* 38–62.

St. John, E., & Starkey, J. (1995). The influence of prices on the persistence of adult undergraduates. *Journal of Student Financial Aid, 25*(2), 7–17.

Summerskill, J. (1962). Dropouts from college. In N. Sanford (Ed.), *The American college* (pp. 627–657). New York, NY: Wiley.

Taniguchi, H., & Kaufman, G. (2005). Degree completion among nontraditional college students: Part-time student barriers. *Social Science Quarterly, 86,* 912–927.

Taylor, J. A. (2000). *Adult degree completion programs: A report to the board of trustees from the Task Force on Adult Degree Completion Programs and the award of credit for prior learning at the baccalaureate level.* Chicago, IL: North Central Association of Colleges and Schools Commission on Institutions of Higher Education.

Thomas, R., & Chickering, A. W. (1984). Education and identity revisited. *Journal of College Student Personnel, 25*(5), 392–399.

Thompson, H. S. (1997). *The proud highway: Saga of a desperate southern gentleman, 1955–1967.* New York, NY: Ballantine Books.

Tierney, W. G. (1999). Models of minority college-going and retention: Cultural integrity vs. cultural suicide. *Journal of Negro Education, 68*(1), 80–91.

Tinto, V. (1975). Dropout from higher education: A theoretical synthesis of recent research. *Review of Educational Research, 45*, 89–125.

Tinto, V. (1993). *Leaving college: Rethinking the causes and cures of student attrition* (2nd ed.). Chicago, IL: University of Chicago Press.

Tinto, V. (1998). Colleges as communities: Taking research on student persistence seriously. *The Review of Higher Education, 21*, 167–177.

Tinto, V. (2006). Research and practice of student retention: What next? *Journal of College Student Retention, 8*(1), 1–19.

Topping, T. (1996). An institutional evaluation of perceptions and expectations of prior learning assessment options (experiential learning). *Dissertation Abstracts International, 57*, 2908.

Turner, B., & Krumenauer, G. (2010). *The value of a bachelor's degree.* WorkSource Quality Information, Oregon Employment Department. Retrieved from https://oregonemployment.blogspot.com/2010/09/value-of-bachelors-degree.html

Tweedell, C. B. (2000, October). *A theory of adult learning and implications for practice.* Paper presented at the meeting of the Midwest Educational Research Association Annual Meeting, Chicago, IL.

U.S. Census Bureau. (2008). *American community survey, 2008.* Retrieved from https://www.census.gov/programs-surveys/acs/news/data-releases.2008.html

U.S. Department of Education & National Center for Education Statistics (2008). *The condition of education 2008* (NCES 2008–031). Retrieved from https://nces.ed.gov/pubs2008/2008031.pdf

Vann, B., & Hinton, B. (1994). Workplace social networks and their relationship to student retention in on-site GED programs. *Human Resource Development Quarterly, 5*, 141–151.

Vasquez, M., & Bauman, D. (2019, April 4). How America's college-closure crisis leaves families devastated: When colleges shut down, people get hurt.

The Chronicle of Higher Education. Retrieved from https://www.chronicle
.com/interactives/20190404-ForProfit

Webb, M. (1989). A theoretical model of community college student degree
persistence. *Community College Review, 16*(4), 42–49.

Wlodkowski, R. J. (1999). *Enhancing adult motivation to learn: A comprehensive
guide for teaching all adults.* San Francisco, CA: Jossey-Bass.

Wlodkowski, R. J., Mauldin, J. E., & Campbell, S. (2002). *Early exit: Understanding adult attrition in accelerated and traditional postsecondary programs. Synop-
sis: Higher education research highlights.* Indianapolis, IN: Lumina Foundation for Education.

Wlodkowski, R. J., Mauldin, J. E., & Gahn, S. W. (2001). *Learning in the fast lane:
Adult learners' persistence and success in accelerated college programs,* Indianapolis, IN: Lumina Foundation for Education.

Woosley, S. (2004). Stop-out or drop-out? An examination of college withdraw-
als and re-enrollments. *Journal of College Student Retention, 5,* 293–303.

Zajkowski, M. (1997). Price and persistence in distance learning. *Open Learning, 12,* 12–23.

About the Authors

Matt Bergman, PhD

Where I came from: I grew up in a small town 25 miles north of Cincinnati. I am one of five children (the baby) of a middle-class family of very successful siblings and parents. While I would be considered a first-generation student (both parents completed some college), I don't feel as much like a first-gen learner because all of my two brothers and two sisters completed 4-year degrees.

I was a very mediocre high school student but felt obligated to attend college mainly to fulfill the dream of playing college sports. Fortunately, many faculty and staff at Union College in Barbourville, Kentucky saw something worth encouraging in me as a freshman. It was the first time that I heard, "Matt, you are good at..." as a student inside or outside of the classroom. This lit the fire that still burns today to be a lifelong learner committed to understanding and embodying knowledge that will advance our citizenry into a higher state of enlightenment. My personal motto is "work hard, spread love, and have fun." I am committed to being a part of something bigger than myself. If I am around a committed group of colleagues and students who are committed to advancing themselves and their organizations, I couldn't care less about the specific workplace.

I found my way to adult learners as a result of my interest in completing a PhD program at the University of Louisville. I have long been an insecure

Unfinished Business, pages 197–199
Copyright © 2019 by Information Age Publishing
All rights of reproduction in any form reserved.

self-doubting person driven to prove I was worthy of a terminal degree. I had no solid plan beyond completing the degree but wanted to prove to myself that I wasn't just another dumb jock.

What I've done since then: I am currently serving as program director/assistant professor in the College of Education and Human Development. My research is focused on adult learner persistence, prior learning assessment, leadership, and degree completion programs. My work has appeared in refereed journals such as the *Journal of Continuing Higher Education, Human Resource Development Review,* and *Adult Learning,* and it has been highlighted in international media outlets including *The Wall Street Journal, The Washington Post, The Chronicle of Higher Education,* and *TIME.* In 2015, my colleagues and I won the E. F. Holton III Outstanding Article of the Year awarded by the Academy of Human Resource Development. My program was the recipient of the 2016 ACHE South's Distinguished Program Award and the 2013 AAACE Malcolm Knowles Award for Adult Education Program of the Year. The program was also acknowledged as a 2014 National Program of Distinction in the American Public and Land Grant Universities' MVP Awards for Campus Based Strategies for Student Success and the 2013 Innovation for Educational Attainment from the Gheens Foundation and 55,000 Degrees based upon local implementation of his research. I was awarded the 2018 ACHE South Outstanding Faculty Award, The Metroversity Outstanding Faculty for Adult Learners in 2015, and have been a Faculty Favorite at U of L from 2012–2018. I am a Fellow for Complete College America and serve as a teacher, administrator, and ambassador of adult degree attainment both locally and nationally.

Joann S. Olson, PhD

Where I came from: I grew up on a small dairy farm in west-central Wisconsin, about two hours east of Minneapolis, Minnesota. I'm the older of two children. Like many (most?) small farmers, we didn't have much in the way of cash flow or resources, but somehow my parents always managed to provide all of our needs and a few more of our wants than you might expect. Being raised on a farm by parents who grew up during the Great Depression shaped my worldview and my work ethic—lessons that I am now grateful for but didn't always appreciate at the time.

I was a good student. I went to college at Michigan State University and was accepted as part of the Honors College, planning to get a degree in chemistry, continue on to a PhD and do cancer research. I loved my time at MSU, but having earned good grades at a mediocre high school meant that

I wasn't as academically prepared as my classmates. I was a first-generation college student, but when I attended college, that wasn't a "thing." Looking back, I can point to several ways my lack of "college knowledge" (Burleson, Hallett, & Park, 2008) created challenges—dealing with financial aid hiccups, choosing a major (Chemistry? What was I thinking!), and building a resume—but the grace of God, a fair amount of dumb luck, and the support of several skilled academic advisors got me through the process. I finished with a degree in employment relations and a double major in psychology. Following graduation, I began working at a computer training company; teaching WordPerfect and other software programs to a wide range of clients was my introduction to the field of adult learning.

What I've done since then: I am currently associate professor and advisor in the adult and higher education program at the University of Houston–Victoria. I have been involved in various aspects of adult education throughout my career, including computer training and leadership development. I earned a master's degree in religious education from Wheaton College and a PhD in adult education from Penn State–University Park. Following graduate school, I spent 2 years coordinating faculty development for an adult degree program that also offered several graduate-level programs. My research focuses on the intersection of higher education and adult learning, including workplace learning of recent college graduates and the experiences of first-generation students (of all ages) in college and following graduation. My work has been published in *Adult Learning, Journal of Career Development,* and *Journal of Continuing Higher Education.* With Anne C. Benoit and Carrie Johnson, I co-edited the book *Leaps of faith: Stories of working-class scholars* (Information Age, 2018). In 2015, I received UH–Victoria's Research and Scholarly Activity Award, and in 2019, I was given UH–Victoria's Distinguished Faculty Service Award. I am active in the Commission of Professors of Adult Education (CPAE) and serve on the board of the Adult and Higher Education Alliance as the editor of the AHEA book series.

About the Contributing
Adult Comebackers

Phillip Young Alier is most known for his long journey to freedom as a Lost Boy of Sudan. If he goes by his family names then you will not even know him at all. His family names include: Amoum, Alier, plus his nickname Hakim (which means "child born in hospital"). He was baptized with his dad, three nieces, his brothers, and his sister-in-law in 1985. His dad's name was Matthew Alier, and he was originally named William, but he changed his name to Phillip. The name Phillip Young came from his aunt's son whom he looked up to and imitated for years. Thus, those names became his permanent new identity. He is originally from Southern Sudan in Jongkuelei, from a tribe called Dinka Bor. This tribe originates from Athooch, Angkuei, Hol, and Baar Jok Ngong. He was born in Mading Bor Town Hospital the headquarters of Jongkulei States.

David Beumer earned his bachelor's degree from the University of Louisville in organizational leadership and occupational development in 2019, at the age of 41. His career experience includes operations, logistics management, marketing, the automotive industry, currently leads a team across the state of Kentucky in the insurance industry while building his own consulting firm. David resides in Louisville, Kentucky with his wife Christi and three daughters Reina, Harleigh, and Cameron and golden doodle named Georgia.

Unfinished Business, pages 201–218
Copyright © 2019 by Information Age Publishing

Rachael R. Black is a biology and pre-AP Biology teacher at Daniel Ninth Grade Campus in Aledo ISD. She graduated from Western Governors University with a Bachelor of Arts in biology. As a student teacher and teacher, she has secured more than $31,000 in grant funds for her campus. In 2017, Ms. Black was nominated for New Teacher of the Year for her district, in addition to earning two nominations for her district's IDEA award (Excellence in Educational Innovation). Her interest in arts and technology integration has been spotlighted in *STEAMed Magazine,* and she continues to encourage community partners and educators to incorporate innovative teaching methods by helping to organize a STEAM Carnival annually. Rachael lives in Weatherford, Texas with her two boys Tristan and Noah.

Jennifer (Jenny) R. Chatman finished her program requirements in organizational leadership and learning in June 2017 and received her bachelor's degree from the University of Louisville in August 2017 with a cumulative GPA of 4.00. Her career experiences include over 20 years in organ, tissue, and eye donation for transplant, education, and research including quality and regulatory, recovery, donor screening, and partner relationships; customer service and sales relationships in credit card processing, data management in car dealership marketing, and she currently holds a position as a program manager in the pharmaceutical field. She is a Certified Tissue Bank Specialist (CTBS) with the American Association of Tissue Banks (AATB), a member of the Golden Key International Honor Society, Project Management Institute (PMI), and American Society for Quality (ASQ). After career and life experiences in the "Washington DC Metro area (McLean, Virginia) and Phoenix, Arizona, she returned to Louisville, Kentucky where she currently resides.

Jeffrey A. Crane is a sales representative for Cox Interior, Inc., a company that specializes in the manufacturing of natural wood products for residential and commercial construction. Jeff sells to builders and homeowners in northern Kentucky and southern Indiana. Jeff has been a sales representative for 22 years. Before Cox Interior, Inc., Jeff spent 12 years as a professional musician. Jeff also managed a thoroughbred racing stable that saddled a horse for the running of the 2003 Kentucky Derby. Some other examples of partnerships Jeff has been a part of include a real estate improvement company and a wholesale lumber supply company. Jeff completed his bachelor's degree at the University of Louisville in the Fall of 2017.

William Dugan is currently a regional OLIF manager in the Spine Division for Medtronic in Florida. Prior to Medtronic, William was a professional salesman for more than 25 years in the medical device industry and the golf industry. His success has been recognized over the years for his dedication, mentorship, and quota achievements from the companies he has represented. As a result, from his experience, he has found his passion, which is developing sales software automation systems that simplifies life for sales professionals and increases profits for organizations. He lives in Boca Raton, Florida with his loving wife of 25 years, Amy. William and Amy and have two daughters that currently reside overseas.

Ellen E. Elliott is the owner and director of Four Directions Counseling and Recovery Center. She is an addictions specialist who has worked in the mental health field for nearly 30 years and provides counseling in various areas including addictions, sexual issues, trauma, childhood abuse, intimacy and attachment, and relationships. Her goal is to assist people in addressing past trauma and creating the lives and connections they long for. In addition to counseling, Ellen provides training related to behavioral addictions and trauma treatment as well as supervision for substance abuse and mental health counselors. As a lifelong lover of learning and culture, she is currently pursuing her doctoral degree in human behavior, completing research in Nepal related to trauma experiences among indigenous populations in underdeveloped countries. When not engaging in her passion for travel, Ellen resides in North Carolina near her daughter and grandson, Cherish and Xander.

Andrew English is a cybersecurity policy and standards consultant for Humana in Louisville, Kentucky, and a cyberspace network operator with Marine Forces Cyber Command in the United States Marine Corps (Current Rank: Gunnery Sergeant). Andrew is an adjunct professor and serves on the cybersecurity development board at Ivy Tech Community College. With Humana he has worked in the Cyber Defense and Intelligence Center, on the Forensic Security Investigations Team, and Information Technology Consulting as part of his current Policy and Standards Team. During Andrew's Marine Corps career, he served in Iraq (2004–2005) performing information technology networking and serving in Major General Richard Natonski's Command Operating Center during Operation Phantom Fury, Iraq (2009) serving as a command operation center watch chief in support of 3rd Battalion 24th Marines Task Force Military Policy mission, Afghanistan (2010) serving as a squad leader establishing the first security posture on Forward Operating Base Delaram II in the Helmand Province during initial base construction under 3rd Battalion 4th Marines, Belize (2016 & 2018) serving as a foreign security forces advisor to the Belize Defense Force and Belize Coast Guard operating under the direction of United States Marine Forces Southern Command, and now as a cyberspace network operator in Andrew current command. Andrew earned an associate degree in criminal justice with

Ivy Tech Community College in 2010, a bachelor's degree in organizational leadership and Learning with the University of Louisville in 2014, and master's degree in human resources leadership and organizational development with the University of Louisville in 2017. Andrew's passion is people and performance management focused on empowering the associate population to balance work and life in a way that drives personal fulfillment and lifelong wellbeing. Andrew lives in Columbus, Indiana with his soon-to-be wife Sandy and their four kids—Connor, Brody, Knox, and Nora.

James C. Ferraris has been an Oregon law enforcement officer since 1978. He currently serves as the chief of police for the City of Woodburn, Oregon, having been invested on December 14, 2015. Chief Ferraris served as deputy chief of the Salem Police Department from 2011 to 2015. From 1983 to 2011, he served with the Portland Police Bureau, holding ranks at PPB from officer to assistant chief of police, starting his law enforcement career in 1978 with the Beaverton Police Department. A vice president and life member of the Oregon Association Chiefs of Police, Chief Ferraris has years of involvement with a variety of nonprofit and civic organizations including Lines for Life, an Oregon nonprofit dedicated to ending substance abuse and suicide, and he has been a member of the Oregon/Idaho HIDTA Executive Board for nearly 20 years. Chief Ferraris is a graduate of the Homeland Defense and Security Program at the Naval Postgraduate School at Monterey, California, and received a Bachelor of Arts degree in management and organizational leadership from George Fox University. He is a graduate of the 201st Session of the FBI National Academy and the 75th Session of the FBI Law Enforcement Executive Development Seminar.

Sean Green completed his BS in organizational leadership at the University of Louisville. He is a graduate of Louisville Male High School (1994–1997) and was inducted into the Male High Hall of Fame in 2016. Before returning as an adult learner, he was a college athlete at the University of Louisville as a baseball pitcher (1997–2000) and was inducted into the University of Louisville Hall of Fame in 2014. He was later drafted by the Colorado Rockies in the 2000 draft. Sean was the first U of L Cardinal pitcher to throw a pitch at the MLB level, and he had a 13-year career in professional baseball and his career spanned 6 years at the major league level split between the Seattle Mariners, New York Mets, and Milwaukee Brewers. He made his major league debut was May 2, 2006 with the Seattle Mariners and he pitched 269 innings at the major league level. Sean was the 2007 recipient of the Seattle Mariner Unsung Hero Award by Sports Writer's Association. He is a father, coach, and business owner and lives with his family in Louisville, Kentucky.

Latrivia Guinn is a program director at Memorial Hermann Amputation Prevention and Wound Care Center. Latrivia is a registered nurse and has worked in a variety of healthcare arenas including home health, outpatient mental health, geriatrics, community health, hospice, and teaching as an adjunct faculty member at Jackson College. She has participated in Sisters of Strength and Black Nurses Rock foundation, was a board member of Save our Youth, and volunteered with various churches to empower youth. She received her certificate as a practical nurse in 2012 and her associate in applied science as a registered nurse in 2013 both from Jackson College in Jackson, Michigan. She completed her Bachelor of Science in nursing from Kaplan University in 2015, her master's in nursing education in 2018, and is currently enrolled in the Doctorate of Nursing program with Walden University. She currently resides in Richmond, Texas with her husband, four children, and one grandson.

Dawn Hall is a service center technician for the Louisville Metro Police Department. In pursuit of her degree, she attended Bellarmine University, Tidewater Community College, Old Dominion University, and McKendree University. She attained her Bachelor of Business Administration—Magna Cum Laude—in 2018, 29 years after she began her educational career. She lives in Louisville, Kentucky with her husband, Glenn. Her three adult children are all in pursuit of various degrees in the Louisville area.

Norris Hamilton is the vice president and associate general manager for Horseshoe Southern Indiana. As VP and AGM, Norris is responsible for the operations divisions of gaming, food, and beverage, security, retail, and environmental services. Norris has worked with Caesars Entertainment in other capacities and jurisdictions during his 19-year tenure with the company. Norris graduated with honors from the University of Louisville with his Bachelor of Science degree in May 2014. He was on the board of directors for the Louisville Urban League where he was a member of the executive committee. He currently sits on the board of directors for the Kentucky Derby Festival Foundation (chair elect), he is a board member of One Southern Indiana, and a graduate of Focus Louisville and Leadership Louisville. Norris currently resides in Sellersburg, Indiana.

Rachel Hensley worked for a nonprofit organization focused on preventing child abuse and reducing the trauma victim's experience after graduating from Oregon State University. While there, she became interested in the research on adverse childhood experiences (ACEs), resiliency, and trauma-informed practices. Her professional and personal experience with the obstacles that students with ACEs face in primary and secondary school has led her to pursue a career as a high school teacher, where she hopes to be an understanding and supportive figure for young adults. She is in the process of earning a master's degree in teaching at Hollins University, to be completed May 2020. Since writing the piece for this book, she has remarried. She lives in Roanoke, Virginia, with her husband, Chris, and two sons, Malachi and River.

Jo Ann Herron is finishing a degree in Religious Studies and Theology from Rockhurst University in Kansas City, Missouri. Graduating from Rockhurst has always been her goal because she believes in the Jesuit philosophy of "Finding God in All Things." She is a recipient of KC Scholars Adult Learner Scholarship. Jo Ann attended Rockhurst back in the 1980s but was unable to complete her degree because of a promotion that relocated her to AT&T Engineering Headquarters in Bedminster, New Jersey. Her background in engineering started in 1966 when she was hired as a key punch operator; responsible for key punching engineering circuit design cards. She worked in the engineering department as a circuit assembler until 1990 prior to being promoted to a process engineer, assistant staff manager for global provisioning. After retirement she was hired at Sprint Headquarters in Overland Park, Kansas and designed repeatable processes for the Sprint Network including Microwave Towers in Puerto Rico and the United States. She retired from Sprint in 2009. She is a volunteer in corrections for the State of Missouri, part-time YMCA employee, mother of three children, grandmother of four, and recent great-grandmother of twins.

Clifford D. Hicks is the internal compliance investigator for Louisville Metro Youth Detention Services, with nearly two decades of experience in youth corrections and law enforcement. He holds a bachelor's degree in justice and public safety administration from Sullivan University in Louisville, Kentucky. Originally from Ohio, Clifford is passionate about contributing to the improvement of the juvenile justice system and attends national training sessions to assist in developing effective, positive procedures and policies. A strong believer in mental and physical wellness, Clifford plays chess, does strength training, and participates in martial arts training in his free time. Clifford currently resides in Louisville, Kentucky with his wife Ashley, daughters Jurni and Crystafer, and has two older sons, Dorian and Kameron.

Althea Jackson is the director of Boards and Commission for Louisville Metro Government. She is responsible for recruiting, vetting, and filling close to 1,000 board and commission seats. In addition, Althea is the host of a weekly radio program titled Metro Matters. While progressing in her

27(+) year career with Louisville Metro Government, she returned to the University of Louisville as an adult learner and obtained her degree in organizational leadership and learning.

Joe Jacoby is most well-known as the three-time Super Bowl champion Washington Redskin and founding member of the legendary offensive line, "The Hogs." A three-time Pro Football Hall of Fame finalist, he is a member of the NFL's 1980s All-Decade Team, 70 Greatest Redskins, and *USA Today's* All Time Super Bowl Team. His commendations include four Pro Bowl selections, two time 1st-Team All-Pro, Redskin Offensive Player of the year, and the Ed Block Courage Award. Joe's most treasured awards are those given in recognition of his community service and charitable endeavors: Kenny Houston Humanitarian of the year, *Washingtonian Magazine* "Washingtonian of the year," Touchdown Club "Golden Timmie Award," two-time NFL Lineman of the Year Finalist, and NFL Man of the Year Finalist. Since retiring from football Joe also garnered numerous off-the-field awards and achievements during his 15+ years as owner of multiple automotive dealerships. He now brings that knowledge and experience to his clients with Joe Jacoby Insurance Solutions under the Capital Group of Companies. Joe helps his clients in the areas of business development, controlling their expense structures, meeting personal and corporate insurance needs, and providing new avenues for revenue growth. Joe also spent much of his post-playing days as a sports talk radio host for ESPN radio. Joe is also a committed advocate for charitable organizations and has spent countless hours working for Youth for Tomorrow, the American Heart Organization, and as a volunteer football coach, among others. Joe is a University of Louisville alumnus and a Louisville ACC Football Legend honoree.

Chad Jones is a dynamic learning and development leader who inspires others through servant leadership. Having earned a Bachelor of Science from Bethel University in 2016 as a returning adult learner, he is presently enrolled at the University of Louisville and in pursuit of a master's in human resources and organizational development, with emphasis on workplace performance and learning. At time of printing, he is employed as head coach of Training & Development at Papa John's International Corporate Headquarters, based in Louisville, Kentucky. Most notably, in 2018, Jones negotiated the development of a fully funded education plan which affords the company's corporate team members the opportunity to attend college with no out-of-pocket expenses. Mr. Jones is a regular contributor to multi-generational learning consortia. A self-taught photographer, he served 3 years, from 2007–2010, as adjunct professor of Fine Art at Eureka College where he created the curricula and instructional learning design for darkroom and digital photography. Jones's photographs have been published in print and electronically in various forums. He continues to expand the boundaries of his photography through wildlife and travel photography. He resides with his wife, Adrienne, in Louisville, Kentucky.

Lawren A. Just is a business owner in Shelby County, Kentucky. She is president and owner of Persimmon Ridge Development, Persimmon Tree Realty, and P.R. Wastewater Management Companies. Lawren has had full responsibility for the land planning of a 935-acre residential development over the past 30 years, including planning, engineering, construction, and sales of the home sites. She is the principal broker of Persimmon Tree Realty Company and not only sells properties but is also responsible for education and growth of three realtors in her agency. Lawren also operates the wastewater management company that owns the treatment facility for the 372 customers in the Persimmon Ridge Development. She is certified by the Kentucky Division of Water as a class II operator in both Operations and Collections. Lawren and her late husband, Elmore Just, built the Persimmon Ridge Golf Courses, which are consistently ranked one of the most challenging courses in the state of Kentucky. In her spare time, Lawren enjoys boating with her husband, Doug Garmon, and spending time with her five children, their spouses, and 15 grandchildren. She is active in several community groups including the National Association of Women Business Owners (NAWBO), local chambers, and boards. She plays the guitar, writes country music, and participates in the music group at her local church.

Michael Keibler is a cooperative education and global engineering track advisor in the J. B. Speed School of Engineering at the University of Louisville. He earned his bachelor's and master's degrees in organizational development at the University of Louisville and is completing his Doctor of Education at Morehead State University. Michael has worked at the School of Medicine establishing an international visiting medical student program for securing clinical elective rotations. He is currently working in the School of Engineering establishing new engineering education abroad programs and developing a global engineering track. His work in international learning and education for students has taken him to Ecuador, Peru, Madrid, and China. Michael has a research focus on identifying forms of cultural intersections that develop authentic global graduates, and international program development. Michael has two children, a son Brandon who is in college and a daughter Katie who looks to pursue a career in medicine following high school.

Rev. Oterias L. Kelley, II is an author and a licensed minister. He holds a degree in business, and has certifications in substance abuse counseling, mediation, and anger management. Reverend Kelley is currently working on degrees in biblical studies and leadership with a concentration on Ministry. Rev. Kelley currently facilitates a mentorship program at Alan B. Polunski Unit in Livingston, Texas. In addition, he is the president and chief executive officer of OLK Ministries in Houston, Texas. Rev. Kelley is a spiritual growth coach and motivational speaker.

Gerald Kinnunen worked for a decade as a senior administrative assistant in the Transfer/Admissions Office at the University of Louisville, assisting students with the transfer experience of a 4-year public institution. He now works for a Fortune 5 company connecting patients and providers that are combating chronic kidney disease. Gerald graduated from the University of Louisville's College of Education and Human Development with a BS in organizational leadership and learning. In his spare time, he enjoys contributing to local social justice movements and advocating for people seeking mental wellness. Some of his hobbies include building a collection of perennial plants, physical fitness, and enjoying two rescue dogs almost lost to black dog syndrome. His favorite quote is, "If I do not know the answer, I will find it, and we will both learn in the process."

Jamie Land is the chief of police of the Elizabethtown Police Department in Kentucky. He began his career in law enforcement as a military policeman in the United States Marine Corps Reserve. He joined the Elizabethtown Police Department in 1998. He has spent the last 21 years with the Elizabethtown Police Department in many different capacities. Chief Land is a graduate of the University of Louisville with a bachelor's degree in organizational leadership and learning. He is also a graduate of the FBI's National Academy, Session 241, as well as a graduate of the Department of Criminal Justice Training Academy of Police Supervision and the Criminal Justice Executive Development Program. Chief Land currently sits on the 911 Services Advisory Council and the Advisory Council for Big Brothers/Big Sisters of Kentuckiana. Chief Land resides in Elizabethtown, Kentucky with his wife Brandi and their son, Beckett.

Amy Lear earned her bachelor's degree from the University of Louisville in organizational leadership and learning at the age of 43. She was awarded the Community Engagement Award from the College of Education and Human Development. Her career paths include information technology, human resources, and marketing, along with mentoring and an advocate for helping others. Amy currently works in the marketing department for a Fortune 500 restaurant company. She resides in Taylorsville, Kentucky with her husband of 28 years, Steve. They have two children, Kevin who has moved on to start his family with his wife Mackenzie, and their youngest Kelsey, 17, who aspires to head off to college next year.

Troy Marables is the vice president, director of human resources for the Presbyterian Foundation and New Covenant Trust Company located in Jeffersonville, Indiana. Troy began his college career at Florida Agricultural and Mechanical University in Tallahassee, Florida, where he studied business administration at their School of Business and Industry for 3 years. After his mother passed in 1992, Troy returned home and began his career in mortgage banking as a supervisor at PNC Mortgage. In 1997, Troy accepted a position with the Presbyterian Foundation where continues to serve. During his career at the foundation, he has served as the manager of Client Services, as a licensed rep for the New Covenant Funds mutual fund family, and as a trust officer for the New Covenant Trust Company. Upon completion of his bachelor's degree in organizational leadership and learning at the University of Louisville, Troy was promoted to the vice president, director of human resources for the foundation and its for-profit subsidiary, the New Covenant Trust Company. He lives in Louisville, Kentucky with his wife, Madalyn, and has two daughters, Victoria and Jocelyn.

Melissa McGarry earned her bachelor's degree from the University of Louisville in organizational leadership and learning in 2015, at the age of 45. She graduated magna cum laude and was awarded the Malcom S. Knowles Award from the College of Education and Human Development. Her career experiences include graphic design, marketing, and publishing positions, along with mentoring at risk youths. She considers herself a lifelong learner and continues to take classes today. She is currently perusing entrepreneurial efforts and resides in Louisville, Kentucky with her husband, Bob, and two teenage children, Kyle and Brooke.

Orman E. Morton, III is an environmental scientist at Brightwater, Inc. located in College Park, Maryland. He is currently certified to perform wetland delineations and has completed three of four levels of the stream geomorphology courses presented by Dr. Dave Rosgen. Orman earned an Associate of Applied Science degree in business management from the Community College of Baltimore County graduating magna cum laude and a Bachelor of Science degree in environmental sciences from Oregon State University graduating cum laude. He spent 6 years as a volunteer with the Anita C. Leight Estuary Center and Maryland Department of Natural Resources before pursuing his degree in the environmental sciences. As a volunteer, he participated in ranavirus monitoring, fish population counts, fieldwork for the Maryland Amphibian and Reptile Atlas, and zooplankton studies. Orman is a member of the Maryland Stream Restoration Association, an association of professionals dedicated to healthy streams through the advancement of stream restoration science. His current work includes watershed assessments, water quality analysis, wetland permitting, stream restoration and monitoring, and biological sampling. Orman lives in Baltimore, Maryland with his three children.

Amobi Okugo is a current professional soccer player and founder of A Frugal Athlete, an online platform intended to promote prudent financial practices and smart career decisions among professional athletes and student athletes. His company has been featured in international media outlets including Market Watch, Forbes, Front Office Sports, Hashtag Sports, Sacramento Bee, and The Undefeated. Amobi was drafted out of UCLA after his freshman year in the 2010 MLS Superdraft to Philadelphia Union. He has amassed more than 150 appearances and 100 starts over his 9-year career playing for Philadelphia Union, Orlando City SC, Sporting Kansas City, Portland Timbers, and Austin Bold FC (USL). While playing, Okugo continued pursuing his degree and graduated magna cum laude from the University of Louisville with a degree in organizational leadership. Okugo is a first-generation Nigerian American and the oldest of four siblings, two brothers, Akachi and Amadi, and one sister Ugonne.

Tommy Phelps began working with HomeDepot Pro fresh out of high school in 1983. Initially, Tommy worked in the warehouse part time and went to school part time to pursue his junior college degree. In 1986 after receiving his AA degree in liberal studies, he was offered a job in sales. He grew a small territory into a multimillion-dollar book of business. Tommy has been a Vision Award winner for excellence in sales six times throughout his career. After meeting the chancellor of Palmetto College during a Rotary meeting, Tommy felt the need to pursue higher learning, and to finish what was started from the early 1980s. After more than 30 years, his college career started back in August of 2013, pursuing a BA in organizational leadership at the University of South Carolina–Palmetto College. Tommy is a member of Rotary International, a former Rotarian of the Year, and club president. Tommy was also an executive board member for senior resources, a nonprofit serving the needs of local senior citizens. His hobbies include boating, hunting, beach time, and all things sports that involve the Gamecocks! He lives in Columbia, SC with his wife and daughter, Caroline.

Raylene Pollio is a diversity and inclusion manager at Brown-Forman Corporation. She joined Brown-Forman in 1996 and was part of initiating the company's diversity strategy beginning in 2008. She has worked closely as an advisor for the company's eight Employee Resource Groups (women, African American, Latino, LGBT, Millennial, Boomer, non-drinker, Veterans), six North American Diversity Councils, and the Executive Leadership Team's Global Diversity Council. She serves as a diversity ambassador within the company while contributing to the development of diversity strategy and promoting a culture of inclusion. She is also a lecturer at the University of Louisville. Pollio has a Bachelor of Science in organizational learning and leadership from the University of Louisville and a Master of Business Administration from Bellarmine University. She is certified as an advanced diversity practitioner from Cornell University. Other certifications include Hogan and Predictive Index assessment interpretation and numerous human resources and diversity training courses. Although originally from western Pennsylvania, Pollio has called Louisville, Kentucky home for more than 20 years. She and her husband, John, have three children, Jade, Claire and John Michael, as well as two grandchildren, Caleb and Preston. She enjoys reading, relaxing with family and friends, camping, theatre, traveling, cooking, and entertaining.

Deb Prather has a passion for helping others, both personally and professionally. She is self-proclaimed "serial learner" and thrives on continuously improving her spiritual, personal, and professional life. At the age of 49, she returned to the University of Louisville to complete her bachelor's degree in workforce leadership/workplace performance and continued by earning a master's degree in organizational leadership and learning. Her path of helping others led her to the International Quantum University of Integrative Medicine where she has earned a bachelor's in holistic health, a master's, PhD, and doctorate in natural medicine. Consequently, utilizing and sharing her knowledge and experiences in person or through self-created eLearning courses, she has helped thousands of people. Thus, her keen interest in helping people figure out what "makes them tick" has been the key to her success as a coach, healer, leader, speaker, and entrepreneur. She continues exploring her next entrepreneurial experience and resides in Louisville, Kentucky with her husband, Billy Joe, their five children and six grandchildren.

Christopher R. Reid is a captain with the Louisville Division of Fire in Louisville, Kentucky. Captain Reid works as a company commander with a fire suppression engine company. His work includes responding to calls for medical and fire emergencies, as well as conducting fire safety programs within the community. Captain Reid is a certified national registered EMT and American Heart Association CPR instructor; he has worked in the department's CPR education and coordination center. He serves in the Army Reserve as a master sergeant health care specialist. He holds a bachelor of science in sociology and has recently received an AAS in fire science. He is originally from Long Island, New York and lives in Louisville, Kentucky with his wife, Stacey, and two children, Alexus and Mckayla.

Kathleen Windell Sailings is a senior account manager at Grand Rounds, Inc. She lives with her husband and five children in New Albany, Indiana. She is an avid runner, fitness guru, and adventure seeker. Alongside being a leader in her organization, she runs marathons and Ragnar races, skis regularly out west, travels the world, and generally makes the most of her life. She is a graduate of Indiana University Southeast located in New Albany, Indiana.

James Sauders is a supplemental insurance salesman and sales coach. He's spent nearly 20 years in sales management, specializing in the development of others and working with small businesses. He's in his senior year at the University of Louisville, earning a degree in organizational leadership and development and on track to graduate with a 4.0 and summa cum laude honors. He plans to continue his education afterwards by earning a master's degree in human resources. He lives outside Paducah, Kentucky with his daughter Emilen.

Brian "Buffalo Stille" Scott is a 39-year-old, Grammy-nominated, platinum-selling recording artist from Louisville, Kentucky. He has earned a *Business First* "40 Under Forty" award as a collegiate licensee and founder of a successful clothing business. Before leaving college as a young man to pursue his dreams, Brian made a promise to his mother that he would eventually return for his degree. In the Spring of 2019, on the eve of Mother's Day, he kept his promise by earning a bachelor's degree in organizational leadership at the University of Louisville, winning the 2019 U of L and Metroversity Adult Learner Undergraduate Award in the process. With his newfound knowledge, this husband and father plans on growing his businesses and starting a non-profit that provides leadership and opportunities for inner-city youth.

Stevie D. Shaw is a district executive with the Boy Scouts of America, Lincoln Heritage Council. Mr. Shaw is responsible for developing and maintaining the organization in the Cherokee District. He meets with community leaders, business owners, and residents in his area to share the organization's mission and to get people involved. He meets with volunteers to train and plan activities for local troops and create initiatives to encourage young people to join the organization. He is responsible for soliciting donations from community members and local businesses that want to support the Scouts and for planning programs and events to raise money. His work with community leaders and volunteers teaches Scouts outdoor and life skills that will help them in their professional and social lives. Mr. Shaw has been very active with organizations that focus on young people, volunteering for the Boys and Girls Club of Kentuckiana, working with the accounting career awareness Program at the University of Louisville, serving as a big brother with Big Brothers Big Sisters of Kentuckiana, and being a mentor for a young male with Louisville Metro's Reimage program. Currently Mr. Shaw has been implementing a podcast focusing on the needs of young people in Louisville. He lives in Louisville, Kentucky with his wife Freida; two children, Brittany and Steven; and three grandchildren Brianna, RayQuan, and ZaKera.

Beki Nixon Sidener is a membership representative and lifeguard at the YMCA of Greater Kansas City. She is a recipient of the KC Scholars Adult Learner Scholarship and is currently enrolled at the University of Missouri, Kansas City where she attended after graduating from Oak Park High School. Beki is a Kansas City musician, singer, and songwriter. She lives in the Northland in Kansas City, Missouri where her immediate family resides, and her joys are simple: home, yard, good friends, and pets.

Amanda Skaggs is a graduate of the University of Louisville. Her passion is traveling and being a lifelong learner. She lives in Louisville, Kentucky with her husband of 30 years. She is a mother of two, Daniel and Andrea, and a grandmother of three, Emily, Jenna, and Bryce. After a loss of sight in 1994, Amanda's resolve was tested in every way. Over time, she regained sight in her left eye and went on to a very successful career. Upon retirement, she decided to complete her unfinished business at the University of Louisville earning the Resilience Award from the College of Education and Human Development at Graduation.

Jeanine Smith was born and raised in Fort Lauderdale, Florida. After a vacation in the fall, she moved to Crossville, Tennessee in 1996. She is a purchasing agent for Amcon Distributing Company. Jeanine lives in Crossville, with her husband of 32 years, their two daughters, and three grandsons. In her spare time, she loves spending time with her family. She is a proud member of Phi Beta Kappa and Alpha Sigma Lambda Honor Society. She earned her bachelor of science degree in organizational leadership and human behavior from Tennessee Technological University in Cookeville, Tennessee in May 2018.

Lisa Spencer earned her associate transfer degree in business management and administration from Shasta College in Redding California in 2018 at the age of 52. Subsequently, in the Spring of 2019, she completed a second Associate of Arts degree in social sciences through Shasta College. She graduated in May of 2019, with two associate degrees while maintaining honors throughout the entire process. Her work history includes more than 20 years of experience in retail and customer service. Lisa plans on continuing her education in the fall and obtain a bachelor's degree in organizational leadership. She is currently working in management in a local retail store and resides in Redding, California with her daughter and grandson, Jennifer and Roman.

Tamra Switzer is a graduate of the ACE Program at Shasta College in California. She started and stopped her journey to her degree multiple times but has persisted to finish what she stared back in 1995. She works full time, goes to school, and is a mother. She is a native Californian and she currently resides in Shasta Lake, California.

Ronald Tiller graduated from Tennessee Technological University with a degree in interdisciplinary studies at the age of 76. He was later recognized as the Tennessee Tech 2011 Outstanding Alumnus. Ron began his college experience after being honorably discharged from the U.S. Army Paratroopers in 1957. During his senior year, he was recruited to go to work for John Deere Company even though he was only 12 credit hours short of his degree. Both parties agreed that it would be permissible for Ron to complete his education via night school, a popular resolution at the time. Ron's career with John Deere became fast paced and he was fortunate to receive several important promotions, which included a relocation of his family alongside having children. This had a direct impact on his night school aspirations and schooling was put on hold. He later retired as general sales manager of consumer products for the Memphis and Kansas City John Deere markets. Subsequent to his retirement, he entered the workforce once again and attained executive status with a smaller farm equipment company spanning an additional 15 years. After his second retirement, Ron and his wife, Marietta, settled down in an East Tennessee retirement community on Tellico Lake. Entertaining their three grown children (all successful college graduates) and their families has been a favorite pastime for all. Ron continues to enjoy lake life as an active water skier and wakeboarder. Ron's message to other adults that have stopped out of their degree programs is to prepare themselves for a comfortable lifestyle by virtue of further academic achievement either through college or a selected vocational trade. Chances are that you will not regret it as long as you have a positive mindset to be successful in your return. One of Ron's regrets was that he didn't return to the academic setting sooner so he could have gone all the way through to his PhD. Ron's return to academics are significant to who he is today, and he would not have the same level of fulfillment without his college degree.

Sharmiesha S. Timlin is an underwriting analyst for Starr Companies in Houston, TX. She has been involved in various functions of adult education, first as a student, then as a student service representative and financial aid advocate. She earned a bachelor's degree in business administration and a master's degree in leadership from Belhaven University. She spent more than 4 years assisting students with financial aid, providing counsel and degree planning to students. Her interests focus on encouraging others to complete their dreams and finish school no matter their age, setting an example for her children and siblings, and assisting friends and family with a desire to return to school to complete their degrees. Her ultimate goal is to become a parenting coach and complete her teacher certification in order to have a positive impact on the children in her life.

Joe Trainer is an enterprise account executive for a Fortune 500 logistics company, YRC Worldwide. Joe has worked his way up from dock operations clerk, supervisor, hub manager, account executive, and terminal manager. His territory includes Ohio, Indiana, Pennsylvania, and New York. Joe has been tasked with handling the company's largest and most sensitive accounts. He lives in Centerville, Ohio with his wife Susie, and three daughters, Natalie, Grace and Kelsey.

LaKeesha Hatchett Turner was born and raised in Louisville, KY. She is currently a 1st grade teacher for Jefferson County Public Schools at Kennedy Montessori Elementary School. Her entire professional career has been dedicated to education, inspiring and encouraging educational and personal growth of the youth of Louisville. She has worked for the Girl Scouts of Kentuckiana as a program facilitator and leader of a program for empowering middle and high school girls and also at the University of Louisville as a financial aid counselor. LaKeesha lives in Louisville with her husband and three wonderful children and is a proud member of Zeta Phi Beta, Inc. She earned her BS in organizational leadership and learning from the University of Louisville in December 2016.

Maria Hope Vazquez is founder and owner of MV Cleaning and graduate of Middle Tennessee State University with a degree in Sociology. Maria began her educational career in 2012 taking GED classes at her local library. In 2013, Maria was accepted at Motlow Community College. Later in 2015, Maria transferred to Middle Tennessee State University. She arrived to the United States in 1988. Aria chose to complete the rigorous requirements to become a U.S. citizen, which was granted to her in 2012. As a third child of twelve, Maria was the first to attend and graduate from college. Maria was baptized as a Christian in 2017 and seeks to continue growing in her relationship with Jesus for which she feels much passion. Maria lives in Nashville, Tennessee and is a very proud mother of two boys, Diego (25), and Elian (18). Diego, persuaded by his mother's example to pursue college, will graduate in the Spring of 2019 and Elian will begin his college career in Fall 2019.

Debbie Webb is a legal assistant at the law firm of Stoll, Keenon, & Ogden PLLC in Louisville, Kentucky, having worked there since 1985 (and she is looking forward to retirement in 2022). Over the years, she has volunteered countless hours with various organizations, most recently with youth soccer. She lives in New Albany, Indiana, has two adult sons (one who lives locally, one who lives in Colorado), and enjoys travelling with family and friends whenever possible.

Cynthia Wentworth is the associate vice president for Advancement Services in the Office of Advancement at the University of Louisville. She is charged with the oversight of operational compliance of policies and procedures instituted and initiated in prospect management and research, gift recording, data management, and technology. Her responsibilities also include the planning, development, implementation, operation, and maintenance of the university's alumni/development information system. She is a member of Council for the Advancement and Support of Education (CASE) and Ellucian Advance User Group. She earned her Bachelor of Science degree in organizational leadership and learning, track in leadership and organizational development from the University of Louisville. She lives in Louisville, Kentucky and has two adult children, three grandchildren, and one great-grandchild.

Nancy Williams is a program manager/lead program coordinator at Louisville Metro Government. Her main focus is to prevent lead-based paint poisoning of children by helping to educate families and administering the HUD Lead Hazard Control Grant (LHCG) for the Office of Housing and Community Development, Develop Louisville. Serving the community and the children in the community is her passion and the LHCG allows her the opportunity to help reduce or even eliminate lead-based paint hazards from the homes of families with children. She graduated cum laude from Columbia College in December 2014 with a Bachelor of Science in business administration. She lives in Clarksville, Indiana with her husband; she has one daughter Kathy, and two grandchildren, Natalie and Eddie.